	Quickfinder tools strategy & design lenses	Page	Strategy	Design thinking				...ect
Ecosystem strategy canvas (page 106)	Design principles	108						
	Initiatives/industry matrix	113						
	Cooperation/industry matrix	114						
	Ecosystem topic areas map	116						
	Customer-centered ecosystem solutions – topic area analysis	118						
	PESTLE ecosystems	120						
	Ecosystem play & win configuration framework	131						
	Ecosystem configuration grid	133						
Design thinking canvas (page 188)	Research/trends/foresight	190						
	Problem statement/HMW question	192						
	Interview for empathy	193						
	Extreme users/lead users	194						
	Persona	195						
	Critical items diagram	196						
	Brainstorming	197						
	Prototype to test	198						
	Exploration map	199						
	Vision prototype	200						
	Final prototype	201						
	Lean canvas	202						
	Requirements for MVP	203						
Lean start-up MVP canvas (page 210)	Minimum viable product (MVP)	212						
	Build – measure – learn	213						
	Innovation accounting	214						
	User stories/user story map/acceptance test	216						
	The pivot	218						
	Usability test	219						
	Willingness-to-pay analysis	220						
	MVP portfolio & MVP portfolio planning	221						
	Transfer of MVPs to MMFs for MVE	223						
Ecosystem design canvas (page 246)	Value proposition statement for MVE	248						
	Identification & description of actors	250						
	Role playing: actors in the system	252						
	Variations in ecosystem maps	253						
	Definition of the value streams	255						
	Exploration of revenue models	258						
	Multidimensional view of business models	260						
	Co-creation as part of the (re)design system	261						
	Prototyping, testing, and improvement of MVE	262						
	Final MVE & avoidance of frequent errors	263						
	Embedding MVE in the ecosystem strategy	265						
Exponential Growth & scale canvas (page 272)	Problem solving by many	274						
	Expanded value proposition	275						
	Building customers and community	276						
	Scalable process, IT, data analytics	277						
	Leverage touch points	278						
	Network effects and ecosystem culture	280						
	Leverage of different actors in the system	281						
	Optimized cost structure & expanded value streams	282						
	Ecosystem reflection canvas (including selected tools)	290						

MW00355229

"Michael Lewrick is a thought leader who has concerned himself full-scale with the development of the design paradigm. His book hits the zeitgeist and is the best definition of business ecosystem design I have read so far."

Larry Leifer, professor of Mechanical Engineering Design (ME310), Stanford University

"Many people have talked about the design of business ecosystems. This book depicts impressively how to approach it."

Ash Maurya, best-selling author and inventor of lean canvas

"The classic definition of a clearly demarcated company has outlived its purpose. Design thinking for business growth and especially business ecosystem design are the winning formula of our age."

getabstract book review, 2021

More books by Michael Lewrick on the subject of design in the business context as well as for personal life and career planning.

Lewrick, Link, Leifer
The Design Thinking Playbook

Mindful Digital Transformation of Teams, Products, Services, Businesses and Ecosystems
ISBN: 978-1119467472

Lewrick, Link, Leifer
The Design Thinking Toolbox

A Guide to Mastering the Most Popular and Valuable Innovation Methods
ISBN: 978-1119629191

Lewrick, Thommen, Leifer
The Design Thinking Life Playbook

Empower Yourself, Embrace Change, and Visualize a Joyful Life
ISBN: 978-1119682240

DESIGN THINKING FOR BUSINESS GROWTH

Copyright © 2022 by Verlag Vahlen GmbH, München. All rights reserved.
Published by John Wiley & Sons, Inc., Hoboken, New Jersey.
Published simultaneously in Canada.

No part of this publication may be reproduced, stored in a retrieval system, or transmitted in any form or by any means, electronic, mechanical, photocopying, recording, scanning, or otherwise, except as permitted under Section 107 or 108 of the 1976 United States Copyright Act, without either the prior written permission of the Publisher, or authorization through payment of the appropriate per-copy fee to the Copyright Clearance Center, Inc., 222 Rosewood Drive, Danvers, MA 01923, (978) 750-8400, fax (978) 646-8600, or on the Web at www.copyright.com. Requests to the Publisher for permission should be addressed to the Permissions Department, John Wiley & Sons, Inc., 111 River Street, Hoboken, NJ 07030, (201) 748-6011, fax (201) 748-6008, or online at http://www.wiley.com/go/permissions.

Limit of Liability/Disclaimer of Warranty: While the publisher and authors have used their best efforts in preparing this work, they make no representations or warranties with respect to the accuracy or completeness of the contents of this work and specifically disclaim all warranties, including without limitation any implied warranties of merchantability or fitness for a particular purpose. No warranty may be created or extended by sales representatives, written sales materials or promotional statements for this work. The fact that an organization, website, or product is referred to in this work as a citation and/or potential source of further information does not mean that the publisher and authors endorse the information or services the organization, website, or product may provide or recommendations it may make. This work is sold with the understanding that the publisher is not engaged in rendering professional services. The advice and strategies contained herein may not be suitable for your situation. You should consult with a specialist where appropriate. Further, readers should be aware that websites listed in this work may have changed or disappeared between when this work was written and when it is read. Neither the publisher nor authors shall be liable for any loss of profit or any other commercial damages, including but not limited to special, incidental, consequential, or other damages.

For general information on our other products and services or for technical support, please contact our Customer Care Department within the United States at (800) 762-2974, outside the United States at (317) 572-3993 or fax (317) 572-4002.

Wiley publishes in a variety of print and electronic formats and by print-on-demand. Some material included with standard print versions of this book may not be included in e-books or in print-on-demand. If this book refers to media such as a CD or DVD that is not included in the version you purchased, you may download this material at http://booksupport.wiley.com. For more information about Wiley products, visit www.wiley.com.

Library of Congress Cataloging-in-Publication Data is available

Names: Lewrick, Michael, author.
Title: Design thinking for business growth : how to design and scale
   business models and business ecosystems / Michael Lewrick.
Description: Hoboken, New Jersey : Wiley, [2022] | Includes bibliographical
   references and index.
Identifiers: LCCN 2021062101 (print) | LCCN 2021062102 (ebook) | ISBN
   9781119815150 (paperback) | ISBN 9781119815181 (adobe pdf) | ISBN
   9781119886365 (epub) | ISBN 9781119886372 (print replica)
Subjects: LCSH: Business planning. | Corporations--Growth.
Classification: LCC HD30.28 .L4944 2022 (print) | LCC HD30.28 (ebook) |
   DDC 658.4/012--dc23/eng/20220113
LC record available at https://lccn.loc.gov/2021062101
LC ebook record available at https://lccn.loc.gov/2021062102

Illustrations: Donika Palaj
Cover design: Donika Palaj
SKY10030563_012522

DESIGN THINKING FOR BUSINESS GROWTH

HOW TO DESIGN AND
SCALE BUSINESS MODELS
AND BUSINESS ECOSYSTEMS

MICHAEL LEWRICK

GRAPHIC DESIGN
DONIKA PALAJ

WILEY

PROBLEM TO GROWTH AND SCALE FRAMEWORK

1 Design thinking

- Determine your potential users, customers, and stakeholders
- Identify the real customer needs with design thinking
- Find solutions that are as elegant as they are simple
- Use systems thinking and data analytics

3 Co-creation

- Retain more customers, users, and lead users
- Get the necessary help from the outside
- Work on teams across departmental and organizational boundaries
- Develop MVPs and build trust in partners and customers

5 Business ecosystem design and agile product and customer development

- Shift your activities from problem solving and finding solutions to finding the right business model with business ecosystem design
- Develop the product and the business model further with agility, e.g. with methods like scrum
- Think in variants when developing business models
- Look at the business models of all actors in the ecosystem in a multidimensional way and create an MVE

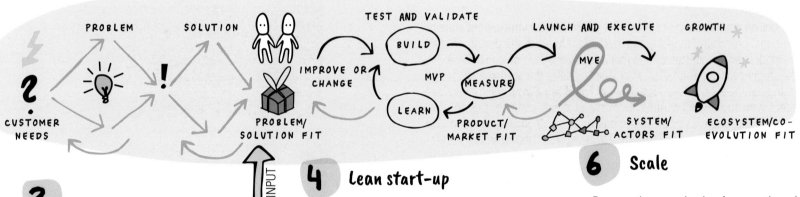

2 Research

- Understand the problem and the situation holistically
- Take advantage of market research instruments
- Validate and supplement your findings

4 Lean start-up

- Use the lean start-up approach to develop your offer further with little capital
- Structure the solution incrementally
- Improve and validate your business model with fast iterations
- Clarify the biggest uncertainties with experiments

6 Scale

- Prepare the organization for growth and scaling
- Establish scalable processes, structures, and platforms
- Check the mindset and skills in your organization and don't just follow a blueprint
- Bring the entire organization one step forward and break new ground

MVP – minimum viable product
MVE – minimum viable ecosystem

Design thinking for business growth offers a mindset that provides the right tools, methods, and procedural models from identifying customer needs to initial prototypes all the way to the scaling of solutions.

This book on applied business design for growth mirrors the current state of definitions, procedural models, and methods related to the design of business models and ecosystems. One major focus is on the design of business ecosystems as a separate discipline that expands the well-known design thinking approaches. While **The Design Thinking Playbook** familiarized readers with the overall context, from the problem statement up to scalable solutions, and was supplemented with the methods described in **The Design Thinking Toolbox, Design Thinking for Business Growth** focuses on a paradigm shift that many companies will face over the next few years in terms of business models, value streams, and growth.

WWW.BUSINESS-ECOSYSTEM-DESIGN.COM

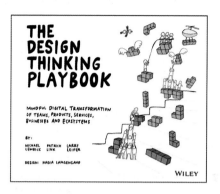

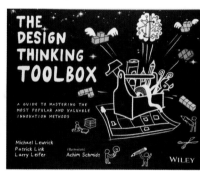

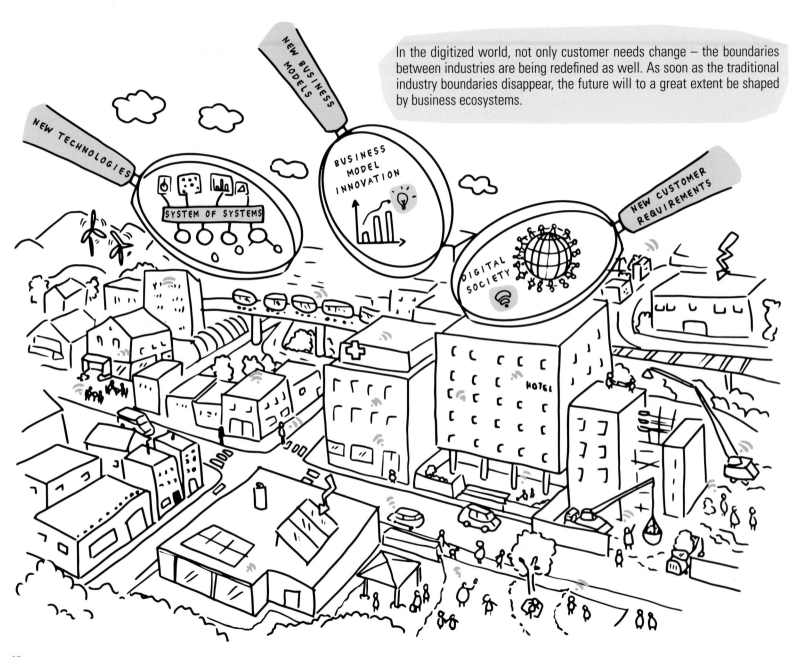

In the digitized world, not only customer needs change – the boundaries between industries are being redefined as well. As soon as the traditional industry boundaries disappear, the future will to a great extent be shaped by business ecosystems.

Foreword

PATRICK VAN DER PIJL
CEO, Business Model Inc., and best-selling
author of *Design a Better Business* and
Business Model Shifts

We, the business users, have long agreed upon the fact that successful companies operate on two levels: EXPLORE and EXPLOIT.

While it's easy for most companies to advance existing capabilities and business models, the tapping of new market areas with new offers and new target customers poses a great challenge.

One possibility for EXPLORE is the initialization of business ecosystems. In such systems, different companies collaborate across the previously known industry boundaries. The common goal of the actors in a business ecosystem is to deliver a unique value proposition to customers.

The structures in such ecosystems are dynamic, and all actors are encouraged to advance themselves and the system constantly. The customer needs, a compelling value proposition and well-thought-out business models that enable the system to grow exponentially constitute the basis for a business ecosystem. New enabler technologies facilitate the implementation of such systems.

> Elements for the preparation of a value proposition are very well known from value proposition design. The validation of prototypes, minimum viable products and ecosystems is vital for later success. In addition, a shift toward new business models is needed that are aligned with the idea of "create, deliver, and capture value."

With *Design Thinking for Business Growth*, Michael Lewrick bridges the gap between the product/market fit and the system/actors fit in the initialization and orchestration of ecosystems.

In my opinion, four decisive features make this book an indispensable companion, especially for users:

- Introducing the principles of business ecosystem design
- Description of a procedural model for the design, development and implementation of ecosystems
- Presentation of the most important design methods and tools
- Description of initiatives and examples of companies that consciously think in business ecosystems

The capability of designing business ecosystems will become one of the key skills for companies in the next decade. This groundbreaking book heralds a paradigm shift in the design of growth, innovation, and new business models.

Good luck and much success with the application of business ecosystem design!

Patrick

Using varying "design lenses"

- Use the appropriate design lens depending on the starting point of considerations about the business ecosystem.
- Concentrate on customer needs and relevant experiences and functions in the early stages.
- Validate the solution with an MVP and use the value proposition to begin with your ecosystem considerations.
- Design the business ecosystem across multiple loops and prepare the organization for exponential growth.

Use momentum in the market and speed

- New ways of working: Use agile working methods.
- Work with short design cycles, prototypes, and iterations.
- Make fail fast a principle in the design of MVPs and MVEs.

Collaboration on interdisciplinary teams

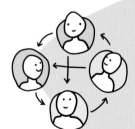

- Transform the organization toward a collaborative culture.
- Be open to co-creation approaches and leverage of existing assets and skills.
- Make use of the design thinking and systems thinking skills of the teams, depending on the situation.

DESIGN THINKING FOR BUSINESS GROWTH MINDSET

The art of letting existing structures go

- Include other actors in the ecosystem as partners on equal footing. They are a part of the delivery of a unique value proposition to the customers whom you share.
- Think in value streams instead of risks.
- Change the perspective from "Yes, but" to "Yes! ... and."

NEW MINDSET.
NEW PARADIGM.
BETTER SOLUTION.

WWW.BUSINESS-ECOSYSTEM-DESIGN.COM

Doubling the heartbeat

- Make it a principle that doing it is more important than talking about it.
- Share initial results, even if they are not final, with potential actors in the ecosystem.
- Always focus on the minimum viability of the product and the ecosystem.

Selection of forward-looking team players, organizations, and companies

- Work together across company boundaries with people who are willing to learn and are optimistic.
- Learn via the people with T-shaped profiles in your own and in other organizations.
- Be willing to accept mistakes and see every instance of failure as an opportunity for reflection and learning.

How to get the most out of the book

The following elements make it easier to find your way in the book:

The book contains simple exercises for better understanding the procedure toward and the principles of business ecosystem design.

Examples of companies and ecosystem and business growth initiatives will be described and presented.

Various known and new methods, tools, and procedural models will be presented. You'll find an overview of all the tools, methods, and frameworks on the first page.

At the end of each logical section, the content is reflected upon and summarized.

Selected tools for the design and documentation of design thinking for business growth initiatives are available for download as a PDF template. Premium templates can be found in the online shop:
www.dt-toolbook.com/shop

Adapt

The rigid management framework has been obsolete at least since the turn of the millennium. So please adapt the procedural models in this book to the specific situation.

For complex projects in particular, such as the design of business ecosystems as part of design thinking for business growth projects, there are countless parameters that allow for leaps, shortcuts, or other pathways.

For all those who work with the new agile tools and who have internalized design thinking deeply, nothing told here is new. But in actual practice, I experience time and again how recommendations for action are painstakingly applied like the instructions from a cookbook to achieve the goal.

It is much more important to have a keen sense of customer needs and to identify the actors in a business ecosystem who fit the desired value proposition and determine the path on which co-creation leads to success. All methods, tools, and procedural models are means to an end. They provide the framework for the business ecosystem design team and indicate the point in the process the teams have reached so that they can quickly find a solid basis for focused collaboration with different actors.

It cannot be pointed out often enough that the tools, methods, and procedural models presented must always be adapted to the respective situation.

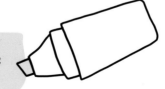

Contents

The focus of this *Design Thinking for Business Growth* book is on the design of business ecosystems and business models. The design of such systems takes center stage and is accompanied by a multidimensional analysis of business models. On the assumption that design thinking for business growth should also be seen as a strategic option, this book shows how, on the basis of customer problems and needs, the foundations for initial solutions can be developed in the form of prototypes, which are then validated as part of the lean start-up approach. The design of the business ecosystem as a basis for growth is developed from the validated value proposition before elaborating on the tools and methods for scaling such systems. This book aims to demonstrate the possibilities of design thinking for business growth and how to become aware of them through well-designed business ecosystems and business models, while supporting the collaboration of different actors on a system with understandable frameworks, tools, and principles.

Ecosystem Strategy   99

Design Lenses Toolbox   171

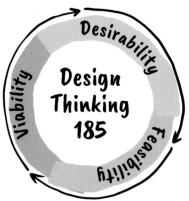

Ecosystem Design 227

Adaptability · Feasibility · Value enhanceability

Scale 269

Captivateabity · Feasibility · Rhythmicability

America · Europe · Asia

Motivation for This Book

Michael Lewrick, PhD, has spent the last years exploring very deeply the mindset that enables us to solve different kinds of problems. He is, among other things, the author of the international best-sellers *The Design Thinking Playbook* and *The Design Thinking Toolbox*, in which he describes the mindful transformation of people, teams, and organizations. He works extensively with universities and companies, and people's self-efficacy in personal and organizational change projects is always at the forefront of his thinking. In recent years, he has expanded his toolbox for designing business ecosystems with an expanded view of design thinking for business growth, described in this book. He is an internationally recognized expert in the fields of digital transformation and the management of innovations, and numerous companies have developed, refined, or scaled innovation, growth, and ecosystem strategies with his help.

Core Statements

Design thinking for business growth and participation in business ecosystems opens up **new growth opportunities** that enable companies to become **much more meaningful to customers.**

Solving real **customer problems** across the entire value chain requires **collaboration between different actors** in a system.

Ecosystems with a **high capital market return** rely largely on the **expansion of growth initiatives as well as on intellectual and ecosystem capital**, which is primarily monetized **from the structures and connections** to the respective actors.

The word *ecosystem* was **originally** limited to the **natural sciences** and referred to a **biological community** of interacting organisms and their physical environment. **Since the 1990s,** it has been used more generally to mean **a complex network or interconnected system.**

Interactions in an ecosystem are **numerous, diverse, and multidimensional,** involving established companies, start-ups, investors, service providers, technology providers, data brokers, payment systems, universities, all the way to government agencies and many others.

To succeed in ecosystems, companies must rethink their **traditional roles and business models** and examine **market opportunities** in collaboration **with actors in other industries.**

Decision makers in particular need to understand **what capabilities** it takes **to design ecosystems**, realize new **value streams,** and assess the risks.

Business ecosystems do not create themselves. The actors in such a system do **not automatically** connect and simply start **radical collaboration**. The reality is **that it is necessary to identify exactly your potential ecosystem partners**, **what their roles** are, **what skills** they bring to the table, and **how any potential co-competition** will be handled.

Why Design Thinking for Business Growth and the Ability to Think in Business Ecosystems Have Become Increasingly Important

The age of business ecosystems is expanding the traditional view of business models and growth. By 2030, more than 30% of global revenue will be generated in business ecosystems. Asia, in particular, has the potential to play a pioneering role here with its high affinity for digital business models. Various studies show that, in addition to the super-platforms already known, new ecosystems making a significant contribution to this development are forming. Worldwide, 15 to 20 dominant business ecosystems will probably set the pace. In addition, it can already be observed today that business ecosystem design plays a particularly important role among the fastest-growing companies in the S&P 500. They include Alphabet, Amazon, Apple, Facebook, Microsoft, Alibaba, and Tencent. Numerous national and local ecosystems will take shape to provide a unique value proposition to customers in niches or in specific regions.

The models, procedures, and mindsets presented in this book have emerged from my work and research in design thinking over the last two decades. I have had the privilege of working in great depth on the management of innovations and technology, the dynamics of high-tech clusters, and the design of business ecosystems.

In particular, I was able to gain deep insights into sourcing initiatives, observe the evolution of data ecosystems, and guide initiatives that reached new dimensions of end-to-end automation through new key technologies and decentralized ecosystems.

In my daily work as an expert in solving complex problems, I consciously live the design thinking for business growth mindset. Being a business and ecosystem designer provides me with an established mindset that helps me solve complex problems based on the needs of customers. Since business ecosystems are usually very complex, I also use systems thinking to shape sub-areas and keep risks under control by applying the minimum viable ecosystem (MVE) approach. This mindset and form of validation is well known to many from the lean start-up world and the associated realization of minimum viable products (MVPs).

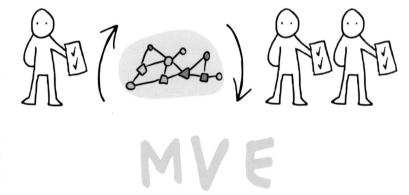

MVE

Thus design thinking, systems thinking, lean start-up, business ecosystem design, and scale methodology constitute the foundation for design thinking for business growth in this book. I have been able to apply and iteratively improve the procedural model for all of them in numerous initiatives.

Especially in my activities as chief innovation officer, later as head of innovation labs at one of the BIG-4 as well as in my current advisory work, the application of business ecosystem design is one of the key approaches toward cross-industry transformation for customers in the banking, insurance, pharmaceutical, technology, and industrial sectors. Many of these companies have the ambition to design, initialize, or orchestrate an ecosystem. Moreover, I am in contact with countless actors who have the ambition of assuming a new market role in existing systems or to advance their capabilities and become a relevant actor in a business ecosystem sooner or later.

The design thinking for business mindset presented in this book, with a strong focus on a procedural model for the design of business ecosystems, helps the participating team members of an ecosystem initiative and the respective actors in the system to get an orientation. It also provides guidance on which aspects should be highlighted in the processing and which factors lead to success. The book also aims at creating awareness that such systems are dynamic structures and are constantly evolving. This is why, in terms of capabilities, market roles, and value propositions, constant reflection and adjustment are needed to ensure value creation for one's own company and the other actors in the system.

The described approach to shaping business growth is not a rigid framework. The depth and breadth of the application is different for each initiative and must be adapted accordingly. Therefore, for complex projects, it is recommended to appoint a skilled facilitator who coordinates the project, has the necessary methodological expertise, and ensures moderation of the respective actors in the system.

I welcome feedback on the application of design thinking for business growth and wish you great success in exploring new forms of collaboration, value streams, business models, market roles, and in building appropriate skills and capabilities.

Michael Lewrick

I welcome direct feedback on the book and a dialog on design thinking for business growth.

www.linkedin.com/in/michael-lewrick

To the
Point !

Design thinking for business growth is the realization of new, unique offerings to customers provided by different actors in an ecosystem.

USING VARIABLE MENTAL STATES...
that allow you to combine design thinking and systems thinking to arrive at scalable offerings, from a problem statement through an MVP/MVE.

APPLYING A DESIGN MINDSET...
that expedites working in iterations and with experiments and puts the function and the customer experience on center stage.

ADDRESS HITHERTO UNKNOWN MARKET OPPORTUNITIES...
that are explored based on customer needs and developed with other actors through co-creation.

AMBITION TO REALIZE A "BLACK OCEAN" STRATEGY... that gives actors in the system the best framework for realizing the value proposition and makes it difficult for rival offerings to stay in competition.

TEN MINDSHIFTS FOR BUSINESS GROWTH

Mindshifts:
10 Shifts Grasp the Topic Quickly

Design thinking for business growth and the associated design of business ecosystems are based on a paradigm shift in the shaping of business models and growth. Essential for this are ten mindshifts that simultaneously constitute the basis for this book and for the design of successful business ecosystems.

Companies that have already undergone major change processes because of the digital transformation are in a better position here since they have already undergone one or another mindshift. However, actual practice shows how dedicated teams for strategy or ecosystem design revert to old ways of thinking time and again. It frequently occurs when they begin to collect ideas about a business ecosystem. Unfortunately, the deliberations all too often pivot on the team's own company with its products and services and not on the customers with their current and future needs **(mindshift #1)**. When it gets really bad, the customer is no more than one actor out of many in the system, instead of them taking center stage. The situation is similar when initial solutions and prototypes of ecosystems are being developed. The design of prototypes, MVPs, and MVEs is an iterative process that aims at receiving a validation of the MVP from potential customers. Secondly, the MVE and the associated value proposition should be validated with little effort expended by the potential actors in the system. Unlike in a linear procedure, the iterative procedure makes it possible to improve the prototypes incrementally, reject them, or develop them further **(mindshift #2)**. In the design of business ecosystems, it is also vital not to lose sight of the other actors and their strengths. Traditional analyses help only to a limited extent here, since the aim is not to learn more about competitors but to create in the best case a symbiosis between the actors. The shared work of different actors in the system constitutes the foundation for the realization of unique value propositions and innovation **(mindshift #3)**. Since business ecosystems are exposed to inevitable dynamics and because the actors in the system constantly advance together, coevolution together with other companies is a natural process. Anybody sticking to silo thinking and clinging to existing structures will not be successful in the short nor the long term **(mindshift #4)**. While before this, companies concentrated on their own core competencies and capabilities to bring a value proposition to the market, it is necessary in the realization of business ecosystems to get away from the consideration of the individual elements, so as to be able to generate a unique value proposition with the consolidated capabilities and expertise in the system **(mindshift #5)**.

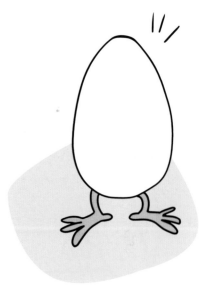

Furthermore, it must be accepted that network structures have a certain level of complexity. Understanding must be heightened for the customers who want to be served via channels that suit them. Instead of decoupling the interactions, business ecosystem design requires a mindset of networked thinking **(mindshift #6)**. The initiators of business ecosystems must understand the value streams and relationships within the network structures. This means: It is no longer isolated financial flows that are looked at but relationships and value streams in systems **(mindshift #7)**. The respective business models must be dealt with in a new way. Instead of looking at one's own business model, the multidimensional view of the business models comes to the fore. Together with the business model of the ecosystem, the initiator or orchestrator must also define potential business models of the other actors in the system and make them correspondingly attractive **(mindshift #8)**. The goal of well-thought-out business ecosystems is to achieve dominant market power and market penetration. This view goes beyond a 100% differentiation strategy and is referred to as the black

ocean strategy **(mindshift #9)**. After all, the business ecosystem with its actors is intended to be superior to other systems and companies because of its configuration. To have such systems grow exponentially in the long term, a sophisticated governance is needed as well as an adequate ecosystem and a leadership approach that is not geared to command and control but to initiate and orchestrate **(mindshift #10)**.

The 10 mindshifts will be described in detail on the following pages. They provide a good foundation for potential design principles that decision makers and business ecosystem teams should put at the center of their work so that design thinking for business growth can be put on solid ground to be successful.

OH WOW!
PARADIGM
SHIFT!

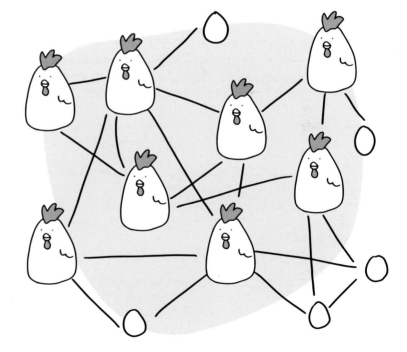

1 Shift: from product-centered/company-centered to customer-centered

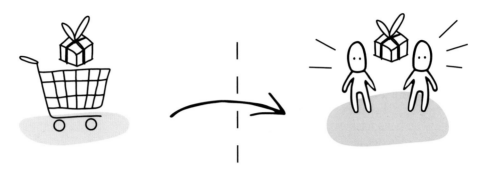

The main focus is not on one's own company or an existing product or service but on customers with their current and future needs and the tasks they want to perform.

2 Shift: from linear to iterative

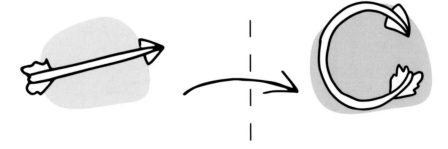

The entire procedure is iterative, i.e. from exploring the customer needs to initial prototypes, minimum viable products (MVP), all the way to an initial functioning system within the framework of a minimum viable ecosystem (MVE).

3 Shift: from analysis to symbiosis

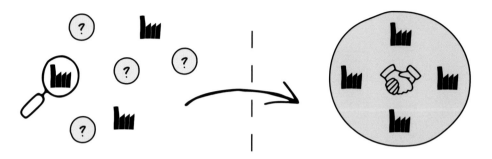

Traditional procedural models of strategy definition are usually limited to the possibilities offered by existing thought patterns about industries, sectors, and competitors. Well-designed business ecosystems perceive other actors from other sectors, including competitors, as partners who are indispensable in providing a unique value proposition to customers.

4 Shift: from silos to coevolution

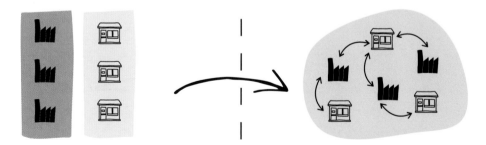

Thinking in product categories, traditional segmentation and core competencies are replaced by a consistent coevolution in the business ecosystem, which enables actors to share in new markets, regions, and customer segments.

5 Shift: from elements to unique value propositions

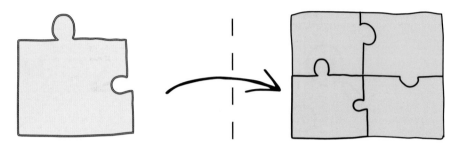

The uniqueness of a value proposition in a business ecosystem emerges through the meaningful linking of different skills, products, and platforms. An individual market participant alone is usually not able to realize and scale such value propositions.

6 Shift: from decoupling to networking

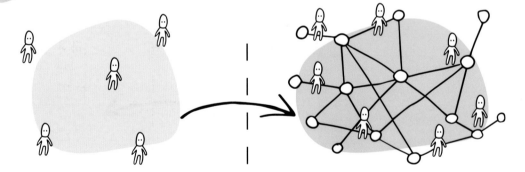

Ecosystems are agile network structures that act in a collaborative and networked way. The top goal of these systems is to serve customer needs in an efficient and effective way through various channels that fit the customer.

7 Shift: from isolation to relationships/value streams

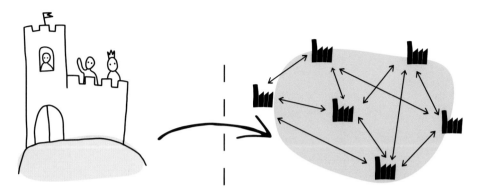

The way of thinking at companies shifts from an internal viewpoint to a holistic understanding of the system with its different value streams and relationships, which are constantly in motion and need to be adapted and realigned depending on customer and market needs.

8 Shift: from the consideration of an individual to the multidimensional view of the business models

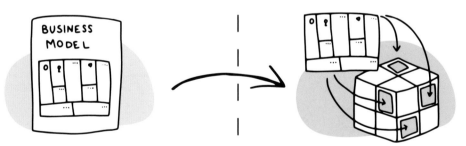

Along with one's own business model, it is important to explore the possibilities and advantages for the other actors in the system by developing a multidimensional view of the business models. Usually, the more attractive the opportunities are for the actors involved to earn money in the system, the greater the willingness to implement the proposed value proposition together and develop it further.

9 Shift: from red/blue ocean to black ocean

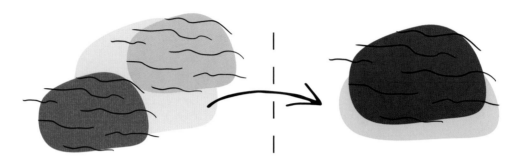

Well-designed business ecosystems are configured in such a way that other systems or individual companies cannot compete with the same or a similar value proposition. Such a strategy is also known as the "black ocean" strategy.

10 Shift: from command and control to initiate and orchestrate

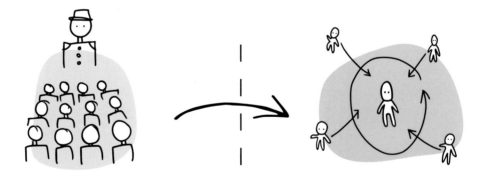

Ecosystem leadership is based on the ideas of initiate and orchestrate. Conventional command and control mechanisms run aground when it comes to the dynamics and complexity of rapidly growing business ecosystems.

To the
Point!

Companies and actors that followed the paradigm shift beyond mere digital transformation focus more and more on the possibilities of digital disruption and innovation in business ecosystems.

Ecosystem players rely on coevolution, symbiosis, and networking and operate beyond traditional customer experience chains. They create systems with unique value propositions.

The successful initiators and orchestrators of ecosystems don't strive for stable, linear growth patterns but for the agile realization of exponential growth.

INTRODUCTION
DESIGN THINKING FOR
BUSINESS GROWTH

Why Design Thinking for Business Growth?

Like other fields of knowledge, the world of design thinking continues to develop and mature. Sub-specializations such as business ecosystem design emerge, and best practices, different approaches, and new tools are limned and come into being. Quite a few things have occurred in the application of design thinking for business growth over the last few years. Entailed in this development was a broadened view that gained great traction and is now used by growth designers and business ecosystem designers as well as in strategic design. Business ecosystem design, for instance, has not yet turned into a formalized field in many companies, so there is still a certain degree of mystery and misunderstanding in the development of such growth strategies. For exponential growth, it is crucial to increase the number of dedicated customers/users rapidly and to apply a mindset of fail fast – learn fast. But design thinking for business growth is about far more than the quick achievement of growth. The goal is to create a lasting experience for the customer/user, develop it further and optimize it, and create network effects, which enrich the ecosystem capital. Data and the application of a hybrid model of design thinking and big data analytics are quite useful in this context. Design thinking for business growth also requires new models for how teams are formed and how close to the customer/market they ought to operate. Successful growth strategies don't come into being by making rash decisions and putting something quickly on the market but by focusing on the problem space, which makes it possible to understand customer needs in the required depth and analyze all available data. A good design thinking for business growth team has all these skills at its disposal and practices a comprehensive way of thinking to give the customer/user the best experience and functions in the end. In brief, design thinking for business growth defines how a single company or all companies in a business ecosystem create, deliver, and capture market values in common.

The interaction of create, deliver, and capture and putting the focus on each of them at just the right time influence the speed of value growth and open up options for later scaling and the realization of exponential growth.

In design thinking for business growth, the teams aim at bringing together the very best from design thinking and systems thinking for exponential business growth.

Design thinking applied during the phase of value creation supports the processes and helps to establish the basis for creating value in the long term by designing products, services, and processes that customers really want. Design thinking for business growth goes beyond familiar, traditional ways of looking at product models, service models, and business models. Alongside the well-known consideration of partners and suppliers, a complete system of ecosystem actors is integrated in the definition of a growth strategy and addressed with special lenses and specific questions in the context of business ecosystem design.

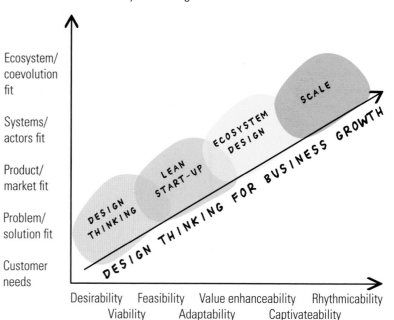

Design thinking for business growth is the next logical step in the evolution of design in a business context (see page 58). The expansion is primarily concerned with the shaping and multidimensional nature of business models and the design of complete business ecosystems. It has an impact on the scope of development and on the strategic focus of design thinking. Companies that think in terms of business ecosystems and strive for exponential growth adapt their way of working and their organizational models. They often become orchestrators of such systems. At the same time, design thinking for business growth affects the strategy of companies. Companies may assume new market roles and redefine competitors and partners. Well-known elements of design thinking and its further development as a culture, mindset, or toolbox are supporting elements to be used for the successful application of design thinking for business growth.

For business growth, the design thinking toolbox is expanded by methods and tools that are known from the lean start-up approach; in addition, there are new tools and methods ranging from minimal viable ecosystem landscapes all the way to minimal viable ecosystems. Frameworks help to scale the systems in question and drive exponential growth. In the growth approach, the design thinking mindset is expanded by three additional design lenses. Further, the selection of future-oriented team players, organizations, and actors needed to deliver a unique value proposition constitutes a vital element. Design thinking as a culture is still the greatest challenge here since design thinking for business growth brings the relevant design teams even closer to the market for them to feel the customers' pulse; simultaneously, it turns the actors involved in the business system into co-innovators who advance the value proposition on their own within the framework of the principles, guides, and the defined ambition. This type of collaboration requires forms of organization that allow for radical ways of collaboration across company and industry boundaries. Companies that have already implemented team-of-teams approaches and define the objectives of organizational units, teams, and individual employees within the scope of OKRs (objectives and key results) have already established important elements of this culture. All this and beyond will facilitate the future interaction in business ecosystems of orchestrators, actors, teams, and employees working on such growth initiatives.

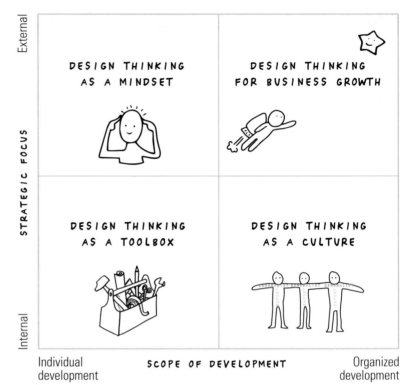

The key questions in design thinking for business growth are, **WHAT** are the customer needs, **HOW** to build and test the experiences and features for a core value proposition, followed by **WHO** are the appropriate ecosystem actors to jointly offer the proposition. These are followed by **HOW** to design, implement, and leverage business ecosystems for growth. In retrospect, it is also very interesting to reflect on **WHY** some ecosystems thrive and others whither with the passage of time.

The following pages provide a definition and a brief introduction to the idea of business ecosystems and how in the context of design thinking for business growth this approach and mindset herald a paradigm shift.

Design Thinking as the Cornerstone of Business Growth

Design thinking for business growth means using methods and tools from design thinking, systems thinking, and multidimensional business model development. It addresses all areas of value creation, value delivery, and value capture. The shaping of business ecosystems has become a new strategic growth path for more and more companies. The goal here is transforming a core value proposition into a real business value for all actors involved in an ecosystem. For ambitious projects with exponential growth, the key to success is meaningful new value creation by thinking in higher-level systems. The growth strategy is developed in iterations; it is driven by customer needs and designed such that the respective minimum viability is achieved with as few resources as possible. The primary goal, however, is always to make the customer/user successful. The design thinking for business growth toolbox (see page 171) is more than building empathy for the customer. It encompasses the permission to think bigger and build ecosystem capital for the system and its actors in the long term.

Design Thinking as the Cornerstone of Business Growth

Conventional strategy development with its analyses of competitors, addressable markets, market segments, and best practices and a planning cycle of three to five years usually results in merely incremental innovations in the business model.

Design thinking for business growth makes use of an iterative procedure, starting from customer needs, going on to experiments with the product all the way to the value proposition and the shaping of a business ecosystem, including a multidimensional view of business models.

Traditional growth strategy

Market analysis

Strategic planning process

Implementation

Idea management

Strategy

Stakeholder analysis

Resource allocation

Design thinking for business growth

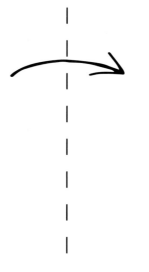

Scaling & exponential growth

Minium viable ecosystem

Business models

Minimum viable product

Prototypes

Customer needs

Focus on the Sweet Spot for New Growth

Considerations about the business model have always been a crucial element for reacting to market conditions and customer wishes. The speed of change is so much higher today, though, and adaptations to the new circumstances must be made quickly and frequently. Following COVID-19 at the very latest, the new generation of decision makers should be aware of how customer needs may change without much notice and to what extent technology can help to generate persuasive value propositions to customers even in difficult market situations. The shaping of and/or participation in business ecosystems gives every company the opportunity to develop innovative business models and rethink the conventional models. Instead of aiming for higher sales of existing products and services, the ecosystem focuses on the customer and their needs. The ever-present circumstances abbreviate the period over which old business models and market roles remain viable. Moreover, technological possibilities have never been so mature and sophisticated as today. For one, they allow for a lean implementation of business models; secondly, they create the foundation for collecting and sharing data optimally and making profitable use of it. Design thinking for business growth provides tools and methods to develop not only one business model but a complete system of value streams and business models. Participating in the business ecosystem not only allows individual actors to shape the business model but also to take part in value creation on several levels.

Design thinking for business growth offers entrepreneurs, decision makers, and those units responsible for the design and implementation of growth in the company a new perspective to think creatively about their business model, the options of designing, all the ways to participation in a business ecosystem, and advancing such growth paths iteratively. The approach emerging from design thinking and systems thinking, coupled with other concepts, allows for new ideas to be tested for their sustainability with few resources. In the future, this will be one of the critical capabilities that will determine success in an accelerating market.

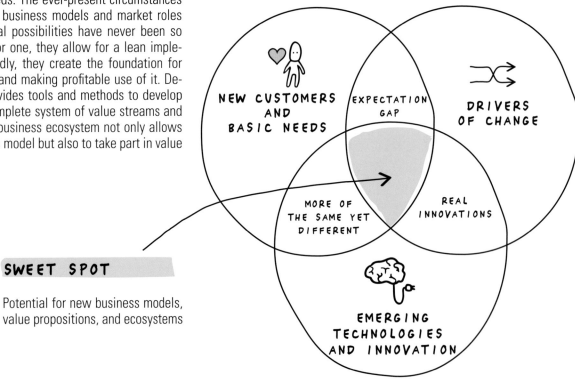

SWEET SPOT

Potential for new business models, value propositions, and ecosystems

The Role of Design Thinking in the Design of Business Models

The design thinking mindset and the philosophy of diverge and converge help the actors involved in a business ecosystem in the design of business models, especially for a multidimensional view of business models. What is important here is that the business model meets a specific purpose, e.g. the wish for a responsible growth strategy. First, the all-dominant question about the customers and their needs must be posed. In the context of value proposition design, this means the question of WHAT shall we offer to the customer. The questions of WHERE is the customer problem/ecosystem *topic area* and HOW to provision and configure channels and ecosystem are important elements; they are augmented by the WHY question in the design of the value streams, namely why the system is profitable in a particular configuration.

These questions of business model design are elaborated in the individual design lenses and are part of the "where to play" and "how to win and configure" framework (page 110). When designing value propositions for business ecosystems, usually more than one user problem is worked on. After all, several products, services, functions, and experiences are often required to ensure that the customer's needs are met. Existing, adapted, and new business models can contribute to the design, application, and implementation.

Design thinking for business growth provides the right tools and methods to look beyond the obvious business models.

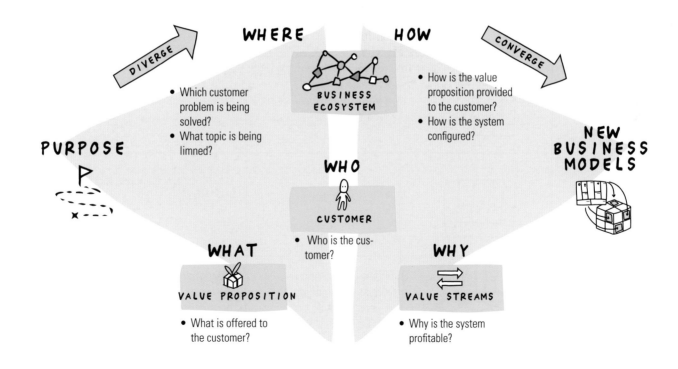

- **WHERE**
  - Which customer problem is being solved?
  - What topic is being limned?

- **HOW**
  - How is the value proposition provided to the customer?
  - How is the system configured?

BUSINESS ECOSYSTEM

PURPOSE

NEW BUSINESS MODELS

DIVERGE / **CONVERGE**

WHO

CUSTOMER
- Who is the customer?

- **WHAT**

VALUE PROPOSITION
- What is offered to the customer?

- **WHY**

VALUE STREAMS
- Why is the system profitable?

There are different perspectives on the shaping of business models. Most sets of methods, e.g. the business model canvas (Osterwalder) and the lean canvas (Maurya), use design thinking principles in the entire approach. In the context of lean start-up, the lean canvas, among many other things, is used in this book, which addresses primarily the WHY with its building blocks of problem, solution, existing alternatives, and unfair advantage. The multidimensional view of business models is particularly important in the design and configuration of business ecosystems and constitutes the basis for the definition of systems that are able to grow exponentially. All three, namely the business model canvas, the minimum viable product concept from the lean start-up principles, and business ecosystem design, encourage teams to draft quick and rough prototypes that can be tested with customers, or customers and potential actors, in the business ecosystem for facilitating quick feedback and rapid learning.

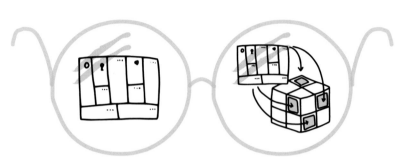

POINT OF VIEW

EXAMPLES OF BUSINESS MODELS	METHODOLOGY	MINDSET	OBJECTIVES
Business model development		• Design thinking • Value proposition design	Optimizing existing business models with a strong focus on the HOW?
Lean canvas		• Design thinking • Lean	Creating new business models with a strong focus on the WHY?
Multidimensional creation of business models		• Design thinking • Systems thinking • Ecosystem design	Disrupting entire industries and creating multiple business models for all participating actors in the ecosystem with a focus on WHERE TO PLAY and HOW TO WIN AND CONFIGURE.

The Hype about Business Ecosystems

No other word is currently used as often in a business context as ecosystems. Over the last decade, many companies, driven by digitization, have opened up and tried out and established collaborative forms of working across company boundaries. Thinking in the way of a business ecosystem is also the result of the necessity to change even more. For one, the framework conditions are changing more and more rapidly, with the result that new skills and capabilities must either be built fast by oneself, or else they have to be rendered by in-house changes and the complementary skills and capabilities of the other actors in the business ecosystem.

Many companies have also found that new technologies make it possible to realize innovative value propositions for customers. Unfortunately, there is often a lack of different elements, like skills, distribution channels, data, or customer access to ensure successful realization. Hence, it comes as no surprise that most goals defined in programs for digital transformation have had little effect so far. If you want to operate in business ecosystems, you have to rethink things far more radically!

The transparency created by digitization has also a disruptive effect on how business ecosystems will be designed in the future.

For companies, the question arises – for both design and implementation – of whether they should initialize a suitable ecosystem on their own or whether they should become a part of an existing ecosystem. In both cases, you will be part of value creation and will realize a value proposition together with the other actors in the ecosystem. Moreover, the business ecosystem approach has the advantage of being able to test different new market opportunities by participating in different ecosystems. In a more traditional, centralized approach, resources and capabilities are usually not sufficient to do so.

A high level of trust in the other actors in the system and common values, ideas, and ambitions of the participating companies constitute the basic prerequisites for taking part in ecosystems. In addition, the initialization of an ecosystem requires financial resources, from the basic idea all the way to the scaling of the system. Alongside money for technologies and interfaces, costs comprise primarily expenses incurred for setup and coordination.

The big challenge is rather to shape the corporate culture toward a participative mindset. Companies should learn to reach out to other actors with the aim to co-create. They must say goodbye to one-sided ownership pretensions. The customer does not belong to a specific company but moves freely in the ecosystem and usually selects between the individual services of the partners involved.

HYPE!

Business ecosystems occur in a global context as much as in local initiatives. Local initiatives are often initialized on the basis of existing connections and partnerships. Global ecosystems are being created, for instance, to disrupt entire industries, create new value propositions, or implement end-to-end automation.

Across the past two decades, new technologies such as the Internet, big data analytics, cloud computing, and blockchain have created new opportunities for ecosystems to emerge in a wide range of manifestations. Innovation ecosystems, knowledge ecosystems, and data ecosystems will be briefly described on page 64.

Business ecosystems have a special character, and they come in all shapes and sizes. For an initial localization of business ecosystems, it seems appropriate to juxtapose the business ecosystem with other extreme manifestations:

VERY STABLE SYSTEMS: Vertically integrated company, usually with static customer/supplier chains.

VERY AGILE SYSTEMS: Open, capital-economy markets without government regulations, in which customers collect and consume various products and services according to their needs.

VERTICALLY INTEGRATED COMPANIES

BUSINESS ECOSYSTEMS

OPEN CAPTITAL-ECONOMY MARKETS

very stable

Very agile

Integrated Companies vs. Business Ecosystem View

From the perspective of a traditional mindset with a more centralized and integrated approach, the ecosystem approach entails various elements that are new to companies. The most important of them is that ecosystems operate beyond the existing industry and company boundaries, meaning that they assume an external focus in terms of value creation. In addition, the mindset is aligned to network effects and overarching network structures instead of 100% focusing on linear value creation. As a result, ecosystems are more exposed to the prevailing market dynamics and changes in technology. This means that the predictability of target states declines, uncertainty heightens, and permanent adjustment becomes a vital capability. Traditional, linear financing models and business model considerations

make way for a multidimensional view of business models and an indirect monetization of investments.

Governance and control of the ecosystem are increasingly decentralized, contrary to the traditional models of full ownership and management. In coordination and collaboration with other actors, different offerings, skills, and services are combined in such a way that the customer enjoys a unique experience with the product or service. This is why such systems are more dynamic and the necessity arises either to develop spirally with the other actors, change, or leave the ecosystem.

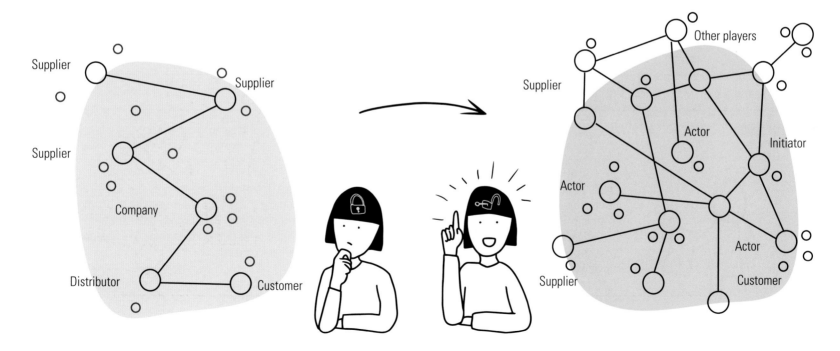

The Top 10 Biggest Challenges for Traditional Companies for Thinking in Business Ecosystems in Terms of Culture, IT, Process, and Capabilities

	FROM...	TO...
1	Internal focus	External focus
2	Linear value creation	Network-oriented value creation
3	Long-term and rigid planning	Iterative procedure and agile adjustment
4	Traditional view of business models	Multidimensional view of business models
5	Direct value and financial streams	Indirect monetization and financial streams
6	Complete control and ownership	Shared control and "membership"
7	Product-centered	Complementary product or service
8	Static view	Dynamic/coevolutionary view
9	Protectionist in terms of data and customer relationships	Transparent and open in terms of data and customer relationships
10	Thinking in market-ready platforms, functions, offers	Thinking in minimum viable products/ecosystems

These new capabilities, mindsets, and technologies to be mastered should not be underestimated. One rule of thumb is that about 20% of a company's core capabilities contribute around 70% of the value added. Conversely, that means that up to 20% of a company's capabilities need to be adapted to exploit the new 70% of first-time value creation in an ecosystem play. Such change is even more complex than what companies know from the digital transformation. Not least because these new capabilities are often lacking in the company itself as well as with the other actors in the ecosystem. Persuasion, orchestration, and collaboration with other actors is part of the governance of business ecosystems.

The multitude of required skills and offers also opens up the possibility for a multitude of actors to contribute their activities.

Why and when should companies deal with business ecosystems?

There are numerous vertically integrated companies, well positioned with their current business models and value chains, for which thinking in business ecosystems has so far not been of great relevance. The picture looks different for companies that sense a disruption by new market participants at present, move in a dynamic environment in which new technologies herald great changes, or for which growth and diversification can only be achieved by spending large amounts of resources. Business ecosystems also offer opportunities to smaller companies because similar resources, experience, and skills can be accessed that are normally available only to large conglomerates. An ecosystem approach makes it possible to react to new and future customer needs.

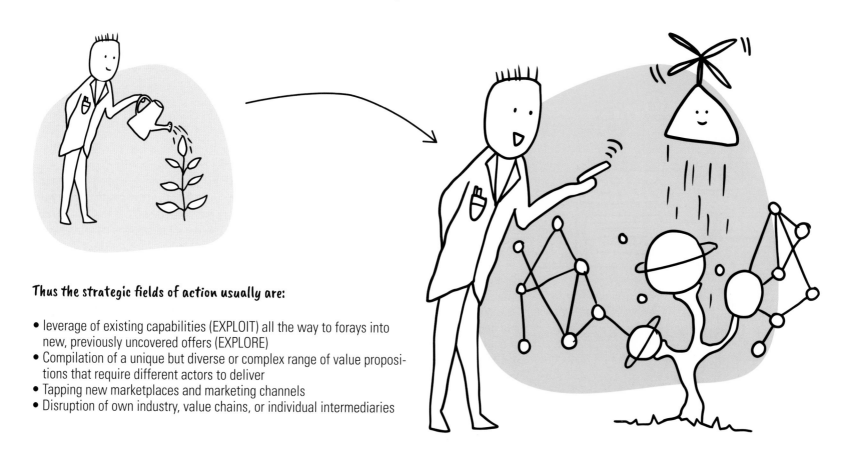

Thus the strategic fields of action usually are:

- leverage of existing capabilities (EXPLOIT) all the way to forays into new, previously uncovered offers (EXPLORE)
- Compilation of a unique but diverse or complex range of value propositions that require different actors to deliver
- Tapping new marketplaces and marketing channels
- Disruption of own industry, value chains, or individual intermediaries

What is the experience like from the customer's point of view?

The customer is given an integrated experience from a large number of actors in the form of a service, a piece of information, or the completely automated processing of a transaction. Thus a business ecosystem consists of a networked set of services that enable customers to satisfy multiple needs. The value proposition created by the ecosystem can be a gateway for customers that allows the use of many services and products – to top it off, this experience should be as free of interfaces for the customer as possible.

Example

For example, via WeChat Messenger, users can not only send a message to a friend but pay for their purchases using cryptocurrencies – all on a single platform. Solutions such as NEST in the smart home segment consolidate different information in a monthly energy balance for customers who also then have the opportunity to compare the results with those of their neighbors.

720°

Ecosystems use network effects that yield a strategic size advantage to the ecosystem as such and, ideally, to all actors in the system. A unique experience for the customer is only possible, though, if there is a **720 degree view of the customer**. Creating a holistic and smart view of the customers is the next stage in a targeted customer interaction.

For this reason, ecosystems integrate data provided by the individual actors. These days, the data is usually evaluated centrally and used for the development of unique offers by the actors. Distributed databases, ledgers, and blockchain are key technologies that will perform this task in a decentralized way and with a new view of data sovereignty in the future. Large volumes of data also allow the mass customization of products and services. An individual experience and an individual product are created for each customer, or products and services are designed that appeal to the masses. This enables ecosystems and their actors, for instance, to expand customer relationships step by step and improve customer loyalty.

Today's technologies make it possible that changing needs of customers are met.

In many ways, the new technologies are the enablers of up-to-date and scalable business ecosystems. Only with technologies such as the Internet and cloud computing was it possible over the last two decades to realize digital marketplaces and platforms. The large and powerful business ecosystems rely on big data analytics as well as on automation and serve their customers through the channel most suitable to them (opti-channel). In some ecosystems, this is already done exclusively by voice control or in the conventional human-machine interaction by text input.

Technologies allow for customers to interact with one another or contact service providers on platforms. In business ecosystems, use of customer and/or transaction data is made possible on various levels. Here the primary focus is on the acquisition and use of proprietary data.

The basis for the respective interactions are the radically, newly designed customer experience chains (the so-called ecosystem journey) that integrate the services of several companies and enable a new type of service delivery that fulfills several tasks for the customer. Technology helps to combine offers and provide them in a transparent way or custom-tailored to the customers. Robotics/automation is used for simple functions. More complex processes require artificial intelligence or machine learning and deep learning approaches. In the next decade, more rapidly than ever, other game-changing technologies will accelerate this process.

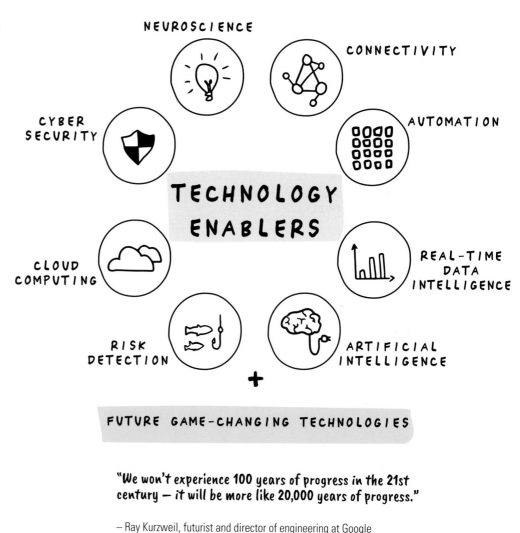

"We won't experience 100 years of progress in the 21st century — it will be more like 20,000 years of progress."

– Ray Kurzweil, futurist and director of engineering at Google

Well-designed and automated business ecosystems reduce the cost of customer acquisition. Moreover, in one transaction, the customer receives a wide range of products and services jointly provided by different actors. The high number of transactions provides the ecosystem and actors with a unique access to data, which can then be used for the design of new products and services or be monetized in other ways. Accurate data on the location, invoicing, movements, and health all the way to data on behavior are in many cases the "oil," the fuel for the further development of ecosystems.

In addition, it has become apparent over the last few years that companies that use network effects are valued higher in the capital market than traditional plant manufacturers, service providers, or 100% technology companies. As mentioned before, companies that think in terms of business ecosystems enjoy higher revenue growth than traditional companies. A study conducted by the BCG Henderson Institute for the period 2012–2017 found that the growth was 1 to 4% higher a year.

Both the initiators of business ecosystems and the actors participating in such systems will increasingly achieve valuation advantages in the capital market in the future, win over potential investors, and ensure their competitiveness. In the world of network effects and data, the valuation of companies is primarily based on user loyalty, which replaces more and more often the familiar top-line metrics. For ecosystems based on blockchain technologies, the reach of the self originated "currencies" in the ecosystem, for instance, may become the benchmark for the future.

Currently, the successful initiators of supra-regional business ecosystems are those companies that already have a digital brand or platform allowing them to develop the ability to think in network effects and scaling. Moreover, these initiators have multiple visions of a feasible future; they have recognized the opportunity to achieve the goal iteratively and in the lean start-up mode via minimal viable products and an active design of the business ecosystem.

REVENUE MULTIPLIES

MULTIPLER	ROLE	EVALUATION CRITERIA
8x	network orchestrator	network size and configuration
4x	technology creator	code and IP
2x	service provider	billable hours, service fee
1x	asset builders	production

"Traditional business models that tend to place the focus on internal skills no longer suffice in a world with highly interconnected ecosystems. Today, successful companies make use of the shared skills of a complete network of partners to achieve a competitive edge."

– Dr. Marco Iansiti, professor at Harvard Business School

Companies that put a great deal of effort into digital transformation today already collaborate within agile structures and across company boundaries. However, for participation in business ecosystems, two more paradigm shifts are of vital importance: the **view of the business models** and the **levers** of such systems **for exponential growth**.

Traditional companies must overcome a metaphorical digital divide. Previously valid assumptions no longer apply such as: product-centered development, traditional hierarchical organizational structures, and a strong focus on market share and physical transaction chains with intermediaries.

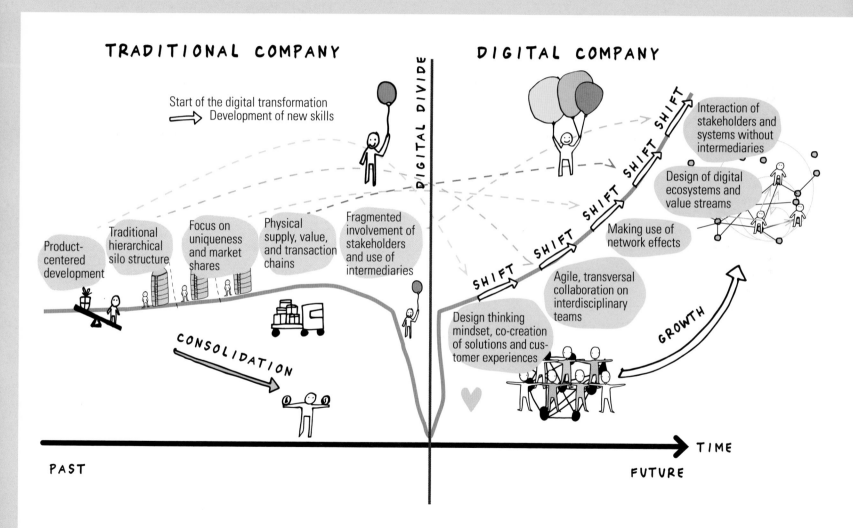

What is the paradigm shift in the design of business models and growth in specific terms?

In the well-known view of a business model, the relevant dimensions considered for a single company or a centralized platform normally are: a view of income and costs; the capabilities and skills of a company; and the customers and customer segments to be addressed, including a defined differentiation for the company's range of offers. These dimensions are not wrong, but they need to be expanded by a multidimensional view. This means that the business model of a business ecosystem is made up of multiple opportunities for the actors. It might even mean that the initiators of a business ecosystem initialize it for the sole purpose of increasing their own market opportunities in the system and gaining advantages from the close (financial) link with the ecosystem, e.g. access to transaction and customer data, which in turn allows conclusions to be made about the behavior or needs of customers. From this, data-driven innovations can be realized in various directions.

Paradigm shift in the view of business models

What is the business model of the company to be successful on the market by means of differentiation?

How can every single actor who contributes his skills to the creation of a unique value proposition profit in multiple ways?

Traditional view of the business model of a company

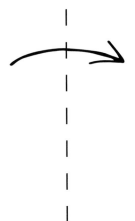

Multidimensional view of the business models in an ecosystem

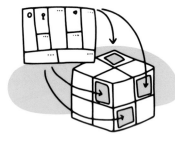

- Differentiation of the company
- A revenue model
- Individual capabilities in the value chain
- Possession of the customer interface

- Contribution to a joint value proposition
- Various possibilities of participation
- Shared capabilities for fulfilling the value proposition
- Participation with the right skills

The second paradigm shift for growth requires a new way of thinking in terms of how to deal with existing business models of companies. Often, existing business models are taken as the starting point and checked whether they can be optimized to boost earnings. But if this way of thinking is applied to ecosystems, it usually leads only to considerations on how existing business models can be expanded by means of an ecosystem approach. This way, only linear growth is realized. The paradigm shift changes the view from 100% optimization toward the design of a superior business ecosystem that is geared to the realization of ecosystem capital and the pursuit of a strategy of exponential growth. Then it must be evaluated whether the existing capabilities or the customer access allow for becoming active in a specific business ecosystem.

Paradigm shift for growth

How can a business model be expanded with an ecosystem play?

How can a business ecosystem benefit the growth of one company?

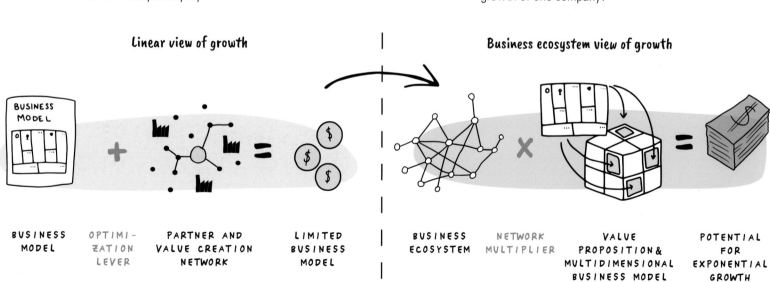

Linear view of growth					Business ecosystem view of growth			
BUSINESS MODEL	OPTIMI-ZATION LEVER	PARTNER AND VALUE CREATION NETWORK	LIMITED BUSINESS MODEL		BUSINESS ECOSYSTEM	NETWORK MULTIPLIER	VALUE PROPOSITION & MULTIDIMENSIONAL BUSINESS MODEL	POTENTIAL FOR EXPONENTIAL GROWTH

New business models and growth in digital or hybrid models require sophisticated business ecosystems that offer added value to the customers in a simple and efficient way. Companies often tend to augment their existing and predominantly linear business models in ecosystem initiatives with well-known business partners. The common ideas about partner management are often based more on the models of sourcing strategies than on the portfolio-based business model view necessary in the digital age: a view that differentiates and simultaneously generates synergies with the core business. In many cases, the willingness to change on the part of top management is simply not given, so it is inevitable that existing business models are protected and short-term financial optimization is given priority over the development of viable systems and innovative business models.

Alexander Osterwalder describes companies that master this balancing act as invincible companies, i.e. organizations that constantly reinvent themselves so as not to become obsolete. Invincible companies explore the future (EXPLORE) while they exploit their market position on existing markets to maximize earnings (EXPLOIT). According to Osterwalder, they live a balanced culture based on innovative strength and implementation power. Competitiveness is realized in the form of well-thought-out business models that cross traditional industry boundaries. The constant exploration of new market opportunities, based on customer needs and across existing industry boundaries, becomes one of the strongest design principles for future growth.

DIMENSION	EXPLOIT	EXPLORE
Focus	efficiency and growth	exploration of new things and radicalness
Uncertainty	low	high
View of finances	safe haven with steady returns and dividends	risk-happy venture capital style with exponential earnings expectations
Culture and processes	linear version, projectable and predictable; low risk of failure	fast and iterative procedure, with fast learning cycles and adaptations arising from failures
Leadership, workflow, and skills	management with a strong focus on organization and planning, on efficient processes to save time and resources	management that focuses on curiosity and sees uncertainty as an opportunity, is able to discern patterns and navigate their teams between the overall picture and details elegantly

Table based on A. Osterwalder et al., *The Invincible Company* (2020)

Why do business ecosystems need to be designed?

Many ecosystems are being created without anybody planning it consciously. Typical examples are start-up ecosystems (see innovation ecosystems, page 63) that emerge due to changed market needs and technologies. Usually, similar start-ups settle in places that offer optimal framework conditions: Well-known examples of this are the FinTech clusters in Singapore or IT security companies in Tel Aviv. As soon as first signs of such systems crop up, a knowledge transfer takes place with universities and established companies. Regions or countries usually promote these conditions.

The business ecosystems in the focus of this book are consciously designed within the framework of design thinking for business growth and are dynamically developed according to the defined rules. The selection of actors and the cooperation among them consciously contributes to achieving a shared goal or creating something new. Many business ecosystems integrate actors from their own industry, non-industry companies, and start-ups and technology partners with a wide variety of characteristics and roles. The primary goal is to create an outstanding value proposition together and design a unique experience for the customer. Actors or platforms of existing ecosystems are also included for implementation.

The active design of business ecosystems requires that all actors involved are open and appreciate collaboration and transparency. Design thinking for business growth demands a new mindset, new methods, models, and procedures that support this goal in the best possible way. Skills and mindsets go far beyond the mastering of new technologies.

Ecosystem leadership, agile teams, and collaboration across organizational boundaries contribute to the success. This is very often a challenge for more traditional industries and companies, both in initialization and in participation in a business ecosystems. In terms of governance, this means that not only actors are integrated who contribute to the effective fulfillment of the underlying customer need. In addition, technology suppliers are also important in order to offer customer requirements smoothly via different channels and interfaces.

To the Point!

Opening up to the outside

In the interaction with other actors, the castle walls must be lowered. This is the only way to ensure that interaction and collaboration actually take place.

Creating transparency of skills and values

A well-functioning ecosystem knows the usefulness of the other actors for innovation and the sustainable realization of the value proposition.

Accepting new market roles in existing or new systems

In most cases, it is probably not possible to be an initiator of the system on one's own. Particularly in decentralized business ecosystems, it will be increasingly more important to assume different market roles in the ecosystem. The primary goal is to elicit a WOW! from the customer with a unique value proposition.

Why Initiators of Business Ecosystems Have the Ambition of Pursuing a Black Ocean Strategy

Differentiation is good – a unique value proposition and a configuration of the business ecosystem that no other system or company can copy is even better. That is the key ambition of a "black ocean" play: to design systems that have no more than three perceptible competitors in the form of companies or other business ecosystems. Companies playing in this league are Amazon and Alibaba in the area of e-commerce, Uber and Didi in the area of mobility, and Google and Apple in the area of operating systems for mobile devices. The examples of Alipay and WeChat Pay as dominating systems for a "black ocean" character are described on pages 300–305.

However, the development of these companies over time also shows how difficult it is to fill the "black ocean" position for a specific value proposition permanently. Uber, for instance, had at times over 80% of the market area (= black ocean). Then it lost considerably in the main market segment, resulting in a market area of around 50% in 2020. This shows how crucial it is to orchestrate a continuous advancement of the value proposition over time and set the right course as part of business ecosystem leadership. Uber has introduced a number of new subsegments in the market that aim at exploiting new customer needs in many ways. Services such as UberX, UberPool, UberEats, and UberMoto have been added in the last 10 years. Large-scale investments have been made in new technologies, some of which would completely disrupt the current business model, e.g. self-driving cars.

RED OCEAN

Existing markets,
strong competition

BLUE OCEAN

Undisputed markets,
low level of competition

BLACK OCEAN

Ecosystem-driven markets,
impossible to compete

In the case of Uber, it happens in the form of co-creation, by way of innovations and ideas coming from actors in the system and through close cooperation with vehicle manufacturers and other technology platforms. In addition, a black ocean strategy needs well-thought-out systems to give the various actors multiple incentives to cooperate with the business ecosystem. The Chinese competitor Didi, for example, as a mobility service provider offers its actors in the system many car-related services. They range from discounts on gas to discounts on new vehicles.

A back ocean strategy has the ambition to create complete new market areas by realizing a unique value propostion for previously unaddressable customer needs.

In the table below, the known advertising strategies for the development of business models in the form of a red and blue ocean strategy of W. Chan Kim and Renée Mauborgne are juxtaposed against the black ocean strategy.

RED OCEAN	BLUE OCEAN	BLACK OCEAN
Competition in the existing market	Creating new markets	Creating completely new market areas
Beating competitors	Avoiding competitors	Realizing a unique value proposition together with other actors (including competitors)
Exploiting the existing demand	Tapping new demand	Solve previously unaddressed customer problems and needs
Direct link between benefits and costs	Undoing the direct link between benefits and costs	Establishing new value streams, business models, and growth opportunities
Alignment of the overall system of the company's activities to the strategic decision in favor of differentiation or low costs	Alignment of the overall system of the company's activities to differentiation and low costs	Alignment of the overall system to co-creation, coevolution, and win-win situations for all actors in the business ecosystem

What a Business Ecosystem Is Not

The concept of ecosystem has assumed a somewhat inflationary character, and it seems as if any initiative in which two companies cooperate is referred to as a business ecosystem. The same applies to the countless platforms and marketplaces that have emerged over the last two decades. In many cases, they are central instances controlled by one company, which is the initiator. As described above, the next generation of business ecosystems needs to open up to the outside, to be transparent about skills and values, and most importantly, to accept new market roles in existing or new systems.

Various studies have shown that a majority of the companies searching for new growth paths would like to assume the role of initiator and orchestrator. This phenomenon can be clearly observed in the case of insurance companies and banks, nearly all of which initialize ecosystems on the subject of housing including renting, buying, and furnishing. Banks also like to serve their customers in the wealth management segment with ecosystem approaches revolving around the topic of wealth and security so as not to lose the customer interface to other players. All these topics are completely valid and have potential for successful ecosystems: coevolution symbiosis and co-competition with the goal of providing the customer in the best possible way with the best offer, the best experience, and the simplest interaction.

Ecosystem design is based on co-creation not only with potential customers but together with the other actors in the system as well. This means allocating the roles according to the capabilities in the system; establishing governance for innovation and growth; and, most importantly, not losing sight of the customers and their needs.

The initial considerations of a business ecosystem usually arise from customer problems that are solved within the framework of design thinking. During the search for a solution and with the implementation of the MVP, design teams frequently come to realize that they need additional actors for the aspired vision. It can also be observed that companies recognize the potential for collaboration as early as during the phase of co-creation to find an initial solution. Conventional considerations and competition analyses on business ecosystems performed as part of the development of strategic options are still dominant, though. In the first phase, projects are limited to a small circle in one's own enterprise. An opening takes place only at a later stage, i.e. the actual design of the business ecosystem.

Advanced business ecosystem orchestrators even aim to get invisible for customers by focusing on more emotional and powerful propositions than selling, for example, just financial products without any relation to the real customer needs and the aim to nudge customers into better financial habits.

Not every collaboration, partnership, and sourcing of partial services should be called an ecosystem, even if it sounds up-do-date and innovative!

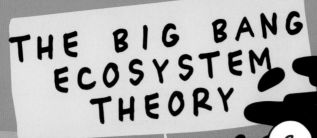

THE BIG BANG ECOSYSTEM THEORY

Administration	Art/culture
Automotive	Marketing/advertising/PR
Banks	Market research
Construction/architecture	Mechanical engineering
Consulting	Media
Education	Medical/pharmaceutical
Chemical	Medical technology
Service	Food/agriculture
Printing/packaging	HR and recruitment
IT	Law
Purchasing	Seminars/trade fairs
Electrical/electronics	Other industries
Energy	Sports/beauty
Finance	Tax consultants/auditors
R&D	Telecommunications
Health/social/care	Textile
Commerce	Tourism/catering
Crafts and trades	Clubs
Real estate	Transport/traffic/logistics
Industrial	Insurance
Internet	Public administration

Traditional industries and offerings are absorbed in new value propositions for customers.

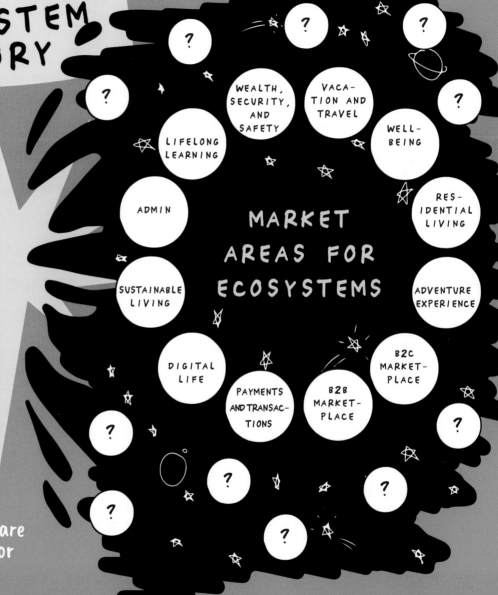

MARKET AREAS FOR ECOSYSTEMS

- WEALTH, SECURITY, AND SAFETY
- VACATION AND TRAVEL
- WELL-BEING
- LIFELONG LEARNING
- ADMIN
- RESIDENTIAL LIVING
- SUSTAINABLE LIVING
- ADVENTURE EXPERIENCE
- DIGITAL LIFE
- PAYMENTS AND TRANSACTIONS
- B2B MARKETPLACE
- B2C MARKETPLACE

To the
Point!

The ultimate challenge to the new generation of business leaders does not consist of designing isolated products but of contributing, in the framework of design thinking for business growth, to the shaping of business ecosystems in which different actors, capabilities, technologies, and platforms across existing industry boundaries create a unique experience for the customer in a simple, inspiring, and holistic way.

The generation of design thinking for business growth is ready to apply the new mindset, change business models, and use the levers for exponential growth.

DEFINITION

Evolution of Design in a Business Context

Before investigating different types of ecosystems in more detail, the timeline shows the evolution of design in a business context. Design thinking for business growth with a strong focus on the design of business ecosystems is the next logical step in the evolution of design thinking, systems thinking, and the shaping of business models. Not least due to the fact that business ecosystems don't create themselves.

The actors in such a system do not automatically connect and simply start collaborating radically. In reality, it is important to understand exactly who are potential ecosystem partners, the roles they are to assume, the skills they contribute, and how to deal with potential co-competition.

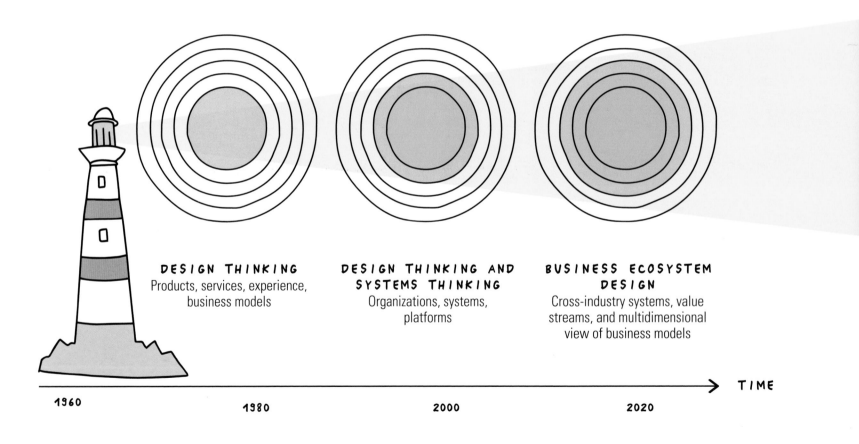

DESIGN THINKING
Products, services, experience, business models

DESIGN THINKING AND SYSTEMS THINKING
Organizations, systems, platforms

BUSINESS ECOSYSTEM DESIGN
Cross-industry systems, value streams, and multidimensional view of business models

TIME

1960   1980   2000   2020

Foundation for the Definition of Strategy and Technology Decisions

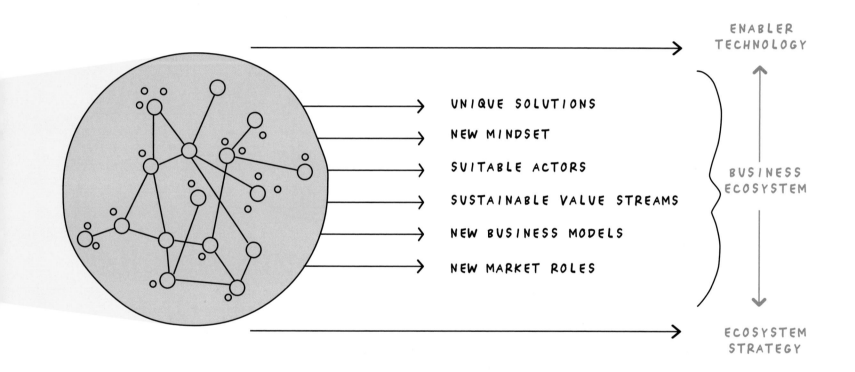

ENABLER TECHNOLOGY

UNIQUE SOLUTIONS

NEW MINDSET

SUITABLE ACTORS

SUSTAINABLE VALUE STREAMS

NEW BUSINESS MODELS

NEW MARKET ROLES

BUSINESS ECOSYSTEM

ECOSYSTEM STRATEGY

Design thinking for business growth and the examination of the business ecosystem often has an impact on the corporate strategy as well as on current and future technology decisions.

Business ecosystem design in the context of design thinking for business growth augments the known methods, tools, and mindsets that are applied today in the context of design thinking and systems thinking. Business ecosystem design and many other design ideas reflect the intention of applying the mindset not only to the design of products and services but to the solution of problems that affect existing systems as well. This includes, for instance, initiatives that aim at applying design thinking to political systems and communities and solving problems that afflict our world. Business ecosystem design scrutinizes existing systems and, through multiple design loops, creates systems that move beyond existing and known boundaries. What's important here is the "design lens," which is enshrined in design thinking, the design thinking, and systems thinking mindset as well as the focus on the customers and their needs. The customer always takes center stage, even if the view changes over the design cycle and the interaction with other actors in the system is more pronounced in the design of the ecosystem. In addition to increasing the frequency of customer interactions, the focus on the exploitation of network effects is crucial for scaling.

Three varying "design lenses," from problem solution to the design of a business ecosystem all the way to the methods for the realization of exponential growth, are presented in detail on pages 172–284.

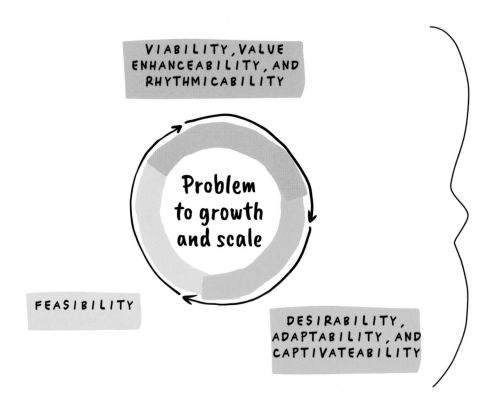

 It is important to point out that the transitions between design lenses are fluid, and a sharp delineation is not possible. Depending on the resolution level of prototypes, MVPs, and MVEs, steps can be accelerated or skipped.

Start ↘

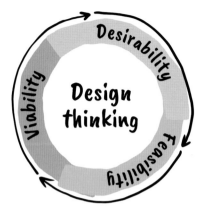

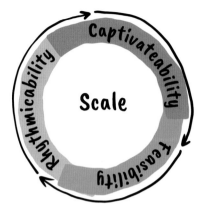

Scale

- **Desirability** – focusing on the customers and their needs
- **Viability** – creation of an innovative and sustainable business model
- **Feasibility** – use of up-to-date, effective, and applicable enabler technologies

- **Desirability** – validation of customer needs on the basis of individual functions and experience
- **Viability** – validation of the business model and value of the offering
- **Feasibility** – testing and validation of selected technology components

- **Adaptability** – focusing on the needs of the actors and their ability to create a value proposition together
- **Value enhanceability** – shaping sustainable value streams and benefits for all actors in the system
- **Feasibility** – specification of technology components and interfaces for the realization of an ecosystem approach

- **Captivateability** – focus on increasing the frequency of customer interaction, share of wallet, and retention to the system
- **Rhythmicability** – exploitation of network effects and scale effects
- **Feasibility** – building out, professionalization, and leverage of the technology components

VISION/FINAL PROTOTYPE

MVP

MVE

BLACK OCEAN

Solution Maturity in Design Thinking for Business Growth

While **feasibility** infuses all design lenses, **desirability + viability** expand into **value enhanceability + adaptability** in the business ecosystem design lens. For exponential growth, **rhythmicability + captivateability** are key. Dynamic systems then come full circle, and we're back at design thinking because customer needs are decisive for the expansion of the value proposition.

Technical feasibility normally does not pose a problem any longer today. Obstacles can be statutory provisions or outmoded core applications that are not compatible with new technologies.

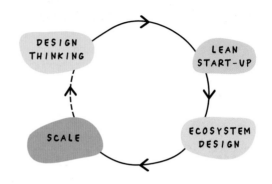

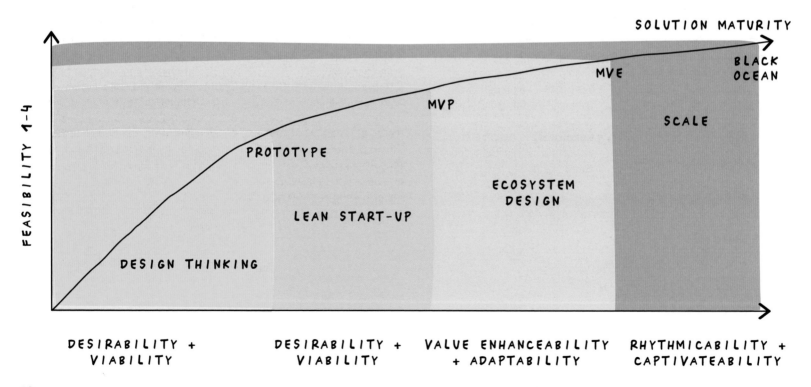

What Types of Ecosystems Are There?

The term ecosystem is used in many ways. Unfortunately, there is no uniform definition based on today's knowledge. We will describe three forms of ecosystems that are part of business ecosystem design. The well-known definitions of (business) ecosystems are often based on the ideas from the 1990s (e.g. Moore, 1996) or reflections on the Internet economy after 2000 (e.g. Stähler, 2002; Zerdick et al., 2001). Some of these approaches have been picked up again in current investigations of the platform economy, e.g. by Kapoor and Agarwal (2017) or Adner (2017).

The threefold division presented here should be understood as a first step for navigating through the conceptual confusion in terms of ecosystems. It also facilitates communication in dealing with other actors because systems can be given a clear name. For the purposes of this book, we divide ecosystems into **innovation ecosystems, knowledge and information ecosystems,** and **transaction and data ecosystems.** A key term in the book is **"business ecosystem design."** Which may refer to one or several manifestations of an ecosystem.

An artful business ecosystem makes use of the resources of every accessible and suitable system as well as of all relevant actors to generate added value for the customer and ecosystem partners.

Innovation ecosystems The purpose of these types of ecosystems is to develop new products, services, or processes through co-creation between all actors. Such initiatives often gather in clusters, e.g. FinTech in Singapore or the IT security cluster in Tel Aviv. The crypto valley in Switzerland or Silicon Valley are other examples. These ecosystems are sometimes supported by government organizations, and various investors such as angel investors and venture companies finance the initiatives and projects at different times.

Knowledge and information ecosystems Ecosystems in this category exploit knowledge and information resources to create value. The knowledge and information sources are usually decentralized and create synergies by swapping values. This large group includes research institutions, universities, and information service providers, trustworthy and secure sources that make information available for automated chains of activities.

Transaction and data ecosystems Transaction ecosystems are based on technological platforms, which coordinate various offerings, technical interfaces, and technologies. Based on such technology stacks are data ecosystems that pursue the goal of combining different data of customers into a centralized or decentralized system to allow a synchronized and integrated 720-degree view of each individual customer. This comprehensive view of data facilitates better decisions regarding price, operation, and marketing. It frequently results in new business models in which synergies are generated even in collaboration with competitors and companies completely outside the industry.

Business ecosystem design in the context of design thinking for business growth is primarily characterized by the fact that a value proposition is developed together with other actors in the system and that customer needs are at the center of all activities. The business ecosystem exploits the resources from all accessible ecosystems or individual actors that are useful for the fulfillment of the value proposition to create added value.

The business ecosystem consciously involves the actors in already known innovation ecosystems, knowledge, information, and data ecosystems as well as existing suppliers, competitors, and non-industry companies. Usually, a company is the initiator of such systems that later exist as traditional partner networks, centralized systems, or decentralized ecosystems depending on the specific design. Consortia, communities, cooperatives, or other forms of business are founded.

Business ecosystems aim at integrating the actors in the best possible way so that all have an advantage. Collaboration does not exclude competition among actors in specific areas. Sustainable business ecosystems are orchestrated market structures that combine flexibility and control. This is achieved by the regular adjustment of value streams, components, and a gradual expansion of the range of offers.

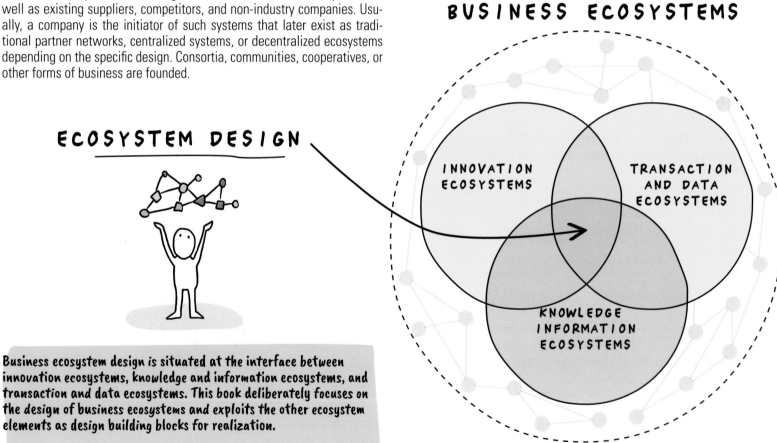

ECOSYSTEM DESIGN

BUSINESS ECOSYSTEMS

INNOVATION ECOSYSTEMS

TRANSACTION AND DATA ECOSYSTEMS

KNOWLEDGE INFORMATION ECOSYSTEMS

Business ecosystem design is situated at the interface between innovation ecosystems, knowledge and information ecosystems, and transaction and data ecosystems. This book deliberately focuses on the design of business ecosystems and exploits the other ecosystem elements as design building blocks for realization.

Business ecosystem design has the ambition of being an integrated discipline, gearing the system to the needs of the customers. Collaboration and orchestration are to create systems that grow exponentially and are dynamic. They can be described as collaborative and tend to be more decentralized.

	DESCRIPTION OF PROCEDURE	MANAGEMENT, ORGANIZATION AMBITION	OUTPUT
BUSINESS ECOSYSTEMS AS AN INTEGRATED DISCIPLINE	collaborative and decentralized	**Initiate and orchestrate** ambition: exponential growth	The value proposition of the ecosystem is aimed at a specific target group and their needs. The systems are dynamic and respond agilely to changes.
TRANSACTION AND DATA ECOSYSTEMS	value driven and data driven	**Build and monetize** ambition: network effects and scaling	Automation and standardization enable the scaling of general value propositions and the collection of data for new products, services, and value propositions.
INNOVATION ECOSYSTEMS	open innovation and business model innovation	**Invent and scale** ambition: differentiation and technology leadership	Predominant output is business model innovations or driven by new technologies; sometimes clustering around key technologies.
KNOWLEDGE AND INFORMATION ECOSYSTEMS	collaboration with qualified organizations and research institutions	**Fund and execute** ambition: intellectual property (IP) and negotiation power	New knowledge emerging through research or based on validated information of trusted entities.

What Roles Can Be Assumed in Ecosystems?

The roles in ecosystems are varied, and so are the respective names they are given. For this reason, a rough and easy-to-understand classification of roles is made at the top level as part of the definition of ecosystems. The key element is the CUSTOMER and their needs. In most cases, an INITIATOR of a business ecosystem sees a market opportunity or wants to develop it due to new or changed customer needs. The ideas are often sparked by new technologies such as cloud computing, IoT, and blockchain. The role of ORCHESTRATOR is still organized centrally in many ecosystems. Depending on the type of system, it may also be decentralized. Often, the initiator takes on this role or else an actor who participates in the system in terms of capital and has better abilities, reach, and possibilities to fill out this role. The other ACTORS in the system contribute to providing the value proposition for the customer, advance it on the basis of the developed rules, and make it available with direct or indirect customer access. It is important that all actors in the system benefit from working and contributing in the system. The capabilities of SUPPLIERS play an equally important role in the implementation and operation of the system. They have no direct impact on rendering the value proposition. Instead, they are enablers for the ecosystem or the necessary technical platforms or decentralized systems. Depending on the specific ecosystem, OTHER PLAYERS can perform different tasks. Such players may be public entities that receive information or validate transactions.

As shown on the grid to the right, the respective roles have a direct or indirect benefit from being a part of the business ecosystem. They are either directly responsible for creating the value proposition or they deliver enabler technologies for the system.

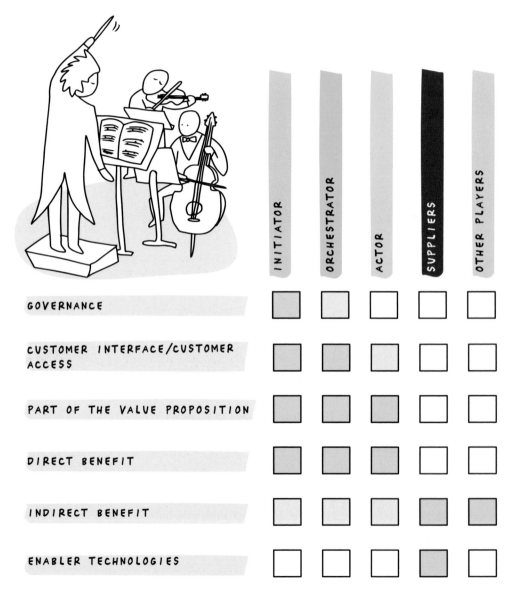

	INITIATOR	ORCHESTRATOR	ACTOR	SUPPLIERS	OTHER PLAYERS
GOVERNANCE	■	■			
CUSTOMER INTERFACE/CUSTOMER ACCESS	■	■	■		
PART OF THE VALUE PROPOSITION	■	■	■		
DIRECT BENEFIT	■	■	■		
INDIRECT BENEFIT	■	■	■	■	■
ENABLER TECHNOLOGIES				■	

CUSTOMER

- Procures service
- Interacts with the ecosystem on a recurring basis
- Shares data about behavior and transactions
- Gets an direct/indirect added value

INITIATOR

- Recognizes customer needs and market opportunity
- Starts initialization of activities
- Provides the budget for initial prototypes and MVP
- Switches to the role of orchestrator or becomes an actor

ORCHESTRATOR

- Coordinates activities
- Defines principles and rules
- Defines framework conditions for growth
- Realizes sustainable governance

ACTOR

- Has skills or offerings that are integrated
- Renders service or partial services of the value proposition
- Innovates on the basis of the principles and rules
- Connects parts of her activities over the course of the project

SUPPLIER

- Delivers technology or technology components
- Provides software or integration layers
- Delivers infrastructure and ensures connectivity
- No customer relationship

OTHER PLAYERS

- Often recipients of information
- Serve as an oracle for the validation of data in automated processes
- Usually no direct customer interface

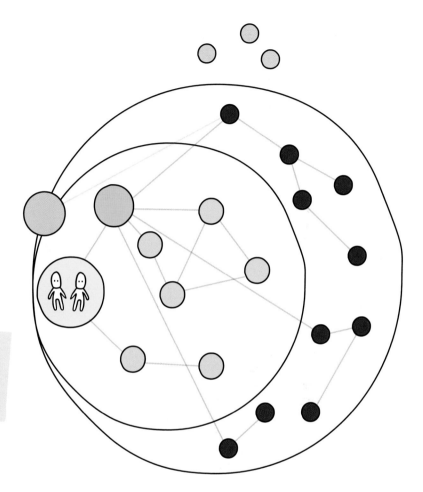

Five to six roles are often sufficient for the definition of a business ecosystem. These roles are normally in charge of different tasks and functions, and their proximity to the value proposition to be provided differs.

How Does a Value Proposition Work?

The key element for a business ecosystem is the value proposition. It is the prerequisite for valuable customer interaction and must be jointly supported and further developed by the actors in the system. A value proposition is embedded in the respective value streams that make a major contribution to the provision of the product or service. This in turn is done in the exchange of value creation and value gain of the individual actors. In complex and dynamic systems, the ecosystem as a whole takes various risks, and so does each individual actor as soon as they become a part of the system.

RISKS

These are risks taken by an entire ecosystem or an actor responsible for a specific value proposition. For example, risks of performance guarantee, risks of outsourcing, and compliance with regulations. **Risk types:** operational, performance-related, financial, activities of other actors due to incentives, or in terms of the system itself or its dynamics.

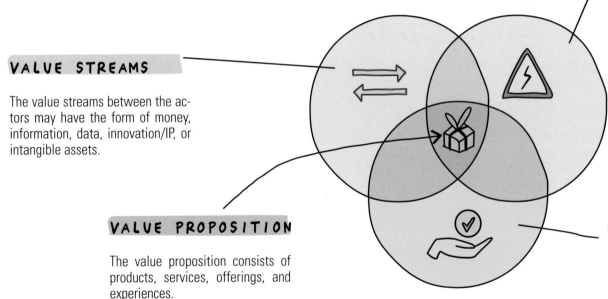

VALUE STREAMS

The value streams between the actors may have the form of money, information, data, innovation/IP, or intangible assets.

VALUE PROPOSITION

The value proposition consists of products, services, offerings, and experiences.

PERFORMANCE DELIVERY

Delivery in the form of activities, resources, and skills required for the fulfillment and delivery of the value proposition.

What Is the Interplay of Value Streams, Value Creation, and Value Gain?

The value creation networks in business ecosystems consist of the actors described above. They often have complementary ranges or compete with one another. Together, they deliver the value proposition described.

Understanding the relationships of the individual actors and their value streams is enormously important for the design of such systems. Only those business ecosystems that create recurring or sustainable values for the actors survive and grow. This type of value design is part of the definition of an MVE and one of the most complex tasks in the design of business ecosystems.

Business ecosystems link actors to value streams. The actors render their added value in a self-developed and orchestrated coexistence.

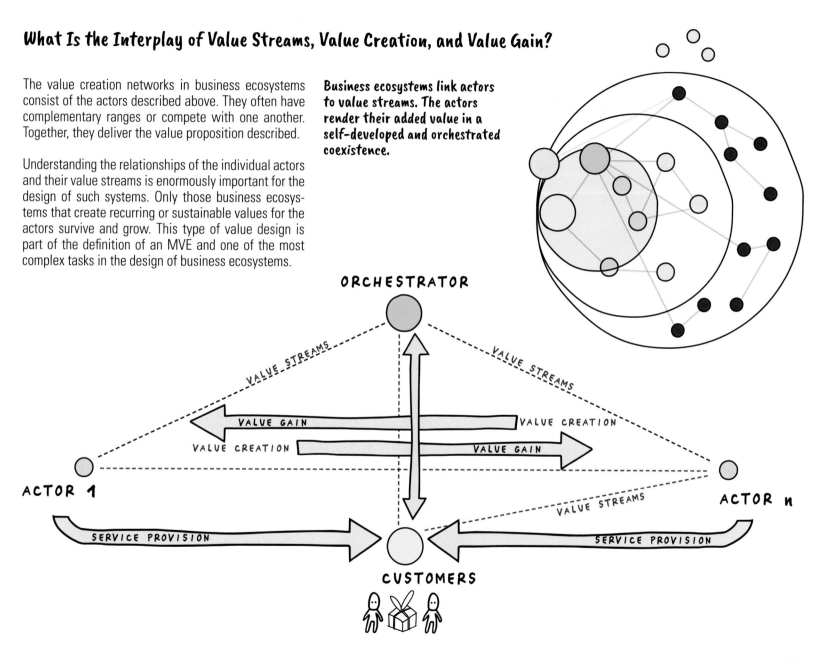

ORCHESTRATOR

VALUE STREAMS

VALUE STREAMS

VALUE GAIN

VALUE CREATION

VALUE CREATION

VALUE GAIN

ACTOR 1

ACTOR n

VALUE STREAMS

SERVICE PROVISION

SERVICE PROVISION

CUSTOMERS

Biological versus Man-Made Ecosystems

Man-made business ecosystems use biological ecosystems (symbiosis, coevolution, cooperation) as an analogy, but their character is quite different in many aspects. A biological ecosystem has one or several states of equilibrium, in which relatively stable conditions exist, and the exchange of populations and nutrients is maintained at a certain level. But the equilibrium is rarely ideal from the point of view of all species. Biological ecosystems operate in cooperation and in competition. Species must correspondingly adapt to remain viable in the long term. This is also basically true for business ecosystems. However, participation in a business ecosystem requires incentives, i.e. market participants will only participate in a business ecosystem if they get something out of it, if they are correspondingly sponsored, or if they have no choice but to change owing to disruption. The design of business ecosystems follows the positive principle of co-creation, value generation for all actors, and a value proposition that is supported by all. Many integrated companies with rigid supply chains have so far not seen a need to change. They operate in special markets and don't sense any threat from new technologies and disruptive offerings. You can compare it to biological ecosystems on an island. Species can live their role here (e.g. birds that no longer fly) since they don't have to fear predators from whom they must flee. Similar to biological ecosystems, the speed of changing and adapting depends a great deal on the size of companies. Some living creatures adapt more quickly to new circumstances such as global warming; some do it more slowly.

The question is the same for living creatures and companies: How quickly can a transformation be carried out, and is there enough time to survive?

Especially large and slowly growing species with a long life span need longer to adapt to new conditions in a biological ecosystem. The analogy to a company is obvious.

"A business ecosystem is just like the natural ecosystem; first, needs to be understood, then, needs to be well planned, and also needs to be thoughtfully renewed as well."

– Pearl Zhu, author of the "Digital Master" book series

Ecology and Biology as a Blueprint

A lot of people have a hard time thinking and acting in business ecosystems since – right with the initial ideas on participation or the building of a business ecosystem – they apply old patterns. In the past, companies were inevitably centralized and hierarchically organized. Today, thanks to new technologies and networked communication, new and more decentralized systems can be realized.

Thus ecology and biology present various blueprints that are useful for the design of business ecosystems and at the same time trigger some of the mindshifts described above. Key concepts such as symbiosis and coevolution are key inasmuch as they need to be increasingly mastered in writing about management and by companies.

Co-creation means nothing more than the joint exploitation of resources and mutual fertilization of ideas in the intertidal zones. The shared work of different actors on the system constitutes the foundation for the realization of unique value propositions and innovation.

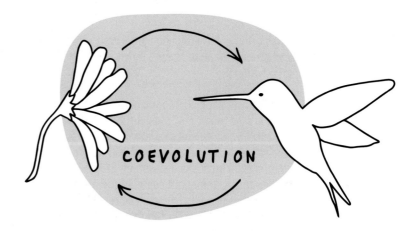

COEVOLUTION

One example of symbioses and coevolution is the collaboration between Apple and Goldman Sachs. Both companies have gradually expanded their activities in the affluent market segment. The affluent target group is, of course, specially coveted; after all, they have financial assets between $250,000 and $1 million at their disposal, depending on the country and the bank. The collaboration could constitute the basis for a larger ecosystem that services the segment of the well-to-do and other target groups. It doesn't take much imagination to see how the individual elements of Apple and Goldman Sachs lead to a symbiosis in an ecosystem, from which, over time, a unique customer experience for wealthy banking customers emerges.

Like living creatures in any biological system, companies can coevolve.

Coevolution of Apple and Goldman Sachs

New business ecosystems often emerge among actors who, at first glance, are not related but complement one another and develop together. At this point, we can speak of coevolution.

Goldman Sachs stands for private banking and the handling of big deals on Wall Street; Apple represents the market for lifestyle smartphones, tablets, and computers, including their own business ecosystem for applications, music, and other digital content. Digital content is one of the important future value streams in the Apple business ecosystem. Step by step, Apple has built out these services to accommodate customer needs, consciously anchoring Apple customers in them, and it becomes more difficult over time for Apple customers to leave this ecosystem. Another anchor is the Apple Card that integrates digital payment options (Apple Pay).

Goldman Sachs is a big name on Wall Street, but up until a few years ago it was not active in the credit card business. The trust of Goldman Sachs and the technology lifestyle approach of Apple made it possible to conquer new market areas at a low risk. While Goldman Sachs took care of the handling and processing in the background, new customer contacts emerge for Goldman Sachs' Marcus Bank. Apple customers have additional benefits, e.g. the reimbursement of up to 3% of the purchase amount of transactions in the Apple Store for digital and physical goods and services. According to Apple, the data has so far not been analyzed and used for advertising purposes.

David Solomon, CEO of Goldman Sachs, called the bank's launch of the Apple Card "the most successful credit card launch ever."

A TRADITIONAL INVESTMENT BANKING INSTITUTE

Goldman Sachs is an investment banking and securities trading firm headquartered in New York. Customers of Goldman Sachs include major companies and governments as well as high net worth individuals (HNWI) who previously primarily availed themselves of the bank's consulting services for mergers and acquisitions, asset management, and brokerage. Since 2018, Goldman Sachs' Marcus Bank has been offering fee-less private loans, interest-bearing online savings accounts, and certificates of deposits.

A LEADING TECHNOLOGY COMPANY

Apple is a technology group with a hardware and a software division that develops computers, smartphones, and consumer electronics as well as proprietary operating systems and application software and provides them to its ecosystem. In addition, Apple handles music, movies, and other digital content. The Apple Card launched in 2019 has been developed for use with Apple Pay on Apple devices such as the iPhone, iPad, Apple Watch, and Macs.

= COEVOLUTION

Example of Coevolution

APPLE PAY - 2014
- Mobile contactless payment system and digital wallet service
- Paying for products and services via near field communication at the POS (in person, via iOS apps, or the Internet)

MARCUS - 2016
- Online platform for open credits and savings accounts for private customers
- Fee-less, fixed-income private loans, high-yield online savings account and certificates of deposit
- Marcus is one building block of an integral and digital wealth product that is currently being integrated into investment management

APPLE CARD - 2019
- Physical credit cards as well as credit cards integrated in the Wallet app
- No user fees
- 1 to 3% daily refund of the cash back by payout to the Apple Cash Card (in the Wallet app)
- Real-time interest estimate
- Real-time protection from fraud
- Interactive functions such as color-coded expense overviews in the Wallet app

U.S. ASSET MANAGEMENT FOR THE "MASS AFFLUENT" MARKET - 2019
- Acquisition of United Capital Financial Advisors, LLC
- Development of an investment platform that realizes interactions with customers via Marcus

APPLE SIGN-IN - 2019
- Secure identification for web services
- Disposable e-mail addresses prevent third parties from reading the Apple ID
- Protection of user data
- Option for anonymous surfing on the Internet

STAKE IN ELINVAR - 2019
- German start-up, founded by former Deutsche Bank bankers
- Digital platform that helps traditional lenders offer their services online
- Goldman holds 13.9% of the stake in the start-up

APPLE CRYPTO KIT - 2019
- Swift API, cryptographic developer tool for creating more security functions for applications with improved support and user-friendliness
- Options for hashing, public and private key generation and key exchange, and integration of encryption in iOS applications

STAKE IN NUTMEG - 2019
- Secure identification for web services
- Disposable e-mail addresses prevent third parties from reading the Apple ID
- Protection of user data
- Option for anonymous surfing on the Internet

What Levels of Complexity of Business Systems Do We Know?

A distinction has already been made between two states, namely stable and agile systems (see page 40). Stable systems can be found in integrated companies with mostly static customer-supplier chains. Agile systems are more open capital-economy markets without government regulations, in which customers collect and consume various products and services according to their needs. Lying in-between are various partner and business networks all the way to decentralized ecosystems.

There are different manifestations within these business systems that are also of varying complexity. New skills are needed for initiation and participation. Over the last few decades, the evolution of business ecosystems has been driven mainly by new technologies. Key technologies were the Internet, blockchain, and big data analytics, reflecting an evolution from simple to complex structures. With respect to the complexity of

business ecosystems, a differentiation can be made between **focused partner networks**, **centralized business networks**, and **decentralized ecosystems**.

The focused partner networks should be assigned to the category of partnerships and value chains since they don't have the character of a real business ecosystem. We will briefly describe them, though, to show the differences.

A business ecosystem goes beyond traditional customer-supplier relationships. It includes all actors who may have a direct or indirect impact on the strategy, sales, products, or capabilities.

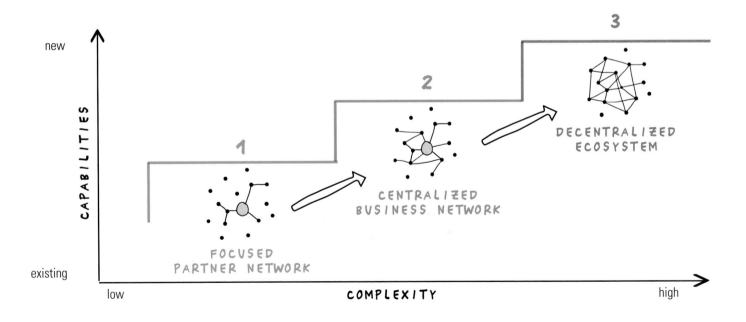

1 ———————

Focused partner networks The most basic form of a business system are value chains, which enjoyed their heyday during the time of the second industrial revolution. Individual market participants focused on their core capabilities, and more products were produced via a value chain. Later (in the third stage of the industrial revolution), activities were expanded to other critical elements in companies. A typical example is outsourcing the operation of the IT infrastructure. This led to standardized infrastructure-as-a-service (IaaS) offerings or software-as-a-service (SaaS) offerings. Usually, the collaboration is based on SLAs. The prices for the services are calculated based on the power relations of the sourcing partners.

2 ———————

Centralized business networks These systems gained in importance in the age of the Internet. The so-called platform economy is characterized by network effects, scaling, and APIs. New business models, e.g. based on data, were realized and monetized by market participants in interactions on the platforms. This form of collaboration is of medium complexity, and most companies know the usual marketplaces or initiatives where they could join. Most often, these centralized business networks work on existing power relations and are based on familiar business models. An initiator of a centralized business network must also expend some thought on how to involve the other actors and what advantages they have and on the business model that allows participants to earn money in the system. In other words, with the platform economy, the multidimensional view of the business models has become a decisive factor for success of the respective systems. Successful companies in the platform economy rely on these levers, e.g. Amazon, Apple, Uber, and Spotify. Moreover, a mindset based on the framework and working methods of design thinking dominates in such companies.

3 ———————

Business ecosystems with a decentralized character Currently, a transition to more decentralized systems can be seen. These systems normally have an orchestrator and meet the customer changed needs. They are very complex and require new capabilities in terms of the design of the business ecosystem, orchestration, and governance, including new leadership skills. The multidimensional view of the business models is becoming a design element critical to success. It makes it possible to realize ecosystems that provide all actors in the system with the necessary benefits. In addition, this view detects potential for exponential growth.

Business ecosystems expand the range of offerings and flexibility for customers by scaling via the actors in the system. Service provision is usually distributed. Customers move freely, and systems are open. This does not exclude two actors providing the same service in an ecosystem. Actors can differentiate themselves through service scope, quality, and pricing.

Transition and Evolution toward the New Business Models and Growth Potential

In addition to the capabilities and complexity of the systems, they can also be plotted on a timeline. The transition to increasingly decentralized ecosystems can be currently seen in the numerous initiatives in which these approaches have either been already realized or are being experimentally tested for new value propositions.

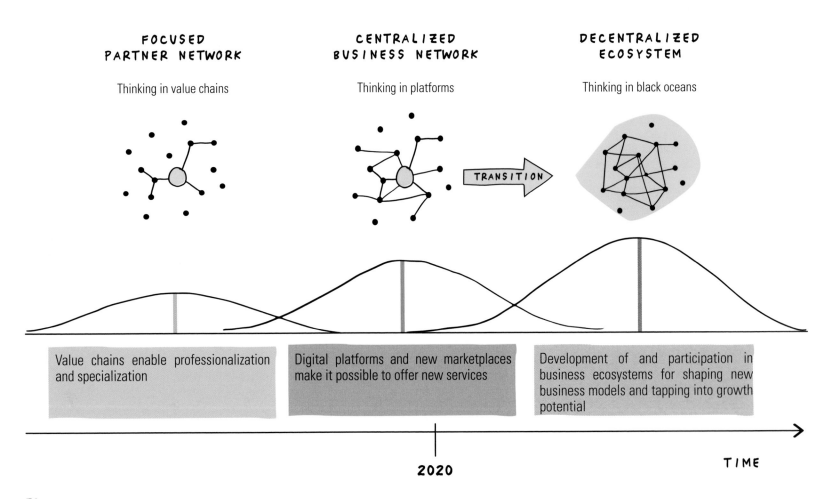

FOCUSED PARTNER NETWORK

Thinking in value chains

CENTRALIZED BUSINESS NETWORK

Thinking in platforms

TRANSITION

DECENTRALIZED ECOSYSTEM

Thinking in black oceans

Value chains enable professionalization and specialization

Digital platforms and new marketplaces make it possible to offer new services

Development of and participation in business ecosystems for shaping new business models and tapping into growth potential

2020

TIME

Integration in the Strategy

For many companies, commitment in a business ecosystem is only of value if this ambition becomes part of the corporate strategy and is linked to the core business. This often is quite a balancing act since an ecosystem strategy is fundamentally different from a traditional view of strategy. Successful ecosystem strategies try to link company values instead of protecting them; they lower the barriers of entry to the system for other actors; and finally, they create a value proposition together with other actors to distinguish their services and products from others'.

The acceleration of this collaboration and its technologies open up new opportunities for superior business ecosystems. Instead of aiming for higher sales of existing products and services, the ecosystem focuses on the customer and their needs

Against this backdrop, we will go into the topic of strategy and ecosystems in greater detail tied in with design thinking for business growth on pages 100–148.

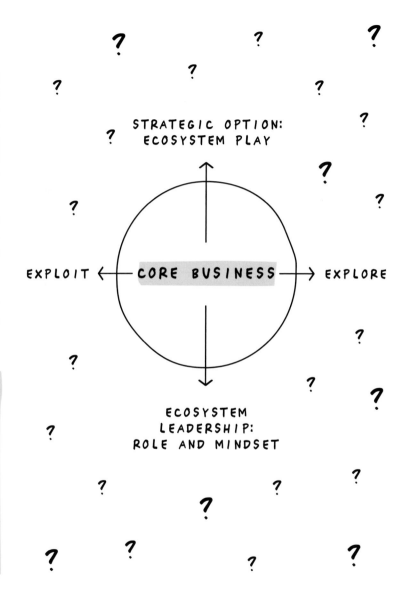

Key questions are:

- What do you want to achieve with the participation in or the initialization of a business ecosystem?
- How can a balanced portfolio be realized using both EXPLOIT and EXPLORE?
- How can existing skills and capabilities, partnerships, and not least customer access be brought to an ecosystem play?
- What skills and leadership approaches need to be rebuilt to assume different roles in an ecosystem?
- How should governance be organized?
- What are the options of scaling and realizing exponential growth?

Learning from Successful Companies

Companies that already applied design thinking for business growth in the platform economy phase make use of principles that contribute to their current and future success. The values and leadership principles demonstrate recurring patterns in the case of Apple, Amazon, Google, Tencent, and Alibaba. Many of these statements are analogous to the design thinking and systems thinking mindset, the basis for the design of business ecosystems.

The most important element for the aforementioned examples of companies is customer orientation. In the case of Amazon, the customer has top priority: "100% customer orientation." Google's set of values also puts the user first.

Companies such as Tencent explicitly focus on the initialization of business ecosystems. For one, open collaboration with other actors is key; a second principal point is the realization of benefits for all actors in the system, based on the multidimensional view of the business models. Tencent sees the basis for the successful implementation of such business systems in cooperative projects with other actors that aim at enabling a win-win situation and exponential growth. Alibaba's mission of "102 years" means longer-term thinking and building a lasting relationship with other participants in the business ecosystem. Alibaba supports competitors and other innovators at market entry, who would not be able to offer their products globally on their own.

APPLE'S 7 LEADERSHIP PRINCIPLES

- **Great products:** Design great products that will change the world.
- **Simple, not complex:** Simplicity is better than complexity.
- **Excellence:** Participation in markets in which a significant contribution can be made.
- **Say no:** Say no to thousands of projects while focusing on a few that are truly important and meaningful to us.
- **Collaboration:** Close collaboration, cross pollination (mutual inspiration) to be innovative in a unique way.
- **Accept mistakes:** Excellence throughout the company, honesty in handling mistakes, and courage to change.
- **Ecosystems:** Ownership and control of the primary technologies behind the products and services.

(Source: Apple's core values according to CEO Tim Cook: https://thinkmarketingmagazine.com/apple-core-values/)

AMAZON'S 16 LEADERSHIP PRINCIPLES

- Customer obsession
- Ownership
- Invent and simplify
- (Leaders) are right, a lot
- Learn and be curious
- Hire and develop the best
- Insist on the highest standards
- Think big
- Bias for action
- Frugality
- Earn trust
- Dive deep
- Have backbone; disagree and commit
- Deliver results
- Strive to be earth's best employer
- Success and scale bring broad responsibility

(Source: https://www.amazon.jobs/principles)

GOOGLE'S SET OF VALUES

- The user is in first place. Everything else follows automatically.
- It's best to do something right.
- Fast is better than slow.
- Democracy on the Internet works.
- You don't always sit at your desk when you need an answer.
- Making money without harming anybody.
- There is always more information somewhere.
- Information is needed across all borders.
- Being respectable without wearing a suit.
- Good is not good enough.

(Source: https://www.google.com/about)

TENCENT'S CULTURE

- **The customer takes center stage:** Listen to customers, meet their needs, and exceed their expectations.
- **All employees are encouraged continuously to improve the company's reputation:** Employees are proud to be employed by Tencent.
- **Grow sustainably and be a recognized player in the digital economy:** Cooperative projects with other actors in the business ecosystem that are geared to win-win constellations constitute the basis of our success.

- **Acting as a responsible corporate citizen:** Making an active contribution to the development of society as a whole.
- **Internet is like electricity:** Provision of basic services that make life easier and more enjoyable for customers/users.
- **Address different needs of different users in different regions:** Offering unique products and services tailored to needs.
- **Building an intact business ecosystem based on open collaboration with partners:** The basic idea is always to strive for a win-win situation for all actors.
- **Business philosophy:** User needs are our first priority.

(Source: https://www.tencent.com/en-us/about.html)

ALIBABA'S VISION, MISSION, AND VALUES

- Make it as easy as possible for customers to do business anytime, anywhere.
- Be first choice with regard to platforms on which data is shared.
- Be a company that has the happiest employees.
- Exist for at least 102 years.

- **Customers first:** The interests of users and paying customers have top priority.
- **Working as a team:** Employees work on teams, are involved in decision-making, and are committed to the team's goal.
- **Anticipate change:** The industry is developing dynamically. Employees are flexible, innovative, and adaptable.
- **Demonstrate integrity:** Trust is an essential element in an ecosystem, and employees comply with the highest standards of integrity and meet all obligations.
- **Be passionate:** Whether serving the customers or developing new services and products – employees are encouraged to act with passion.
- **Show dedication:** A great deal of commitment to understand and meet the needs of Chinese and global customers and SMEs.

(Source: https://www.alibabagroup.com/en/about/overview)

To the Point!

Taking the comparison with biology, an ecosystem refers to an adaptive, resilient, and extensive network of organisms. These organisms are in various interrelationships with one another — from symbiosis to collaboration all the way to competition.

In the business context, business ecosystems are relatively free cooperative projects of several company actors that collaborate beyond industry boundaries. The networks can be physical and real or else virtual.

When designing such systems, various "design lenses" from the design thinking for business growth toolbox are helpful. They are based on design thinking, lean start-up, systems thinking, and scale mindset.

Companies from the platform economy and existing marketplaces provide indications for which values, leadership principles, and visions contribute to the success of complex systems.

EXERCISE

START THINKING IN ECOSYSTEMS. NOW!

A 60-Minute Introduction to the Design of Ecosystems

Exercise

The basic principle of design thinking for business growth can be understood best through experience. The following exercise demonstrates selected steps for examining the design of a business ecosystem. The starting point to this exercise could not be better since a team of experts has done good groundwork and has already solved a customer problem. In addition, the solution was selected from various options, and the problem/market fit was tested by an MVP (minimum viable product). This is where you come in with your design thinking for business growth. The task is to design a suitable ecosystem that can be tested in the form of an MVE (minimum viable ecosystem) in the market. As you can see from an article in the *Pharmacy Today* journal, the selected design challenge is taken from the health care sector. It could have been a challenge from the area of media, financial services, agriculture, or pharmaceuticals since business ecosystem design is currently needed in many industries to solve customer problems and develop efficient systems.

The exercise should give you a sense for the design of a business ecosystem. It shows how a simple business ecosystem can be developed in 60 minutes. The steps are flagged with a time indication so the exercise can be completed in the specified time — timeboxed. The book has little space for writing, so it's best for you to take a notepad, pencil, and a couple of Post-its to start the exercise. Solution ideas are outlined below the free spaces. They aren't by any means model solutions; there are countless ways to solve this ecosystem challenge.

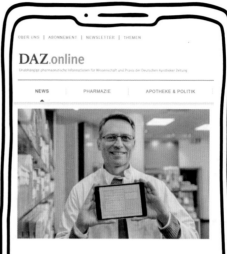

Although there is no fixed date yet for the launch of a nationwide application of digital prescriptions, the e-prescription is definitely in the offing. Pharmacies need new hardware and software, the market of patient apps is already booming, software firms and data centers need to change their processes and products.

> A business ecosystem goes beyond traditional customer-supplier relationships. It includes all actors who may have a direct or indirect impact on the strategy, sales, products, or capabilities.

(Source: DAZ Online [www.deutsche-apotheker-zeitung.de]
Photo: imago images / Westend 61)

The Original Design Challenge

Exercise

6 MIN
Start: Read this double page

"How can a better digital health care experience be designed for patients that simultaneously allows for cost reductions in the health care system?"

After various iterations, in-depth interviews, and user interactions, it has become obvious that patients want a simple way of handling prescriptions. The person (user profile) delivers information on the pains, gains, and jobs to be done. The needs of patients constituted the basis for the development of different prototypes and the construction of a minimum viable product (MVP), which is shown on the opposite page.

Persona: Current situation of a typical patient (user profile)

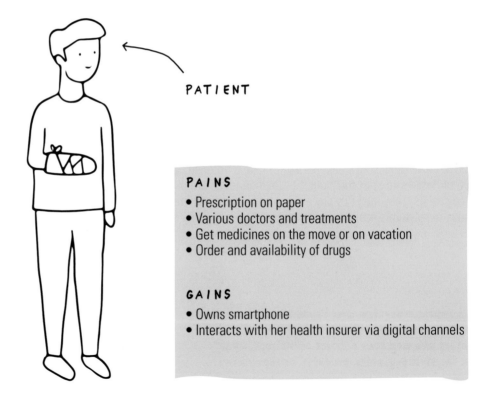

PATIENT

JOBS TO BE DONE

When patients are at the doctor's office, they want to know whether the prescribed drugs are incompatible with other active ingredients so that they can take the medication without worries.

When the patient leaves the doctor's office, they want to get the drug from the closest pharmacy so their pain is quickly alleviated and healing begins as soon as possible.

If the patient has an annual prescription, they want to receive their medicine during vacation or when they're on the move.

PAINS
- Prescription on paper
- Various doctors and treatments
- Get medicines on the move or on vacation
- Order and availability of drugs

GAINS
- Owns smartphone
- Interacts with her health insurer via digital channels

Critical items diagram: The vision prototype and the tested MVP for an electronic prescription, based on critical experiences and functions for patients/users:

Exercise

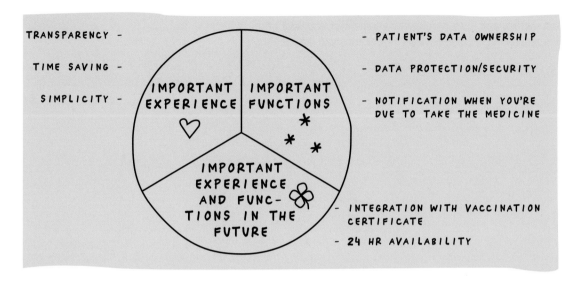

TRANSPARENCY –

TIME SAVING –

SIMPLICITY –

IMPORTANT EXPERIENCE

IMPORTANT FUNCTIONS

IMPORTANT EXPERIENCE AND FUNCTIONS IN THE FUTURE

– PATIENT'S DATA OWNERSHIP

– DATA PROTECTION/SECURITY

– NOTIFICATION WHEN YOU'RE DUE TO TAKE THE MEDICINE

– INTEGRATION WITH VACCINATION CERTIFICATE

– 24 HR AVAILABILITY

Value proposition: The electronic prescription allows patients to hand in their prescription for the medicine they need at any pharmacy and receive a reminder for the correct dosage. In addition, the information helps to avoid incompatibilities with other medicines.

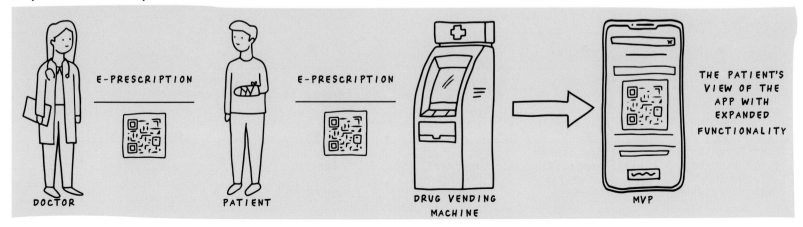

DOCTOR   E-PRESCRIPTION   PATIENT   E-PRESCRIPTION   DRUG VENDING MACHINE   MVP   THE PATIENT'S VIEW OF THE APP WITH EXPANDED FUNCTIONALITY

85

1. Brainstorming: Start your business ecosystem considerations with brainstorming: Who are the actors currently involved in a conventional prescription?

Look at the patient's entire ecosystem journey and think which actors come in contact with the prescription for handing it in, clearing, and billing. Include obvious interactions and interactions running in the background.

Exercise

5 MIN

SOLUTION IDEAS

DOCTORS	PATIENTS	PHARMACIES	ONLINE PHARMACIES	PHARMACEUTICAL COMPANIES
INTERMEDIARIES FOR BILLING, PHARMACY HEALTH INSURER	INSURANCE COMPANIES PHARMACIES, FAILURE OF PAYMENTS FRAUD	ACCIDENT INSURANCE COMPANIES	HEALTH INSURANCE COMPANIES	...

2. Visualize: Draw a sketch of the current system = ACTUAL state

Exercise

Show how the prescription makes its way to and from the actors. Highlight the problem areas of the current system.

8 MIN

SOLUTION IDEAS

- Susceptible to fraud and high transaction costs
- Long processing times due to intermediaries
- Data inconsistency and discrepancy, isolated technology platforms
- No or inefficient information for patients
- ...
- ...

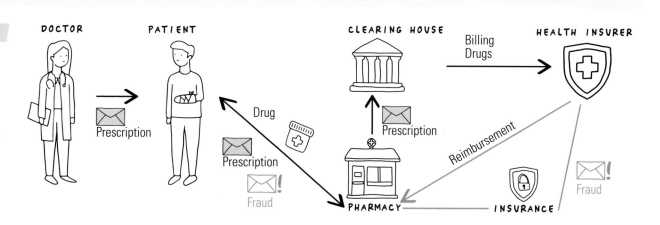

3. (Re)design: Business ecosystem

What might a business ecosystem that is superior to the current system and allows the featured MVP to be realized look like?

3.1 Design 1 to 2 variants of a business ecosystem and enter the respective value flows (data, money, information).

DESIGN

REDESIGN

6 MIN

- Which actors are missing?
- Which ones might be eliminated by new technologies?
- Is the system sustainable?
- Do all actors have advantages?
- Which actors are mandatory?
- What might be their concerns?

SOLUTION IDEAS

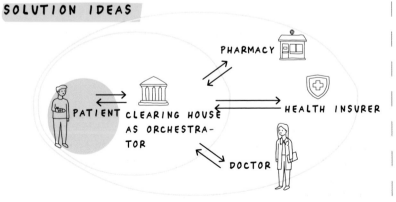

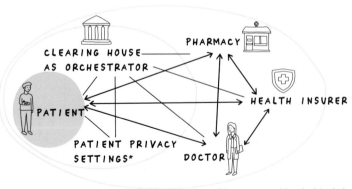

*(data ownership via blockchain)

3.2 Think about the benefits each actor has from participating in the ecosystem (preferred variant) and what motivates them to become a part of that system.

Exercise

ADVANTAGES:

6 MIN

SOLUTION IDEAS

PATIENTS
- Have up-to-date prescriptions always with them
- Quick preorder from pharmacy
- Quick pharmacy finder
- Display which drugs are in stock and where they are available
- Easier to use

HEALTH INSURERS
- Prevention of multiple billing -> savings

DOCTOR
- Paperless prescription
- Forgery-proof prescription
- Transparent overview of drugs with a wide range of analysis options

PHARMACIES
- No expenditure with the billing
- No fee accounting
- Improved liquidity
- Loyalty programs and pharmacy finder integrated in the patient app

FRAUD PREVENTION AT THE DOCTOR'S OFFICE
- With two-factor authentication, for instance, the creation of prescriptions by third parties can be prevented (e.g. by the doctor's assistant)
- Prescriptions that were created without authorization can be identified and analyzed by the doctor (date, patient, medicine)

FRAUD PREVENTION AT DOCTOR'S AND PHARMACY
- Fraud mainly exists in the case of expensive drugs, especially chemotherapeutics, pain killers, and other addictive drugs
- Multiple billing of prescriptions is not possible

FRAUD PREVENTION AT THE DOCTOR'S, PHARMACY AND PHARMACEUTICAL INDUSTRY
- Secret agreements favoring some drugs in prescriptions can be detected and analyzed

4. Multidimensional view of the business models: Look at the possible business models as well as the actors in the system

4.1 Core

What is the business model of the overall system? How are setup costs and operations financed?

BUSINESS MODEL OF THE OVERALL SYSTEM

 8 MIN

SOLUTION IDEAS

BUSINESS MODEL

POTENTIAL REVENUE	POTENTIAL EXPENSES
• Advertising of pharmacies	• Incentives for doctors to participate in the system
• Provision, connection to health insurance companies	• Operation blockchain, patient app
• Financial participation of health and accident insurers	• Integration in the software used at the doctor's office
• Integration of pharmaceutical companies (legally problematic)	• Marketing costs for raising the awareness of actors
• Transaction fee of pharmacies	• Marketing end consumer (patient)
	• Further development of new added value for patients

4.2. Actors

What additional business models can be implemented by which actors in the system? Which actors in the system may need to be convinced with other incentives since they are indispensable to the success of the system?

BUSINESS MODEL OF ACTORS
AND OTHER INCENTIVES

8 MIN

SOLUTION IDEAS

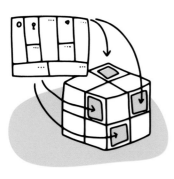

POSSIBLE INCENTIVES FOR DOCTORS

- Free web-based software for the doctor's office for easy and fast entry of prescriptions
- Suggestions for treatments and information on intolerances
- Real-time view of cost assumption for different drugs

INCENTIVES FOR HEALTH IN-SURERS AND ACCIDENT INSUR-ANCE COMPANIES

- Better treatment of patients/quicker recovery owing to optimized prescription
- Cost savings with the checking of cost acceptance and with billing
- Potential for further services for patients

INCENTIVES FOR HOSPITALS

- Updated view of prescriptions and dosing (if patient makes it visible)
- ...
- ...
- ...

5. MVE requirements: Think about how the actors in a minimum version interact with one another and which technologies could be used.

Exercise

What are the requirements for implementing the MVE? Which technologies are enablers for the realization of the desired ecosystem?

 6 MIN

SOLUTION IDEAS

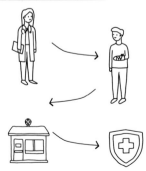

- **Doctor** writes a prescription/the relevant formulation on the blockchain with the patient's ID.

- **Patient** receives a QR on their mobile application and goes to the pharmacy to pick up the medicine.

- **Pharmacy** hands the drugs to the patient after verifying the patient ID and QR scan.

- **Health insurer and accident insurer:** The invoice for the prescription is directly transmitted and paid; or information on the estimated treatment cost is stored directly on the blockchain.

⟹ Centralized billing and clearing offices can gradually be replaced by blockchain.

6. Storytelling: Why should actors become a part of the ecosystem?

Exercise

How can actors in the system be convinced that they should participate and be a part of the value proposition to be provided?

- What are the individual benefits for each actor that should be highlighted?
- What needs of customers/users are satisfied?

6 MIN

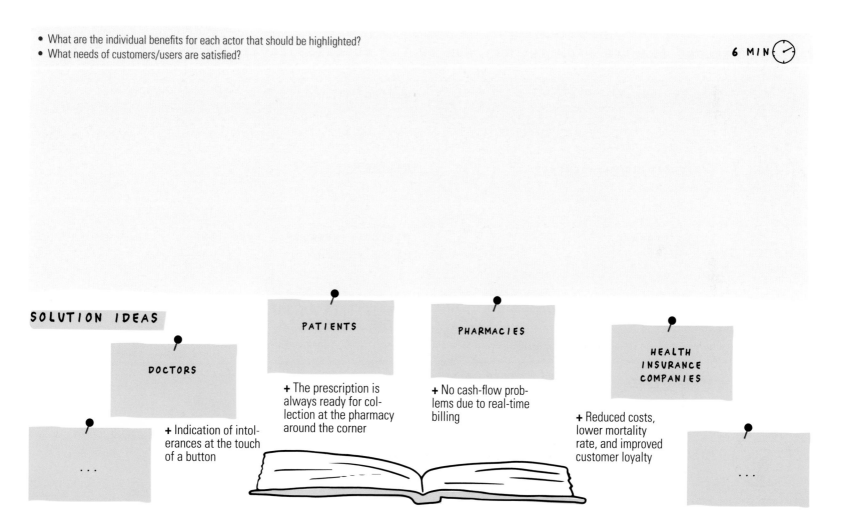

SOLUTION IDEAS

DOCTORS

PATIENTS

PHARMACIES

HEALTH INSURANCE COMPANIES

...

+ Indication of intolerances at the touch of a button

+ The prescription is always ready for collection at the pharmacy around the corner

+ No cash-flow problems due to real-time billing

+ Reduced costs, lower mortality rate, and improved customer loyalty

...

What Are the Learnings from the Exercise?

Exercise

Subsequent reflection helps to take along specific learnings from the dry run and place them in the context of similar business ecosystem challenges.

TYPICAL LESSONS LEARNED FROM THE DRY RUN ON THE BUSINESS ECOSYSTEM DESIGN   5 MIN

 TARGET IMAGE?

 FUNDING?

 STAKEHOLDERS/MANAGEMENT?

 SCALING?

 VALUE STREAMS

 CRITICAL EXPERIENCE FUNCTIONS FOR CUSTOMERS?

 INITIATION?

 CAPABILITIES OF THE ACTORS IN THE SYSTEM?

 OPERATIVES?

 NEW TECHNOLOGIES?

 MINDSET?

 COLLABORATION?

SOLUTION IDEAS

 A clear target image of the ecosystem helps in the communication with potential actors in the system.

 Ecosystems only work if all actors in the system benefit from it.

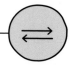 Outlining value streams helps to understand the overall system.

 Buy-in of all actors is important to build the ecosystem.

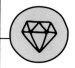 Try, fail fast, and learn – from the first prototype to the MVP all the way to the MVE – is the work motto.

 Business ecosystem design needs a new mindset that consciously gets away from traditional ways of thinking.

 Building and orchestrating an ecosystem requires financial resources.

 Well-designed ecosystems can be scaled faster.

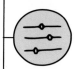 Focusing on individual key experiences and functions based on customer needs helps to boost the probability of success.

 New ideas and approaches emerge as soon as you know the capabilities of the actors and can start a dialog.

 New technologies (e.g. the cloud, AI, and blockchain) help make systems efficient.

 Collaboration between business and technology is essential.

95

Use of the dry-run exercise for "design thinking for business growth" in the context of training in design thinking, strategic design, and ecosystem design

The realization of a business ecosystem as MVE follows the basic idea of an MVP, i.e. the system is tested with a small budget and a very limited number of actors (e.g. one per role) and then optimized until the most promising system can be validated.

The above exercise is very good for training in business ecosystem design and an excellent example of the transition from an MVP to an MVE.

Use of design thinking tools (such as critical items diagram) in the definition of critical functions and experiences

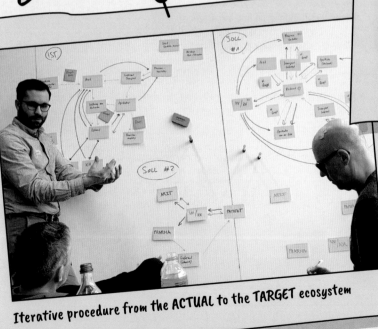

Iterative procedure from the ACTUAL to the TARGET ecosystem

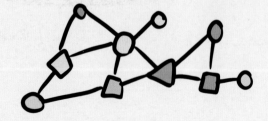

Discussion about the optimization of the system with a multidimensional view of the business models

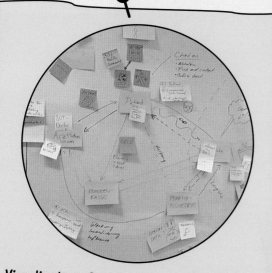

Visualization of value streams and network structures

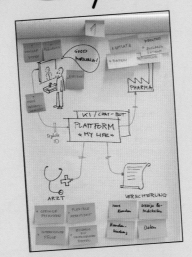

Development of different ecosystem variants

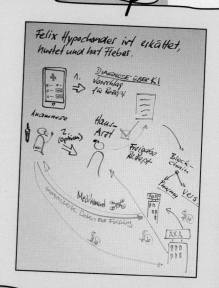

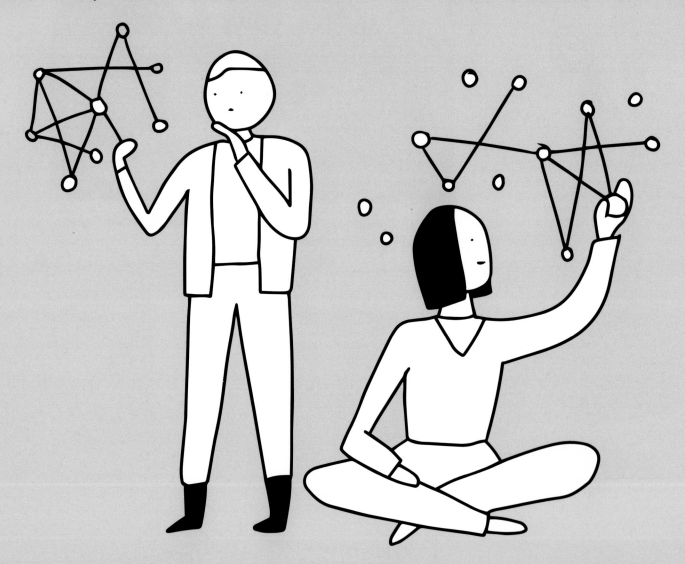

DESIGN THINKING FOR BUSINESS GROWTH AS A BASIS FOR THE DEVELOPMENT OF STRATEGIC OPTIONS

ECOSYSTEM STRATEGY

Awareness of Ecosystems as a Strategic Option

Many companies that have understood the mechanisms of a business eco-system play focus their attention solely on the design of a unique value proposition for the customers and think about growth strategies that make it possible to break out of the traditional industry silos.

In an ecosystem play, it has never been easier for companies to penetrate fields of action outside their domain. The reasons why this is more easily doable today than in the past are obvious: Cloud computing and associated technologies make it possible to bring together a large number of interactive platforms and solve customer problems in a holistic manner. Big data analytics, artificial intelligence, and distributed ledger technologies also allow for end-to-end automation and simultaneously make custom-tailored offers to customers as part of mass customization.

In addition, a collective capability has established itself allowing for easy access to external resources and capabilities. In simple terms, traditional boundaries between the industries are in the process of disappearing, which signals a fusion of industries and ranges of offers that had previously been unrelated to one another.

As a result, services, products, and brands of formerly isolated units are combined into comprehensive business ecosystems by the actors. Many companies, including those leading in the industry, will sooner or later be confronted with this global phenomenon. They will have no choice but to find new ways to accommodate the paradigm shift described above. Otherwise they run the risk that even their core business will be disrupted by the new competitors.

The opportunities and chances of participating in or initializing a business ecosystem are usually greater than the risks. However, it takes investment, good governance structures, and a new mindset to succeed in such a growth path.

Many decision makers therefore ask themselves:

What capabilities, products, and customer interfaces does the company have and how can they be used outside the known industry boundaries and structures?

In short: Who are we, and what role can the company assume in an ecosystem play?

Thinking in ecosystems is probably uncharted territory for most decision makers. Up to now, they have focused too much on what they did in the past and not on what the customers they serve really need. The customer experience was usually limited to the function of the product.

Today offers and entire platforms merge into larger ecosystems. Digital providers of payment solutions offer car sharing; department stores open their doors to e-commerce giants; and insurance companies no longer only take care of people's financial wellness but, across industries, of their mental fitness as well. Car makers become orchestrators for car-sharing and suppliers of micromobility. All this clearly shows that actors increasingly search for market opportunities across industry boundaries to be able to meet new or changed customer needs.

Progressive market actors have realized that this entails great opportunities and growth options while at the same time requiring cooperation and collaboration to create new values for customers.

Integration of Business Ecosystem Initiatives in the Corporate Strategy

The definition of the corporate strategy has undergone various phases over the last 70 years. They range from the traditional "plan and execute" approaches all the way to influences from the "blue ocean" and "value migration" movements. What they have in common is a linear development of the strategy that is based on an ambition as well as comprehensive market and competitor analyses, from which the individual business units derive detailed implementation plans and measures. Those who apply this process and planning cycle to the definition of a business ecosystem strategy will quickly reach their limits since the speed, coevolution, and framework conditions are more dynamic. We know from experience that these factors make traditional plans superfluous.

The development of a target image for an ecosystem requires an experimental procedure that makes it possible for the value proposition to be advanced together with other actors in the ecosystem, to pursue data-driven innovation, and to adjust the value streams according to the needs of the actors. The strategy process is more like an enabler to promote co-creation, provide the necessary funds for experiments, and finally to shape the environment together with the other actors.

Initial high-resolution prototypes, emerging from iterative and agile approaches, often form the basis of a business ecosystem. Starting with a customer need, initial prototypes are developed, tested, and gradually improved through iterations. The vision prototype, for instance, aims at the imaginative power of the business ecosystem design team to realize a visionary version of a service, product, or business model before the requirements for an MVP are defined.

With traditional approaches, it is inevitable that the fields of activity for an ecosystem approach were gained from competitor analyses. However, success usually fails to materialize since the customer needs were not taken into account nor was a jointly supported value proposition worked on together with other actors in the system.

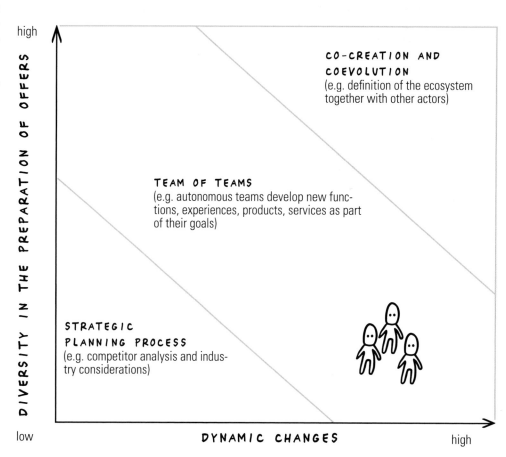

CO-CREATION AND COEVOLUTION
(e.g. definition of the ecosystem together with other actors)

TEAM OF TEAMS
(e.g. autonomous teams develop new functions, experiences, products, services as part of their goals)

STRATEGIC PLANNING PROCESS
(e.g. competitor analysis and industry considerations)

high — low · **DIVERSITY IN THE PREPARATION OF OFFERS**

low · **DYNAMIC CHANGES** · high

The Crucial Question Regarding a Business Ecosystem

Since each starting point in the definition of a growth strategy is different in the context of a business ecosystem, the main question should be:

"WHAT DOES THE CUSTOMER WANT?"

- **What are the deep-seated needs and wishes of the customers?**
- **Which customer problem can be solved?**
- **Which tasks does the customer want to complete?**

If the strategy work starts with the customer, there must be an in-depth understanding of the potential customers before starting to think about the business ecosystem. The design thinking mindset is very useful here because it helps to achieve, through iterations, solutions that meet the customer needs.

The final prototypes and critical items from design thinking deliver the requirements for MVPs. One or several MVPs constitute the basis for designing a business ecosystem. Depending on the problem statement, it is necessary to consider whether a first prototype should already be developed with potential partners, whether opening up to the outside is possible only upon the definition of the MVP requirements, and whether other actors should be involved even later in the project with the initial MVP for the ecosystem considerations.

In actual practice at companies, often only very select partners are involved in the first phases. The opening is mostly done after the MVP since this – due to a higher level of maturity – gives more certainty about the potential solution for decision makers and the design teams.

The iterative procedure via the "design lenses" and with the typical questions for each phase will be examined in greater depth starting on page 172.

This foray on the integration in the corporate strategy makes sense since the questions that crop up when selecting strategic options are fairly typical. In addition, the **ecosystem play** option competes with other strategic options. Applying the **problem to scale and growth framework** yields the content for the **ecosystem play and win configuration framework**. The goal is combining well-known strategy tools with iterative approaches. For pros in ecosystem design, it is often enough to work with the design lenses since their goal is to design a superior system that goes beyond the familiar ideas of addressable markets.

THINK FROM
THE CUSTOMERS'
POINT OF VIEW

Problems to Growth and Scale Framework

New mindsets, working methods, and agile tools help — from a problem statement to the inclusion of customer requirements — to realize initial prototypes and MVPs that make it possible later, when we begin to design the ecosystem, to bring unique value propositions to life for the customers.

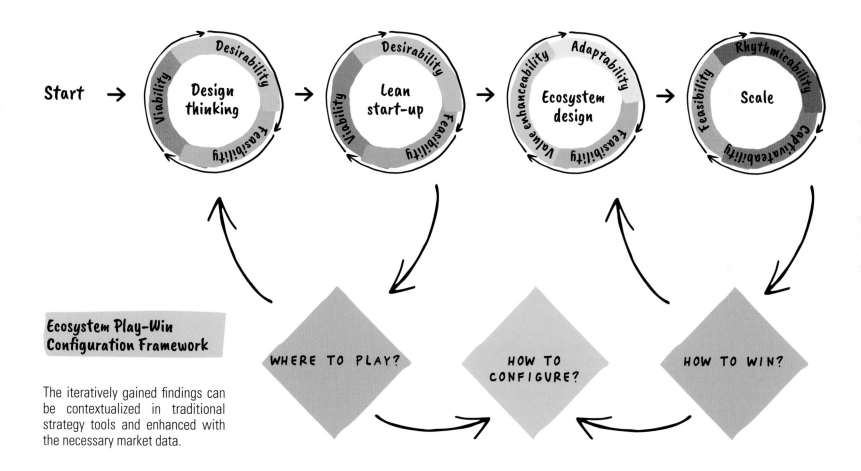

Start →

Design thinking
Desirability · Viability · Feasibility

Lean start-up
Desirability · Viability · Feasibility

Ecosystem design
Adaptability · Value enhanceability · Feasibility

Scale
Rhythmicability · Feasibility · Captivateability

Ecosystem Play-Win Configuration Framework

The iteratively gained findings can be contextualized in traditional strategy tools and enhanced with the necessary market data.

WHERE TO PLAY?

HOW TO CONFIGURE?

HOW TO WIN?

Strategy Documentation

For the ongoing documentation of the results from the design lenses and the general strategic issues, it is advisable to use the ecosystem strategy canvas, which deals with the key questions of where to play, how to configure, and how to win. The canvas helps to capture all the necessary elements, from customer needs to governance all the way to scaling activities.

A good starting point is to use the existing resources and tools for internal and external analysis. The focus here is mainly on creating *actual* analyses, roughly drawing up topics and capturing the wider context in a PESTLE (which stands for political, economic, social, technological, legal, and environmental factors) analysis in conjunction to a potential business ecosystem. Although these preliminary works are valuable, they don't replace the first design lens, namely design thinking. The research to be conducted should be seen as a complementary element; it allows for the comprehensive understanding of the problem and the situation as well as for the validation of initial assumptions that are still unclear. It doesn't do any harm to the work on strategy and design to prepare and establish the design principles as a team together with the project sponsors at an early stage. The design principles are guidelines for the team. They offer quick orientation with regard to open questions and help with decisions on the next steps. The principles can be worked out for a specific ecosystem initiative or else be defined in general terms for ecosystem projects.

The primary task of the ecosystem strategy canvas is to document the ongoing activities arising from the design lenses. Each iteration in each respective design lens brings new insights into customer needs, functions, business models, and value streams. In this way, the strategy canvas will be fleshed out and developed dynamically and in an evolutionary way. Even after realization, elements will change, so it is all the more important not to lose sight of the larger target image of the ecosystem.

Typical Activities

WHERE TO PLAY? **HOW TO CONFIGURE?** **HOW TO WIN?**

Design Thinking Canvas — **188**
Documentation of the customer needs, jobs to be done, first prototypes, MVP requirements

Lean Start-Up Canvas — **210**
Documentation of the value proposition; new skills regarding IT, data, infrastructure, AI; final design of the minimum viable products (MVPs), minimum marketable features (MMFs); backlog of products and services

Ecosystem Design Canvas — **246**
Description of the validated ecosystem vision based on minimum viable ecosystems (MVE); definition of the roles in the business ecosystem; business model of the business ecosystem and models of the respective actors

Growth and Scale Canvas — **272**
Shaping network effects and examination of new partnerships, initiatives, technologies, and strategies for the realization of exponential growth.

Key Questions about Strategic Design

 Value Proposition

- What products, services, or experiences are offered?
- Who is the target customer?
- How do customers benefit from the products, services, or experiences?
- What makes the offer unique?

HOW TO CONFIGURE?

- Which role is to be assumed in the business ecosystem?
- What capabilities are needed regarding IT, data, infrastructure, AI, and APIs?
- What are the MVPs and MMFs to be verified?
- What is the backlog of products and services?
- How is governance organized?
- What organizational setup should be chosen to set up the business ecosystem and have it grow?

PLAY　　**CONFIGURE**　　**WIN**

WHERE TO PLAY

- Which customer problem is solved? Which topic area is covered by the ecosystem?
- What reach (regional, national, international) does the target ecosystem have?
- What existing skills and capabilities, technologies, products, and services are used for the business ecosystem?

HOW TO WIN?

- What is the vision of the business ecosystem?
- What is the business model of the ecosystem?
- What opportunities do other actors have to implement their familiar or new business models?
- How can the system grow exponentially?
- What new skills and capabilities, technologies, products, and services are required for future growth?

ECOSYSTEM STRATEGY CANVAS

WHERE TO PLAY?	HOW TO CONFIGURE?		HOW TO WIN?
ANALYSIS OF THE TOPIC AREA AND THE ENVIRONMENT How can the topic area be described? What are the environmental factors that affect the topic area?	**VALUE PROPOSITION** What value does the offer have for the customer? What product, service, or experience do the customers get? What can the other actors do to deliver the value proposition?		**ECOSYSTEM VISION** What is the vision? How is the goal to be achieved?
CUSTOMER NEEDS CUSTOMER PROBLEM Where is the problem? How has it been solved up to now? Who has the need?	**CAPABILITIES REGARDING IT, DATA, INFRASTRUCTURE, AI** What skills and capabilities exist? What skills need to be expanded? What skills are contributed to the business ecosystem by other actors and suppliers ?	**ROLES IN THE BUSINESS ECOSYSTEM** What roles are there in the system? Which actors take on what role?	**BUSINESS MODEL OF THE ECOSYSTEM** How does the ecosystem make money? - - - - - - - - - - - - - - - - **MULTIDIMENSIONAL VIEW OF THE BUSINESS MODELS** How do the other actors in the ecosystem make money?
CUSTOMER INTERFACE, CUSTOMER RELATIONSHIPS Through what channels should the customers be served? (e.g. multi-channel, opti-channel) What is the relationship with the customer? (e.g. personal, digital, automated)	**MINIMUM VIABLE PRODUCTS, MINIMUM MARKETABLE FEATURES, BACKLOG OF PRODUCTS AND SERVICES** Which function and experience should be dealt with first? Which products, services, and experiences complete and supplement the value proposition over time?	**ORGANIZATIONAL DESIGN GOVERNANCE** How should setup, operation, and growth be embedded in the organization? How does governance take place, and who takes care of it?	**GROWTH AND SCALE** How is scaling to be realized? Which new skills are needed? How is growth financed?
EXISTING PARTNERSHIPS, INITIATIVES, TECHNOLOGIES, AND STRATEGIES Which existing partnerships can be used? Which existing technologies can be used? What are known and obvious market opportunities? EXPLOIT	EXPLORE		**NEW PARTNERSHIPS, INITIATIVES, TECHNOLOGIES, AND STRATEGIES** What new partnerships are needed? What new technologies are needed? What unknown market opportunities can be explored?

INPUTS FROM THE DESIGN LENSES

ECOSYSTEM DESIGN CANVAS

PAGE 246

Template download

DESIGN THINKING CANVAS

PAGE 188

EXPONENTIAL GROWTH AND SCALE CANVAS

PAGE 272

WHERE TO PLAY?	HOW TO CONFIGURE?		HOW TO WIN?
Topic area	Value proposition		Ecosystem vision
Customer needs/ customer problem	Skills regarding IT, data, infrastructure, AI	Roles in the business ecosystem	Business model of the ecosystem — — — — Multidimensional view of the business models
Customer interface, customer relationships	Minimum viable products, minimum marketable features, backlog of products and services	Organizational design, governance	Growth and scale
Existing partnerships, initiatives, technologies, and strategies	New partnerships, initiatives, technologies, and strategies		
	EXPLOIT	EXPLORE	

LEAN START-UP MVP CANVAS

PAGE 210

The ecosystem strategy canvas helps to capture the results of the design lenses in the documentation of the individual strategic analyses.

DOWNLOAD TOOL
https://en.business-ecosystem-design.com/strategy

Using Design Principles in the Shaping of Business Models

Design principles help business ecosystem design teams to obtain guidelines for a specific ecosystem design in the form of clear statements. Especially if the collaboration crosses company boundaries (co-creation), it makes sense to develop these principles together and accept them as a cross-company team. The principles should be developed for the particular purpose and adapted to the project. These principles are of great help in the development of strategies for cutting-edge, complex, and networked systems.

The design principles help the business ecosystem design team to:

- put a clear focus on a specific mindset or the requirements for the ecosystem or a topic area as early as at the beginning of the project.
- provide the team with a uniform understanding of the task so that everybody is on the same page.
- provide guidance so that decisions of the business ecosystem design team can be made faster.
- define general characteristics that should be treated with a higher priority.
- develop a guideline that ensures that future ecosystem projects are created on the same overarching principles.

1 — BASKET OF INGREDIENTS (= DESIGN PRINCIPLES)

2 — PROJECT-SPECIFIC

3 — GENERAL

Procedure and template, design principles:

1. Invite all participants to write design principles on Post-its and put them in the "basket."
2. As soon as the "basket" is full, sort the design principles on the pyramid, e.g. by dividing them into three groups. The sorting is done according to the rule: the higher up on the pyramid, the more project-specific the principle. General design principles for business ecosystems are located at the bottom of the pyramid.
3. Once the assignment of the design principles is completed, a vote can be conducted, e.g. with glue dots. The aim is to reduce the design principles to a maximum of three per section, i.e. a maximum of nine per pyramid.
4. It's best to put the selected and adopted design principles in a place where the business ecosystem team is often confronted with them and to which it has quick access.

4 — DESIGN PRINCIPLES FOR ECOSYSTEM PROJECTS

DOWNLOAD TOOL
https://en.business-ecosystem-design.com/strategy/design-principles

To the Point!

The focus should primarily be on the development of business ecosystems based on the relevant design lenses.

For incorporation in traditional frameworks of strategy development, it is advisable to adapt the methods and procedural models in question to the requirements of a customer-centered design thinking for business growth approach.

The combination of an iterative development of the systems and the contextualization in traditional strategy frameworks allows for communicating and evaluating business ecosystems as a strategic option.

Ecosystem: Typical Questions Related to the Company and <u>the Environment</u>

Since dealing with business ecosystems is something entirely new for many companies, an inventory of existing strategies, capabilities, and partnerships often marks the beginning of the ecosystem considerations (questions relating to one's own company and the environment). This actual inventory is indeed commendable since it helps to harmonize later target images of one or several ecosystems with existing initiatives or partnerships.

In addition, there will always be various options in terms of topic areas and the configuration of a business ecosystem. Most companies will operate in the future in different business ecosystems where they assume different roles, e.g. that of initiator, orchestrator, or participating actor. Classic strategy tools such as the PESTLE analysis or "right to play/how to win" help to contextualize the strategic options for business ecosystem projects and thus make them accessible to decision makers and management bodies.

Typical Questions Regarding One's Own Company

- What are the company's strengths and weaknesses (SWOT analysis)?
- What is the core business today?
- What skills and capabilities exist in the company?
- What is its current market role? What market role can be assumed without supplementing one's own business? What market roles are conceivable for the company in the future?
- How high is the value of customer and transaction data?
- What kind of data can the company provide and which data does the company require for a comprehensive view of customers?
- To what extent is the mindset of the decision makers open for participation in a business ecosystem?
- Do employees have the ability to think in business ecosystem structures, business models, and value streams?
- Are there any business relationships, partnerships, or shared networks with other companies that can be used? What companies are they?
- What functions, manifestations, and initiatives are in place or are being planned that can pay into a specific ecosystem topic?

Establishing or participating in a business ecosystem is a strategic option and a vital element that will affect the business model and the future decision on technologies.

The Required Capabilities — from the Decision for an Ecosystem Play All the Way to the Realization of (Exponential) Growth

The skills and capabilities required for the shaping of a business ecosystem cover a wide range. Along with understanding customer requirements, they include the ability to realize initial prototypes together with other companies and test them in MVEs. Participation as an actor in an ecosystem also requires the capability of thinking in business ecosystems, assuming new roles in a system, and creating the technical prerequisites for connecting with the other actors.

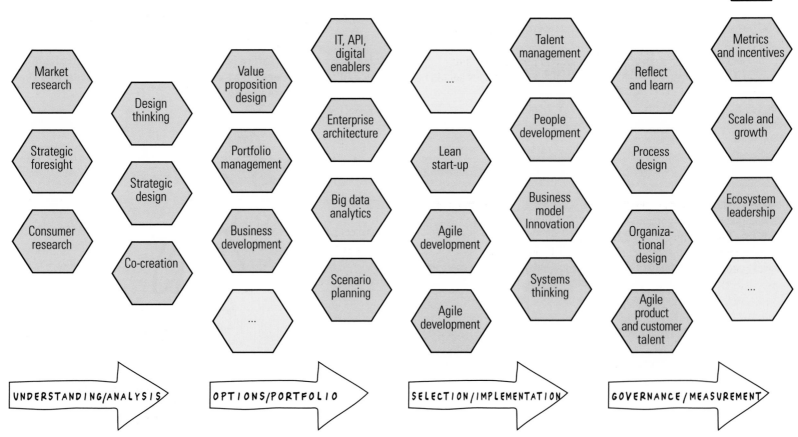

UNDERSTANDING/ANALYSIS
- Market research
- Strategic foresight
- Consumer research
- Design thinking
- Strategic design
- Co-creation
- ...

OPTIONS/PORTFOLIO
- Value proposition design
- Portfolio management
- Business development
- IT, API, digital enablers
- Enterprise architecture
- Big data analytics
- Scenario planning

SELECTION/IMPLEMENTATION
- ...
- Lean start-up
- Agile development
- Agile development
- Talent management
- People development
- Business model Innovation
- Systems thinking

GOVERNANCE/MEASUREMENT
- Reflect and learn
- Process design
- Organizational design
- Agile product and customer talent
- Metrics and incentives
- Scale and growth
- Ecosystem leadership
- ...

Initiatives/Industry Matrix

Since dealing with business ecosystems is a complex matter, it is a good thing first to make an inventory of all initiatives currently implemented and planned in the company. Thus a view of existing internal initiatives or resources can mark the starting point for ecosystem considerations. The initiatives/industry matrix helps to classify the existing activities and to reach a better understanding of the *actual* situation.

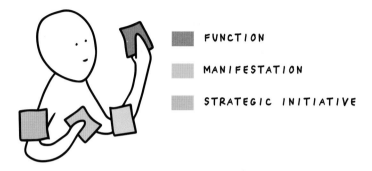

■ FUNCTION

■ MANIFESTATION

■ STRATEGIC INITIATIVE

The initiatives/industry matrix aids the business ecosystem design team to:
- outline which other strategic initiatives are planned in the future;
- include in their deliberations what new products and services should be launched;
- identify which programs, products, or initiatives are being planned in individual submarkets, other regions, or countries.

Procedure and template design principles:
1. Initially, all initiatives across the entire company can be written down by the responsible persons or, if a workshop is held, by workshop participants from the different departments.
2. Subsequently, the initiatives are placed on the matrix. The axes may vary depending on the company and its focus. The X axis is used for general labeling (function, manifestation/initiative), and the reach is divided into one's own industry or cross industry.

Initiatives that already are of a networked and cross-industry character are especially intriguing.

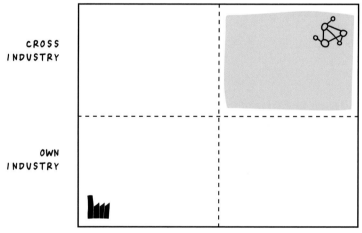

CROSS INDUSTRY

OWN INDUSTRY

Isolated   **FUNCTION/ MANIFESTATION/ INITIATIVE**   networked

DOWNLOAD TOOL
https://en.business-ecosystem-design.com/initiatives

Cooperation/Industry Matrix

Tool

Another starting point often chosen is the examination of existing partnerships and cooperative projects. In many cases, the company doesn't even know where long-standing cooperation already exists that would provide quick customer access, data, or technology for the design of business ecosystems.

.

The cooperation/industry matrix aids the business ecosystem design team to:

- analyze which partnerships and connections with other companies are already in place;
- determine whether these connections with other companies are in the same industry, industry-related, or completely outside the sector;
- identify which capabilities and skills may already be on hand in an existing partner network;
- check whether there are suitable suppliers, for instance, among the partners and business relationships.

Procedure and template:

1. Initially, all cooperative projects, supplier relationships, and partnerships can be written down by the responsible persons or, if a workshop is held, by workshop participants from the different departments.
2. Subsequently, the connections to other companies are placed on the matrix. The axes may vary depending on the company and its focus. The X axis is used for general labeling (focus/diversification), and the reach is divided into one's own industry or cross industry (as in the tool presented on the previous page).

■ PARTNERSHIP

■ COOPERATION

■ SUPPLIER

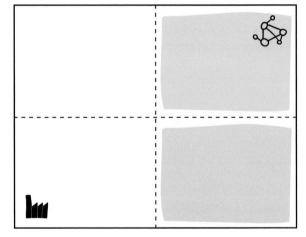

CROSS INDUSTRY

OWN INDUSTRY

FOCUS   DIVERSIFICATION

Some partnerships and cooperative projects are more used for "exploit" (left side of matrix); while others are designed to drive diversification in terms of the industry and the services to be provided.

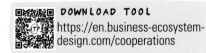

DOWNLOAD TOOL
https://en.business-ecosystem-design.com/cooperations

Ecosystem: Typical Questions Related to the Company and the Environment

Many questions about the company environment are usually raised and assessed as part of the ongoing definition of the corporate strategy. Since conventional strategy exercises are usually rigid and only geared to consider the familiar dimensions of one's own sector, it is recommended to use all of the findings from the design lenses systematically for strategy development. In this way, considerations that are limited to corporate alliances or individual corporate acquisitions for goal attainment can be avoided.

For the use of tools such as the PESTLE analysis, it would be wise to adapt the questions to the requirements of business ecosystems. In general, com-panies have various options to position themselves in emerging ecosystems. However, there is a risk that they fall right back into the old ways of constantly striving for negotiating power. The customer needs, existing capabilities, and the appetite for new disruptive business models must take center stage. When conceiving an ecosystem, existing fences separating regions and countries should be discarded since many digital services and experiences do not have such artificial boundaries.

Typical Questions Regarding the Environment

- Which business ecosystems emerge locally and which globally?
- How do individual industries develop, and where does new value creation occur in cross-industry structures?
- What do other industries do in terms of business ecosystems, and how can the services, products, or data provided by the company create added value in the respective system?
- How large is one's own industry/sector in the respective ecosystems, and how high is the penetration rate of the integrated network economy?
- How large is the growth potential in the individual systems?
- To what extent have local and international competitors themselves begun to initialize or participate in business ecosystems?

Establishing or participating in a business ecosystem is a strategic option and a vital element that will affect the business model and future technology decisions.

115

Map of Topic Areas

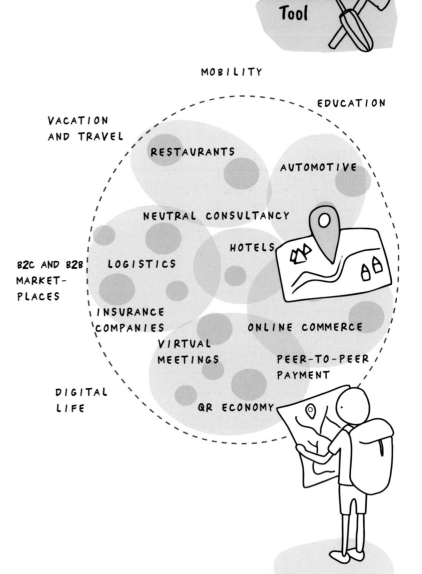

A map with the different topic areas of business ecosystems can be used to show the ecosystems in a particular region, including the firms participating in it, or to make an inventory to find out who acts as initiator or orchestrator. Such maps with topic fields, including a reference to the respective actors, also help at a later time with the discussion of different options of ecosystems. Usually, the maps are used to represent the individual industries, capabilities, and ecosystem spheres in relation to the customer needs. When using this visualization tool, the dimensions should always be adapted to the objective and the strategic considerations of the ecosystem since otherwise, maps become confusing quite quickly.

The topic areas map helps the business ecosystem design team to:
- visualize the current situation of a business ecosystem in one topic of specific initiators or competitors;
- explore the relationships and respective participation of actors in one or more business ecosystems;
- outline and discuss a planned value proposition through different dimensions and potential actors.

Procedure and template design principles:
1. You can start with those companies that appear as the initiators of such systems and represent their activities, topics, and connections to other actors.
2. Another variation is to look at what capabilities and skills are needed for a particular topic area, which are then plotted on the map. The exploration of the customer needs or carrying out a (re)design of a business ecosystem yield more inputs for the map.

Classification of Different Ecosystem Options into Topic Fields

Tool

TOPIC AREAS MATRIX

	Administration	Education	Wealth and security	Health	Housing	Vacation and travel	Adventure/expe-rience	Marketplace	Payment/transactions	Digital life	Sustainable life	...
Administration												
Automotive												
Banking			■									
Construction/architecture												
Consulting												
Education		■										
Chemical												
IT/digital platforms												
Energy												
Insurance			■									
Research				■								
Health care/pharmaceutical					■							
Real estate												
Industry												
Art/culture			■									
Mechanical engineering												
Media												
Agriculture												
Law												
Tax consultancy												
Telecommunications												
Tourism/catering												
Transport/traffic/logistics												

■ INITIATOR

■ ORCHESTRATOR

■ STRATEGIC INITIATIVE

DOWNLOAD TOOL
https://en.business-ecosystem-design.com/topic-area

117

Customer-Centered Analysis of Topic Areas

If a good overview of existing ecosystem initiatives is already available, once it has been recognized that the customers with their new or changed needs are essential, the topic field exploration can begin with a what-if question. The greatest market opportunity is to design and implement an ecosystem that is geared to the capabilities of one's own company, to co-creation, and the needs of a large number of potential customers and users. Possible starting points for exploration range from basic needs such as energy, food, and water all the way to more complex needs such as belonging to a community or exploiting one's own potential to the fullest. What if such experiences, functions, or products were made possible by a combination of actors and skills? What systems would emerge?

The topic areas map aids the business ecosystem design team to:

- outline new topics roughly starting from the basic needs;
- leave existing industry boundaries behind;
- start the creative process with an initial round of ideation;
- think in holistic solutions instead of concentrating on individual functions, products, or services;
- create new topic areas that so far have not been identified by pure analysis of existing ecosystems.

Procedure-Inclusive What-If Questions

Step 1: What are the current needs?

The first question is: "What are the current needs?" It examines the status quo, the current reality. The "What if..." question should be based on a solid assessment and empathetic understanding of what is happening today before beginning to explore potential topic areas.

Step 2: What if?

The question "What if?" automatically generates ideas. It leads directly to potential topic fields for business ecosystems. This questioning technique helps to think consciously outside the box.

Step 3: Where might a "Wow!" be created for the customer?

Based on first ideas for topics, corresponding assumptions can be made that are later reviewed over the course of design thinking.

Step 4: What works?

The last question is usually answered in an iterative process through design lenses # 1–3 and is validated by customer feedback.

WHAT IF OUR POTENTIAL CUSTOMERS...

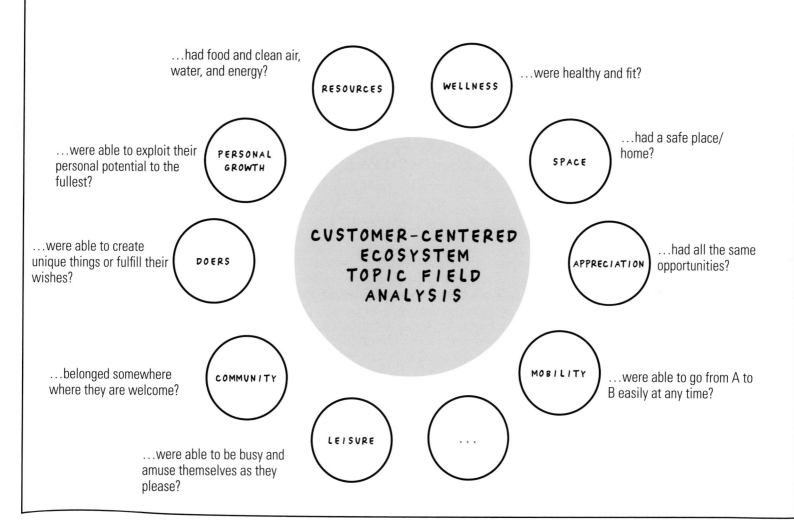

...had food and clean air, water, and energy?

RESOURCES

WELLNESS

...were healthy and fit?

...were able to exploit their personal potential to the fullest?

PERSONAL GROWTH

SPACE

...had a safe place/ home?

CUSTOMER-CENTERED ECOSYSTEM TOPIC FIELD ANALYSIS

...were able to create unique things or fulfill their wishes?

DOERS

APPRECIATION

...had all the same opportunities?

...belonged somewhere where they are welcome?

COMMUNITY

MOBILITY

...were able to go from A to B easily at any time?

...were able to be busy and amuse themselves as they please?

LEISURE

...

PESTLE with Questions for Ecosystems

Tool

The result of a PESTLE analysis is often used as input for other business management tools such as SWOT analysis, SOAR analysis, risk assessment for the design of business models, or as we do in this book, as the basis for the contextualization of a business ecosystem strategy.

This framework has many variations that examine different combinations of external factors specific to particular industries. For example: PEST, STEE-PLE, STEER, and STEEP. An adapted standard PESTLE analysis was used as the foundation for general business ecosystem considerations.

POLITICS

Political or politically motivated factors that might affect the project.

For example:
Government policies, political stability or instability, bureaucracy, corruption, foreign trade policies, tax policies, trade restrictions, labor law, environmental law, copyright and consumer law, fair-competition regulation, subsidies, and funding initiatives.

Typical questions:
- Which government policies or political groups might be beneficial or harmful to the success of the ecosystem?
- Is the political environment stable or likely to change?

ECONOMIC

Macroeconomic forces that might affect the project.

For example:
Economic trends, growth rates, industry growth, seasonal factors, taxation, inflation, interest rates, international exchange rates, international trade, labor costs, consumers disposable income, unemployment rate, availability of loans, monetary policy, raw material costs.

Typical questions:
- Which economic factors will affect our further courses of action?
- Is the ecosystem affected by the current economic performance?
- How do changes in similar industries or ecosystems affect prices, revenues, and costs?

SOCIAL

Social aspects, attitudes, and trends that affect your business or the business ecosystem and your target market.

For example:
Attitudes and shared beliefs about a number of factors such as health, work, leisure time, money, customer service, imports, religion, cultural taboos, environment, population growth and demography, family size/structure, immigration/emigration, lifestyle trends.

Typical questions:
- In what way do the consumers' values and beliefs affect their purchasing behavior?
- Do human behavior or cultural trends play a role for the business ecosystem?
- How do customer needs change?

The PESTLE analysis aids the business ecosystem team:

- to understand the market and business position of the company's own actors better; to plan strategically and conduct market research.
- to find a topic area or an ecosystem strategy and ways to design the ecosystem.
- to get an overview of external influences that might affect an ecosystem initiative.
- to make more certain and informed decisions.
- to map a decision-making document for management bodies.

Procedure and template

- For each dimension, the typical questions in relation to politics, economics, in social, technological, legal and environmental terms will be addressed.
- The answers help explore any risks and opportunities in an early project phase.
- The results of the PESTLE analysis should be made available to all teams involved in the design of the ecosystem and in the definition of the ecosystem strategy.

TECHNOLOGICAL

Technology that has an influence on how products and services are made, sold, scaled, and communicated.

For example:
Technology and communication infrastructure, access of consumers to technology, emerging technologies, automation, laws addressing technology, research and innovation, intellectual property regulation, technology, and development of competitors.

Typical questions:
- What innovations and technological advances are available or will be available in the future?
- How might they affect the design, governance, and scaling of the ecosystem?

LEGAL

Current and future legal and regulatory requirements that affect the ecosystem.

For example:
Laws in the fields of consumer protection, work, health and safety, antitrust, intellectual property, data protection, tax and discrimination; international and national trade regulations and restrictions, advertising directives, product labeling and safety standards.

Typical questions:
- What regulations and laws apply to the desired value proposition and new business models (e.g. in terms of data)?
- Do they help or hinder the project?
- Are the laws and regulations understood in all the dimensions in which the business ecosystem will operate?

ENVIRONMENTAL

Environmental influences that affect the ecosystem, the services provided, the environment, and the natural resources used.

For example:
Weather, climate change, carbon footprint, environmental requirements, environmental laws and goals, recycling and waste disposal policies, endangered species, support for renewable energy.

Typical questions:
- How does the physical environment affect the ecosystem and vice versa?
- What are the ramifications of the climate, weather, or geographical location?

DOWNLOAD TOOL
https://en.business-ecosystem-design.com/pestle

Environmental Analysis 2.0

When using tools from traditional methods of strategic analysis, a new way of thinking is required and an adapted model must be used.

In particular, the relationship between a company and its environment is different since business ecosystems can be shaped. The variety of services is likewise not limited to elements customary in the industry. Business ecosystems are more open, diverse, and multidimensional than the known environmental analyses, industry analyses, and competition analyses.

THINK OUTSIDE YOUR OWN INDUSTRY

APPLY ECOSYSTEMS THINKING

DIMENSION	TRADITIONAL APPROACH TO THE ANALYSIS OF ENVIRONMENTAL FACTORS	MODEL FOR THE ANALYSIS OF ENVIRONMENTAL FACTORS ADAPTED TO ECOSYSTEM DESIGN
ROLE OF THE THE ENVIRONMENT ANALYSIS	analysis as the basis for strategic decisions	basis for design principles for the realization of new value propositions and value streams
NATURE OF THE THE ENVIRONMENT ANALYSIS	given	carried out as part of the exploration in different design lenses (e.g. minimum viable ecosystem)
RELATIONSHIP BETWEEN COMPANY, ECOSYSTEM, AND ENVIRONMENT	the company searches for suitable adaptations to environmental factors	an initiator/orchestrator chooses or shapes the environment that matters most in the end: the business ecosystem
KEY ELEMENT FOR STRUCTURING THE ANALYSIS	sector/industry view	ecosystem thinking
DIVERSITY OF SERVICE DELIVERY	industry-focused	together with other actors, regardless of whether they belong to the same industry

Basic **ACTUAL** analyses of one's own capabilities, of ecosystems already existing and of other companies with their initiatives and existing partnerships help understand the environment and in-house capabilities better.

In particular, the relationship between a company and its environment is different since business ecosystems can be shaped and the environment does not have to be accepted as given.

The pure analysis, without the iterative exploration of customer needs, tactics, and strategies, will not lead to success.

For a well-configured ecosystem, both dimensions are needed as well as a clear statement as to where the playing field is and how it is to be played to be successful.

WHERE TO PLAY?   HOW TO   HOW TO WIN?
                   CONFIGURE?

HOW TO WIN AND CONFIGURE?

Big Playing Field for Business Ecosystems

Corporate reality today shows that normally both are used in business ecosystem initiatives, i.e. a mixture of EXPLOIT and EXPLORE. This means that companies rely on existing skills and capabilities as well as as on activities concerning the core business and existing business models. These are the things they can bring to an ecosystem as participating actors. New revenue streams can be realized this way or a larger market area addressed. Finally, it is helpful for companies to place their competitiveness on a broader basis and to leverage existing business models. Usually, such considerations result in the initialization of ecosystems only for linear growth, though, due to the fact that it's not the ecosystem and the multipliers and other actors that take center stage but the transfer of one's business model to a business ecosystem.

As an alternative, companies can create new systems that are of an exploratory nature due to a unique value proposition and new configurations of business models, including those of the partners. Configured correctly, these ecosystems have the potential to become a successful "black ocean" strategy. The superiority arises from the design of the business model, for example, that makes participation attractive to all desired actors. The basic business model and the attractiveness of all business models that are used by the actors in the system surpass the familiar differentiations according to price, technology, customer access, or the leverage of a brand known in the market. Such ecosystems usually emerge as a "greenfield approach," far removed from traditional corporate structures and mindsets. For companies that use EXPLORE to initialize a new business ecosystem, prospects for exponential growth are good since it is the ecosystem that is decisive for the outcome, not the established products, services, and business models. The experience gained from various initiatives helps to document the moves that worked particularly well in a playbook for business growth. They can be correspondingly repeated if they work well and fit the new situation. If it doesn't work, improvise! The failure of past moves fuels the alternation of planned moves and improvisation. The pattern can be applied to business ecosystem design.

There are countless ways to contribute existing capabilities to an ecosystem, to scale and monetize radically different value propositions in a redesigned business ecosystem.

TOUCHDOWN!

Where to Play / How to Win Matrix

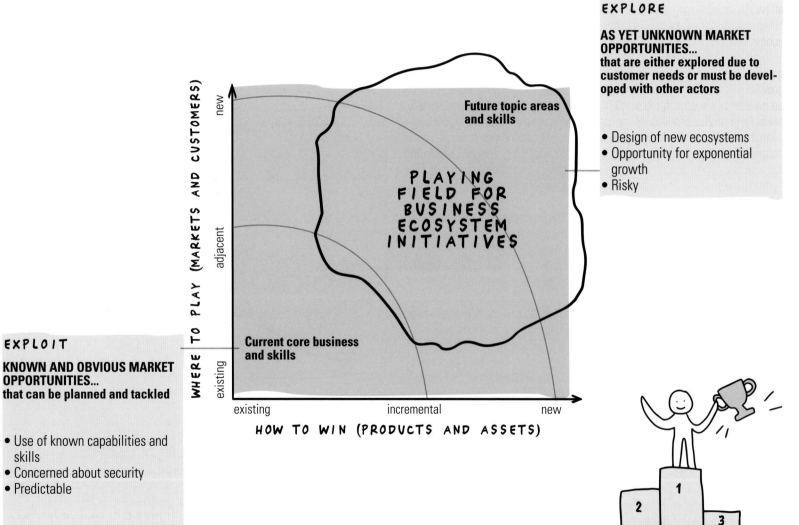

WHERE TO PLAY (MARKETS AND CUSTOMERS)

new

adjacent

existing

HOW TO WIN (PRODUCTS AND ASSETS)

existing — incremental — new

Future topic areas and skills

PLAYING FIELD FOR BUSINESS ECOSYSTEM INITIATIVES

Current core business and skills

EXPLORE

AS YET UNKNOWN MARKET OPPORTUNITIES...
that are either explored due to customer needs or must be developed with other actors

- Design of new ecosystems
- Opportunity for exponential growth
- Risky

EXPLOIT

KNOWN AND OBVIOUS MARKET OPPORTUNITIES...
that can be planned and tackled

- Use of known capabilities and skills
- Concerned about security
- Predictable

Companies that bank on EXPLOIT and stick to their existing focus have a hard time generating exponential growth. Their growth through an ecosystem will be increased by a factor of 2 at the most. Traditional companies often have a very high proportion of tangible and human capital. Both don't allow for achieving greater margins and exploiting new growth opportunities. By contrast, companies, that have understood the importance of ecosystem capital, consisting of the interaction of all actors in the system, and generating win-win situations through a multidimensional view of the business models have corresponding opportunities to realize exponential growth. The research of Staeritz and Torrance (2020) found that their return on investment is usually above 20%, with margins of over 40% and a price-sales ratio of 10x. Traditional sectors, with the exception of industries with a large share of intellectual capital (e.g biotech, software providers), are far below these figures. Banks, for instance, usually have a return on capital of 1.5%, margins of 7–8%, and a price-sales ratio of 1.5x. The situation is similar for insurance companies. Traditional retailing must be satisfied with margins of 5–6 %, a return on investment of less than 3%, and a price-sales ratio of 1x.

Ecosystem players such as Amazon make increasing use of the ecosystem capital lever as a supplement to the existing mix of business models. Companies such as Ping An (originally a conventional insurance company) have managed to evolve into an ecosystem orchestrator in 10 years. Many of the currently successful ecosystem actors pursue a balanced portfolio of EXPLORE and EXPLOIT. Steady evolution and the expansion of intellectual and ecosystem capital can be observed here, as demonstrated impressively by Ping An's growth chart. See the example on page 307.

Configuration of Traditional Enterprises vs. Ecosystem Orchestrators (Capital/Business Model)

Example

High proportion of human capital, tangible capital, and financial capital

Ecosystem capital as a growth lever

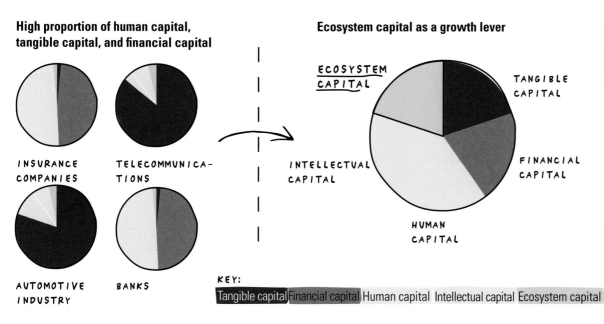

INSURANCE COMPANIES

TELECOMMUNICA-TIONS

AUTOMOTIVE INDUSTRY

BANKS

ECOSYSTEM CAPITAL

TANGIBLE CAPITAL

INTELLECTUAL CAPITAL

FINANCIAL CAPITAL

HUMAN CAPITAL

KEY:
Tangible capital | Financial capital | Human capital | Intellectual capital | Ecosystem capital

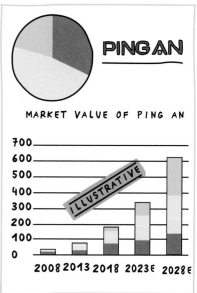

PING AN

MARKET VALUE OF PING AN

ILLUSTRATIVE

2008 2013 2018 2023E 2028E

S-Shaped Developments: Possible Evolutions in an Ecosystem Play

There is no established or standardized pattern for the classification of business ecosystem strategies. From the drafting and observing of various initiatives, some patterns could be derived that can be presented in selected dimensions. Based on this, some strategic manifestations can be typified, for example: **"engaged participant"**, **"focused challenger"** or **"life cycle approach."** These variations will be described in detail on page 142 et seq.

It is also intriguing to reflect on where companies currently stand and how their S-shaped development toward being an actor, integrator, or orchestrator of ecosystems is going. Many enterprises are currently still busy coping with the digital transformation, although there has been an acceleration of this ambition in recent years. As part of this transformation, companies have already launched various measures to improve customer interfaces, use big data analytics gainfully, and to intensify collaboration with technology start-ups. This provides a good basis for establishing the company in digital marketplaces via APIs or integrating more comprehensive data about customers (including from external providers).

Collaboration with technology start-ups is perceived as a field for experimentation and learning. Frequently, the following step opens up a role as solution integrator/bundler in a life cycle approach. The focus here is on the aggregation or integration of services from company partners, which usually takes the form of providing a digital marketplace/platform for the respective range of offers. Increasingly, companies rely on the EXPLOIT approach. Starting from there, companies are venturing into completely new ecosystem initiatives. The advantage of such a greenfield approach is that work is usually done consistently on a new value proposition, while existing business models, products, and services remain in the background.

As an alternative, enterprises take a direct path to being an initiator or orchestrator of a business ecosystem. Normally, such a radical step is only taken by companies and business leaders who have mentally performed and internalized all mindshifts.

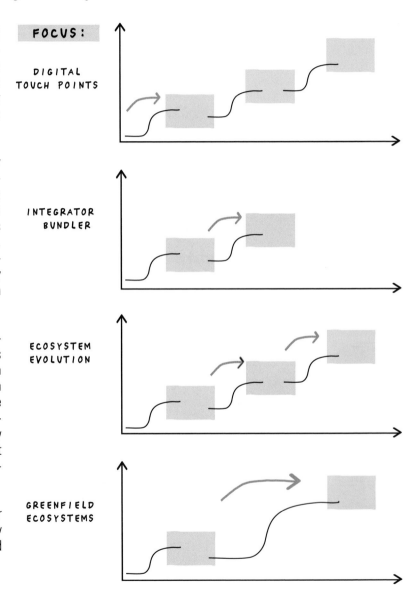

FOCUS:

DIGITAL TOUCH POINTS

INTEGRATOR BUNDLER

ECOSYSTEM EVOLUTION

GREENFIELD ECOSYSTEMS

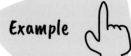
CUSTOMER-
CENTERED
OPEN
ECOSYSTEMS

COMPANY-
CENTERED
CLOSED
ECOSYSTEMS

TRADITIONAL COMPANIES WITH A STRATEGIC FOCUS ON DIGITAL TRANSFORMATION AND DIGITAL CHANNEL EXPANSION

ECOSYSTEM PLAYER WITH A STRATEGIC FOCUS ON THE ROLE OF SOLUTION INTEGRATOR BUNDLER IN A LIFE CYCLE APPROACH

ECOSYSTEM PLAYER, E.G. WITH A STRATEGIC FOCUS ON THE ROLE OF INITIATOR AND ORCHESTRATOR, BASED ON THE GREENFIELD APPROACH WITH NEW TECHNOLOGY

COMPLEXITY AND ACCESS TO NEW VALUE STREAMS

LOW

MEDIUM

HIGH

- Focus on improving digital customer interfaces
- First initiatives in the area of big data analytics
- Sponsoring and interaction with innovation ecosystems (e.g. start-up initiatives)

- Focus on the aggregation or integration of the services provided by business partners
- Provision of a digital marketplace/platform for the offering
- Use of new business models with new direct and indirect value streams

- Active role as a business ecosystem orchestrator
- Use of state-of-the-art information technology
- Definition of multiple value streams and business model options
- Data-driven service and product development with further options of monetizing data

Opening up and taking a path toward the various ecosystem roles will affect the respective business model, with all the consequences associated with it. Again, there exist many possibilities and manifestations, which can differ greatly depending on the business ecosystem. Consequences with regard to resources, skills, organization, and value proposition are shown in the table.

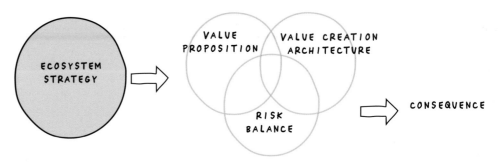

SELECTION OF...	EXAMPLES	POSSIBLE CONSEQUENCES
CUSTOMER INTERACTIONS	• Addressing new customer groups/segments • Use the means of price discrimination • Type of customer interaction via physical, multidimensional, or 100% digital channels	• Intensity of competition • Types of customer segments • Number of touch points, user experience design
CUSTOMER INTERFACES, CUSTOMER RELATIONSHIPS	• Definition of the width and depth of the offers per segment • Decentralized, hub-and-spoke, or point-to-point support and customer relations	• Automation possibilities • Know-how of experts • Physical and digital presence
CAPABILITIES IN TERMS OF IT, DATA, INFRASTRUCTURE, AI	• Use of resources of low strategic importance • Development of in-house technology	• Availability of resources on the labor market • No need for partners in technology development
ROLES IN THE BUSINESS ECOSYSTEM	• Function as initiator • Role of orchestrator • Participating actor with specific or general tasks	• Amount of pre-investment for prototypes and MVPs • Degree of responsibility for growth • Degree of opening, adaptation, and provision of skills
PRODUCT AND SERVICE PORTFOLIO ELEMENTS	• Full service with a wide and deep range of offers • Specific offerings or amplification of existing offers	• Number of different actors in the system • Complexity of orchestration • Satisfying individual or a variety of customer needs
FEATURES OF ORGANIZATIONAL DESIGN	• Interaction/co-creation with new actors • Direct marketing/bundling	• Bargaining power of the stakeholders • No need for distributors
COMPETITIVE STRATEGIES (OCEAN)	• Continuation of a red ocean strategy • Strong differentiation via blue ocean strategy • Realization of a black ocean strategy with a unique value proposition	• Degree of differentiation • Opportunities for growth • Radicalness of current and future innovations

Contextualization of Strategic Options in the "Ecosystem Play and Win Configuration Framework"

As described above, questions and so-called choice cascades from strategy work can be used as a basis to contextualize options, thus making the evaluation of different fields of action in terms of ecosystems more accessible to decision makers and decision-making bodies. A well-known tool is the strategy methodology of "playing to win" by AG Lafley and Roger Martin, which can be used for such a purpose. The framework is based on a number of questions that are interrelated and can be adapted to ecosystem initiatives as shown here in the example.

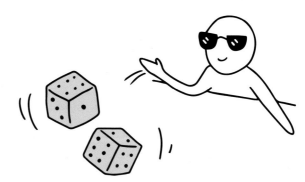

The strategy consists of a coordinated and integrated approach of various options:

A winning aspiration:
The purpose of the ecosystem, the motivating aspiration of all actors, is to be successful.

Where to play:
A topic area where the goal can be achieved.

How to win:
The manner in which you can win in the chosen topic area.

Core capabilities:
The capabilities and expertise required for achieving the chosen target image.

Management systems:
Governance that makes it possible to expand existing capabilities, build up new capabilities, and achieve the prioritized target image.

How to configure:
Enhancing the understanding of roles in the ecosystem, including the shaping of customer interactions and offers.

ECOSYSTEM PLAY AND WIN CONFIGURATION FRAMEWORK

Tool

DEFINITION OF MARKET OPPORTUNITY, MARKET AREA, AND CUSTOMER NEEDS

DEFINITION OF THE CAPABILITIES, ROLES, AND GOVERNANCE

DEFINITION OF THE PROCEDURE, TACTICS, AND STRATEGY

TOPIC AREA ENVIRONMENT ANALYSIS

CAPABILITIES

ECOSYSTEM VISION

EXPONENTIAL GROWTH

WHERE TO PLAY?

Customer needs

Customer interaction

Customer relationships

Value proposition

HOW TO CONFIGURE?

Strategic focus
Customer interaction
Customer relationships
Capabilities and skills (e.g. IT, data)
Product and service portfolio
Organizational design
Competitive strategy
Roles

HOW TO WIN?

Product and service portfolio

Roles in the business ecosystem

Organizational design; governance

Multidimensional view of the business models

EXPLOIT Existing partnerships, initiatives, technologies, and strategies

New partnerships, initiatives, technologies, and strategies **EXPLORE**

Ecosystem Configuration Grid
From "Where to Play" to "How to Win and Configure"

Tool

The specific dimensions for "how to configure" should be developed individually for each ecosystem. The manifestations presented on the following pages are of an illustrative and exemplary nature. Configurations of business ecosystems from a company's point of view — according to the aforementioned criteria — are shown on pages 142–145.

The ecosystem configuration grid map aids the business ecosystem design team to:
- carry out the critical configurations for the business ecosystem;
- develop a configuration that matches the initiative and role (e.g. initiator or active participant);
- address the elements critical to success, from strategic focus to customer interaction all the way to organizational design;
- describe configuration elements accurately to reach clarity on the intention and goal attainment.

Procedure and template ecosystem configuration grid:
1. The results from the definition of market opportunity, market area, and the respective customer needs (where to play) help to shape the configuration.
2. The configuration is closely linked to the actual definition of the project, the chosen tactics, and strategies (how to win).
3. After all, the configuration should contain all the elements required to make, step by step, an ecosystem vision a reality; the dimensions and manifestations are selected and described to fit the initiative.

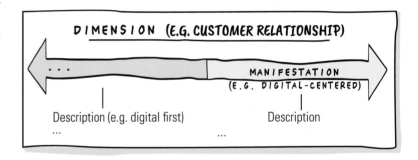

DIMENSION (E.G. CUSTOMER RELATIONSHIP)

MANIFESTATION
(E.G. DIGITAL-CENTERED)

Description (e.g. digital first)
...

Description
...

The dimensions and manifestations should be selected so they match the focus of a business ecosystem.

DOWNLOAD TOOL
https://en.business-ecosystem-design.com/win-configure

How to Win and Configure: Strategic Focus

Many established companies pursue a strategy that is well balanced between EXPLOIT and EXPLORE and operate in these dimensions for participation in or initialization of business ecosystems. The EXPLORE path is more
in line with the approach and the mindset needed for the establishment of
new ecosystems with unique value propositions; ecosystem initiatives and
participation of an EXPLOIT nature tend to pursue the goal of marketing
products and services via an additional channel or marketplace. You'll find
a comparison of EXPLOIT and EXPLORE in the table on page 50.

Example

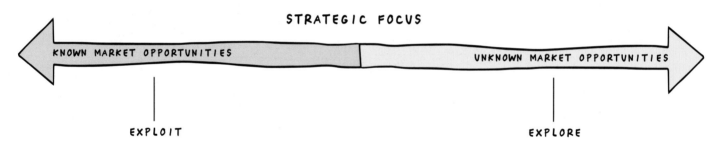

STRATEGIC FOCUS

KNOWN MARKET OPPORTUNITIES — UNKNOWN MARKET OPPORTUNITIES

EXPLOIT

Focus on existing capabilities,
products, customer interfaces, and
markets, or expansion of existing
business models into an ecosystem.

EXPLORE

Focus on emerging customer
needs, new behaviors, and markets
as well as product and service
groups, or assuming new roles
and business models that offer an
ecosystem.

How to Win and Configure: Customer Interaction

The selection of the right customer interaction is another frequently used feature of business ecosystems. The dimensions of customer interactions cover a wide range. The selection presented here distinguishes between human centered and digital centered. Many services and products require an actual, face-to-face contact person, while other services and products can be purchased 100% digitally without any problems. Many ecosystems begin with a focus on "digital first" and later build out supplementary physical touch points such as "experience centers" or "representations" for the purchase of products or services. Other ecosystem initiatives are learning from physical touch points and supplementing their offering with digital interaction later.

Example

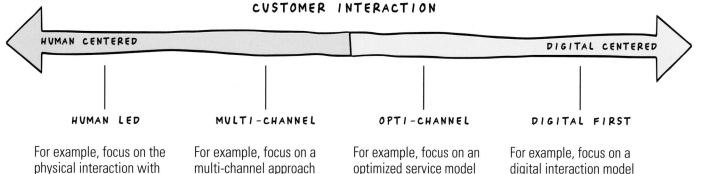

CUSTOMER INTERACTION

HUMAN CENTERED ← → DIGITAL CENTERED

HUMAN LED	MULTI-CHANNEL	OPTI-CHANNEL	DIGITAL FIRST
For example, focus on the physical interaction with customer across all transaction types and segments.	For example, focus on a multi-channel approach with digitally supported or fully automated customer interaction across all transaction types and segments.	For example, focus on an optimized service model with custom-tailored interactions based on the needs of each individual customer.	For example, focus on a digital interaction model that minimizes physical interaction, unless physical interaction is an integral part of the value proposition.

135

How to Win and Configure: Customer Interface, Customer Relationship

In addition to customer interaction, business ecosystems can establish and practice different forms of customer relationships. Contrary manifestations can be imagined here: "digital and automated" versus "digital and personal." Here too, numberless variants are possible, and they differ greatly depending on the ecosystem and the value proposition. Point-to-point relationships, for instance, make use of personal customer interaction for specific issues, where the involvement of experts is called for. For automated interactions, more decentralized approaches are used, e.g. by means of intelligent voice bots and chat bots.

Example

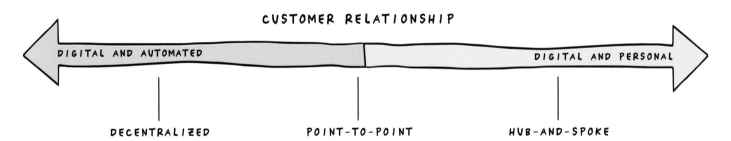

CUSTOMER RELATIONSHIP

DIGITAL AND AUTOMATED ← → DIGITAL AND PERSONAL

DECENTRALIZED

For example, focus on a consistent digital customer interface without a personal contact person who is responsible for the customer relationship.

POINT-TO-POINT

For example, focus on targeted personal customer interaction for specific issues by subject matter experts (SMEs).

HUB-AND-SPOKE

For example, individual service model with specific contacts for particular target groups, issues, or types of transaction.

How to Win and Configure: IT, Data, Infrastructure, AI

The strategic dimensions of EXPLOIT and EXPLORE are already applied by many to deal with skills in terms of IT, data, infrastructure all the way to artificial intelligence. Companies that focus on EXPLOIT often tend to build out IT and data capabilities slowly and gradually. Greenfield approaches, by contrast, implement their initiatives on new technology platforms and exploit the full potential of digitization. Every type of legacy system or the lack of APIs all the way to data analytics skills slows down implementation and reduces scalability.

Example

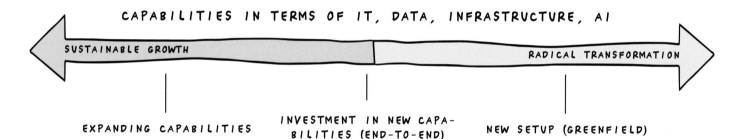

CAPABILITIES IN TERMS OF IT, DATA, INFRASTRUCTURE, AI

SUSTAINABLE GROWTH ⟵ ⟶ RADICAL TRANSFORMATION

EXPANDING CAPABILITIES

For example, investments in digitization or replacement of critical skills for the design of new functions and customer experiences, all the way to new value propositions.

INVESTMENT IN NEW CAPABILITIES (END-TO-END)

For example, as part of a comprehensive transformation of capabilities across large parts of the value chain with cutting-edge and innovative technology.

NEW SETUP (GREENFIELD)

For example, building an entirely new technology platform on the greenfield that operates as a separate company or business unit and exploits the full potential of new digital capabilities.

How to Win and Configure: Product and Service Portfolio

The dimensions of the products and services on offer in the ecosystem are based, for one, on the value proposition and secondly, on the planned steps and stages for the creation of the business ecosystem. At the beginning, so-called killer experiences and functions are frequently used, which aim at binding customers to the system and serving their needs in the best possible way. Again, the offers, from setup to the target image, can take on most diverse forms here. Examples of the product and service portfolio range from full-service offerings to bundles and such offers that focus on the life cycle of customers and companies.

Example

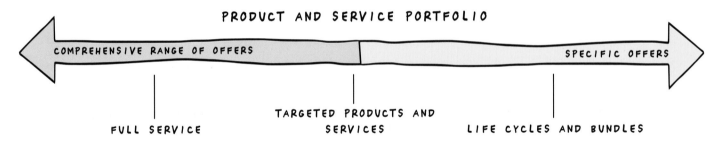

PRODUCT AND SERVICE PORTFOLIO

COMPREHENSIVE RANGE OF OFFERS ⟵ ⟶ SPECIFIC OFFERS

FULL SERVICE

For example, a very wide and deep range of products and services to be delivered by your own company and other actors in the ecosystem.

TARGETED PRODUCTS AND SERVICES

For example, the development of specific offers tailored to fit defined customer needs and sub-segments, either as completely new offerings or as an expansion of existing components of the range.

LIFE CYCLES AND BUNDLES

For example, design of various services and products that focus on the needs of the customers in different phases of their lives (cradle to grave).

How to Win and Configure: Organizational Design

Designing the organization is usually strongly influenced by the chosen governance and the way in which new capabilities, e.g. IT, data skills, are built and used. The characteristics range from customer-centered approaches with transversal teams all the way to traditional approaches that are integrated into the known structures of business units. Experience shows that for the successful realization of a business ecosystem a customer-centered model should be chosen and the organization should be aligned with it.

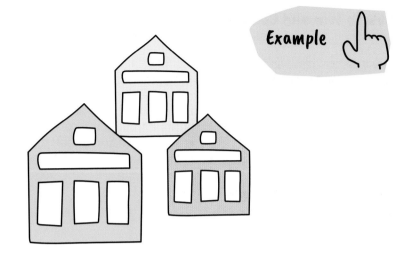

Example

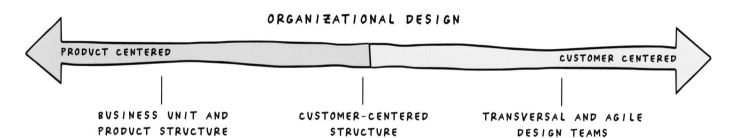

ORGANIZATIONAL DESIGN

PRODUCT CENTERED ← → CUSTOMER CENTERED

BUSINESS UNIT AND PRODUCT STRUCTURE

The organizational structure for participation in ecosystems follows the known product areas and business units of an enterprise.

CUSTOMER-CENTERED STRUCTURE

The structures and processes are designed in such a way that large parts of the organization can concentrate on designing a unique customer experience, including the digital channels and new incentives as "anchors" in the recurring customer interaction.

TRANSVERSAL AND AGILE DESIGN TEAMS

The structure of the organization is shaped by the transversal collaboration of different design teams that allows for greater agility, thus being able to address customer needs and market requirements better and respond to them quicker.

How to Win and Configure: Competitive Strategy

Example

Red, blue, and black ocean strategies are different views on the design of competitive strategies. The basic idea is that there are three different ways of achieving growth and sustainable corporate success. Red ocean describes the more traditional view, while blue ocean aims at developing new markets that truly provide differentiating and relevant benefits to the majority of customers and/or non-customers. Black ocean strategies pursue an even more radical path. The strategy aims at the creation of business ecosystems that, owing to their configuration, actors, and the provision of a unique value proposition, gives rivals little leeway to compete.

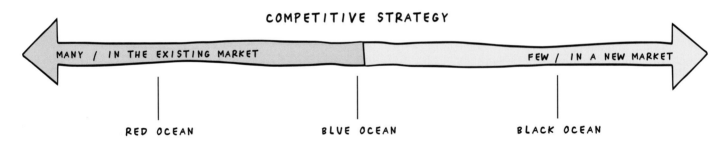

COMPETITIVE STRATEGY

MANY / IN THE EXISTING MARKET   FEW / IN A NEW MARKET

RED OCEAN

For example, focus on competition in an existing market, or exploiting existing demand with the aim of beating competitors.

BLUE OCEAN

For example, focus on the establishment of a new market, or tapping new demand with the aim of dodging competitors.

BLACK OCEAN

For example, focus on a unique value proposition that could not be delivered by an individual company, or satisfying new customer needs with the aim of generating an ecosystem consisting of co-competition and coevolution with other actors.

How to Win and Configure: Roles in the Business Ecosystem

The roles in the business ecosystem range from initiator to orchestrator all the way to actor in the system. Often, more roles are defined that are relevant to a specific business ecosystem. Usually, three of the roles on the list are of the greatest strategic importance and should be analyzed and defined accordingly in the context of the ecosystem strategy. Companies may have several roles in different ecosystems. They participate in ecosystems and at the same time actively build a new business ecosystem in a different environment. There are additional roles such as supplier and, as they are described here in the book, other players acting as technology enablers, for instance, or as validation points for information.

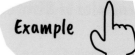
Example

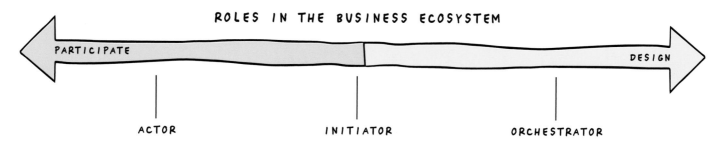

ROLES IN THE BUSINESS ECOSYSTEM

PARTICIPATE — DESIGN

ACTOR

An actor in a business ecosystem usually has capabilities or offerings that are integrated in the development of the value proposition. The actors also have the task of innovating within the framework of the principles and rules. They adjust parts of their activities, business models, and strategies according to the project.

INITIATOR

An initiator has discovered a new customer need, for instance, and begins to initialize activities. In many cases, the initiator provides the budget for initial prototypes and MVP. Often, initiators switch into the role of orchestrator or become the actor in their own system.

ORCHESTRATOR

The job of this role is coordinating the activities. Principles and rules are laid down for this; the framework conditions for exponential growth are defined. The orchestrator wants to achieve sustainable and targeted governance.

Examples of Strategic Manifestations

Each configuration of a business ecosystem is different. Three scenarios are outlined below to show how these scenarios lead to a different configuration. The first strategic manifestation is the simplest form of configuration of how to become active in a business ecosystem. As a participating company, in the role of active participant/innovator, capabilities and skills are brought to the ecosystem; within the limits of the principles and defined values, there is then the option to co-innovate in the system (see page 143). Participation in a business ecosystem can take any form imaginable. For example: An initiator can take on the role of participating actor once the ecosystem has been established.

The second example of a configuration is that of an initiator of a digital ecosystem initiated by an established company (see page 144). This initiator wants to challenge the market with the business ecosystem and the value proposition entailed in it. Focused challengers are usually companies that want to serve a particular market segment with very targeted offerings in an ecosystem play.

The third example is that of a company assuming a major orchestration role in the business ecosystem (see page 145). On the assumption of digital first, a business ecosystem is designed around a defined life cycle. Normally, the value proposition is linked to certain events (e.g. live events). In such business ecosystems, the potential of big data analytics is taken into account in the design of the value streams and the ecosystem at an early stage of development.

Examples of configurations are infinite. And configurations change over the course of time since they are dynamic constructs. The following examples are only snapshots of business ecosystems that are currently evolving or have already been established in the market.

ACTIVE PRACTITIONER

FOCUSED CHALLENGER

TRUSTED LIFE CYCLE PLAYER

The examples are illustrative and are intended to show how numerous and varied the combinations are. Ecosystems are complex and are constantly evolving. For this reason, the examples are only snapshots from the process of "how to win and configure."

Examples of Strategic Manifestations: Active Participation/Innovator

The role of the participating actor is usually characterized by the company bringing in-house capabilities to a business ecosystem. The contributions may consist of customer contacts, products, or the provision of channels to customers. Within the framework of the principles and rules, an actor in such a system has the opportunity to innovate and design.

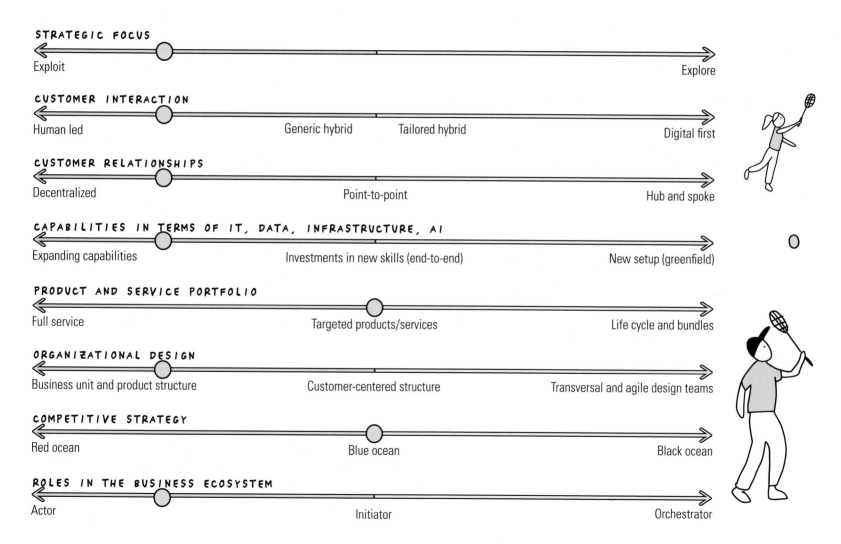

STRATEGIC FOCUS

Exploit ←————————○———————————————————————→ Explore

CUSTOMER INTERACTION

Human led ←————○———————————————————————→ Digital first

Generic hybrid   Tailored hybrid

CUSTOMER RELATIONSHIPS

Decentralized ←————○——————————————————→ Hub and spoke

Point-to-point

CAPABILITIES IN TERMS OF IT, DATA, INFRASTRUCTURE, AI

Expanding capabilities ←——○——————————————→ New setup (greenfield)

Investments in new skills (end-to-end)

PRODUCT AND SERVICE PORTFOLIO

Full service ←————————————○————————————→ Life cycle and bundles

Targeted products/services

ORGANIZATIONAL DESIGN

Business unit and product structure ←——○————————→ Transversal and agile design teams

Customer-centered structure

COMPETITIVE STRATEGY

Red ocean ←————————————○————————————→ Black ocean

Blue ocean

ROLES IN THE BUSINESS ECOSYSTEM

Actor ←————○————————————————————————→ Orchestrator

Initiator

Examples of Strategic Manifestations: Focused Challenger

Design of a digital ecosystem that is initiated by an established company to challenge the market with this offering (challenger) and serves a particular market segment with targeted products. The design is customer-centered, and the interaction offers a custom-tailored value proposition based on needs together with the option to transfer the role of the orchestrator to another actor, for instance.

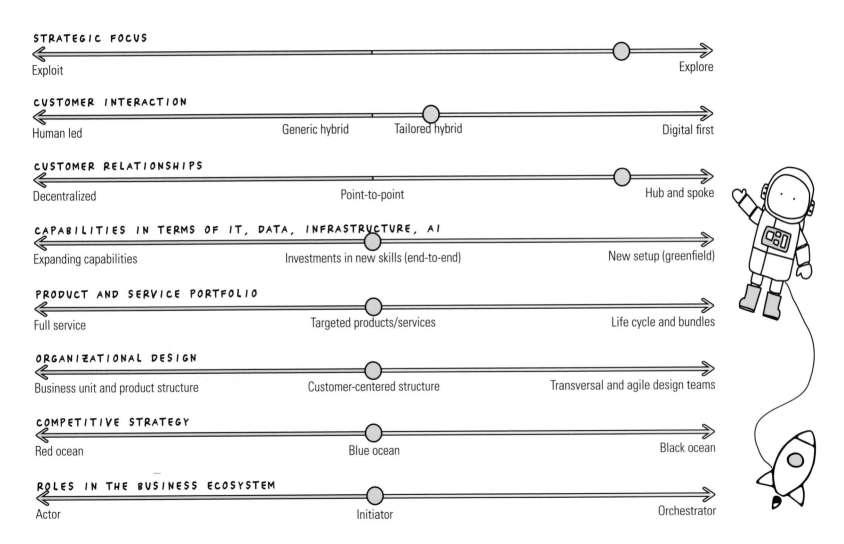

STRATEGIC FOCUS

Exploit   Explore

CUSTOMER INTERACTION

Human led   Generic hybrid   Tailored hybrid   Digital first

CUSTOMER RELATIONSHIPS

Decentralized   Point-to-point   Hub and spoke

CAPABILITIES IN TERMS OF IT, DATA, INFRASTRUCTURE, AI

Expanding capabilities   Investments in new skills (end-to-end)   New setup (greenfield)

PRODUCT AND SERVICE PORTFOLIO

Full service   Targeted products/services   Life cycle and bundles

ORGANIZATIONAL DESIGN

Business unit and product structure   Customer-centered structure   Transversal and agile design teams

COMPETITIVE STRATEGY

Red ocean   Blue ocean   Black ocean

ROLES IN THE BUSINESS ECOSYSTEM

Actor   Initiator   Orchestrator

Examples of Strategic Manifestations: Trusted Life Cycle Player

Greenfield approach with the aim of establishing an ecosystem on the assumption of digital first with regard to customer support. The life cycle of a customer or a service may constitute the basis for this. The ecosystem offers the appropriate (neutral) expertise as needed for a trustworthy response to customer inquiries. Data and agile internal structures help to develop new and individualized products quickly.

STRATEGIC FOCUS

Exploit ⟵————————————————○————————————————⟶ Explore

CUSTOMER INTERACTION

Human led ⟵——————————————————————————————○———⟶ Digital first

Generic hybrid   Tailored hybrid

CUSTOMER RELATIONSHIPS

Decentralized ⟵————————————○————————————————⟶ Hub and spoke

Point-to-point

CAPABILITIES IN TERMS OF IT, DATA, INFRASTRUCTURE, AI

Expanding capabilities ⟵——————————————————————○———⟶ New setup (greenfield)

Investments in new skills (end-to-end)

PRODUCT AND SERVICE PORTFOLIO

Full service ⟵——————————————————————○———⟶ Life cycle and bundles

Targeted products/services

ORGANIZATIONAL DESIGN

Business unit and product structure ⟵——————————————————————○———⟶ Transversal and agile design teams

Customer-centered structure

COMPETITIVE STRATEGY

Red ocean ⟵——————————————————————○———⟶ Black ocean

Blue ocean

ROLES IN THE BUSINESS ECOSYSTEM

Actor ⟵——————————————————○————————————⟶ Orchestrator

Initiator

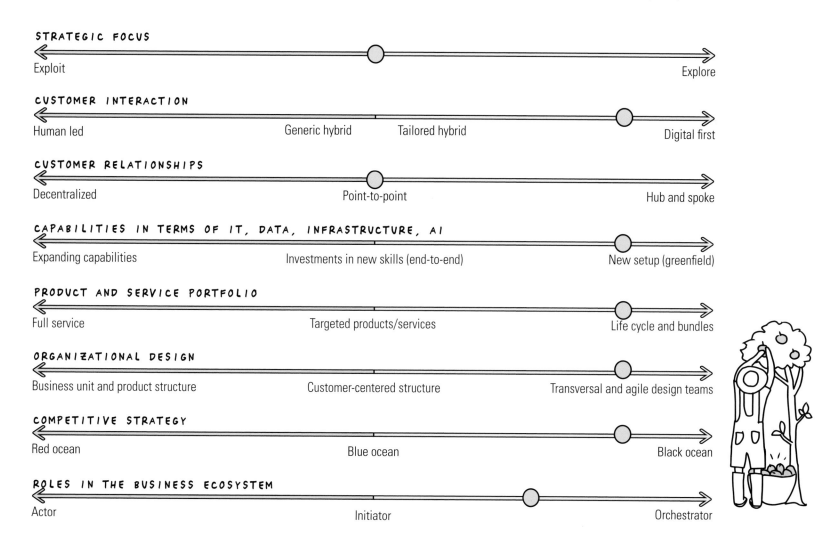

The explanations in this section of how to perceive business ecosystems as strategic options show how momentous ecosystem approaches and the application of design thinking for business growth are for the entire company. The complexity of such initiative requires new approaches in the strategy development all the way to the right governance for such growth paths. In addition, business ecosystem design affects the forms of collaboration within the business and across companies. Entailed in it are the major mindshifts (page 24) and paradigm shifts (pages 48–49).

The governance of an ecosystem has nothing in common with the established ideas of partner management in businesses. It is more about the orchestration of employees and other actors in the system. They must be enabled to be innovative, change quickly, and exploit the full potential of an ecosystem for all those involved. In addition, business leaders must be willing to accept the risks of change, modify organizational structures, and direct the parameters of future ways of working in the right direction. The collaboration of people and technology as a team is one of the key drivers for an efficient use of resources to be more determined and responsive. A business ecosystem play needs a good mix of different skills. They range from technology knowledge all the way to a new kind of leadership. This is the only way to achieve the target images of a business ecosystem and finally exponential growth. The topics of ecosystem leadership, communication of target images, and use of the team-of-teams approach will be briefly outlined on page 155 et seq. An overview of future ways of working and co-creation approaches is given on page 159 et seq. so that all dimensions, from the mindset to capabilities all the way to team structures of agile working required for successful ecosystem initiatives, are covered. It has also proven useful to define the design principles before the teams start activities in the lenses. This tool was already presented on page 108 in this chapter.

Experience from various business ecosystem initiatives shows that the biggest challenges for companies are to move beyond existing market and product segmentations. This is accompanied by the change of business models with direct and indirect revenue sources. Furthermore, this requires appropriate governance structures that allow the step-by-step implementation of the defined ecosystem strategy. The illustration on the right summarizes the most important elements, building blocks, and capabilities.

UNLOCK EXPONENTIAL GROWTH

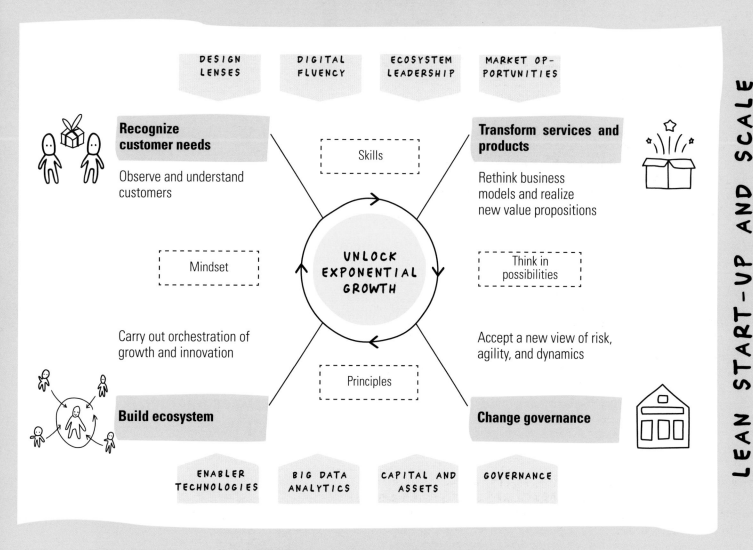

BUSINESS ECOSYSTEM DESIGN

DESIGN THINKING AND SYSTEMS THINKING

LEAN START-UP AND SCALE

CORPORATE STRATEGY

DESIGN LENSES

DIGITAL FLUENCY

ECOSYSTEM LEADERSHIP

MARKET OP-PORTUNITIES

Recognize customer needs

Observe and understand customers

Transform services and products

Rethink business models and realize new value propositions

Skills

Mindset

UNLOCK EXPONENTIAL GROWTH

Think in possibilities

Carry out orchestration of growth and innovation

Accept a new view of risk, agility, and dynamics

Principles

Build ecosystem

Change governance

ENABLER TECHNOLOGIES

BIG DATA ANALYTICS

CAPITAL AND ASSETS

GOVERNANCE

To the Point!

The procedure via the ecosystem play and win configuration framework and the associated objectives and strategies show how market opportunities can be realized in different configurations.

The configuration of the business ecosystem shows the roles, capabilities, and governance of the system. The dimensions of the configuration should be defined so they fit the ecosystem initiative and be continuously adapted so all the elements are directly or indirectly connected.

Each turn of an adjusting screw in the configuration has consequences for other dimensions. The dynamics are comparable to a mobile that is constantly moving and whose parts mutually affect one another.

WHERE TO PLAY?   HOW TO CONFIGURE?   HOW TO WIN?

ECOSYSTEM LEADERSHIP

Ecosystem Leadership

Ecosystem leadership is a key task in design thinking for business growth and the participation in business ecosystems since either existing skills must be exploited in the best possible way or new skills must be built. In addition, in most cases, a new mindset must be established beyond the boundaries of the company. This does not only mean the development of an ecosystem strategy and the determination of various strategic options but also the way in which business models are viewed in a multidimensional way; how the ecosystem governance of the orchestrator is set up; how core competencies will be used; how value streams should be defined for the benefit of all involved; and finally, what the organizational model should look like. The key to success is the mindful transformation of teams, organizations, and companies as described in **The Design Thinking Playbook.**

The convergence of technologies, customer wishes, and ecosystems has never happened faster than today. It's time to rethink previous mindsets, values, and risk assessments. But ecosystem innovation is more than just defining new business models. Prototypes of entire systems are needed, i.e. minimum viable ecosystems (MVEs) by which key risks are tested before the appropriate roles are assumed, e.g. that of orchestrator or actor.

In terms of transformation, "minimum viable" means that all important elements for a well-functioning ecosystem must be thoroughly examined. Transformation is the constant here, not least because business ecosystems are constantly evolving dynamically.

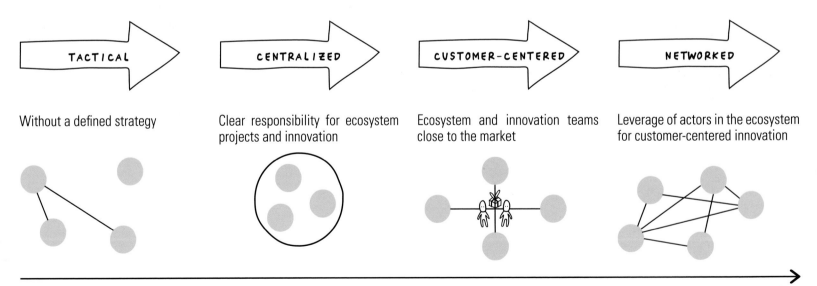

TACTICAL — Without a defined strategy

CENTRALIZED — Clear responsibility for ecosystem projects and innovation

CUSTOMER-CENTERED — Ecosystem and innovation teams close to the market

NETWORKED — Leverage of actors in the ecosystem for customer-centered innovation

ECOSYSTEM LEADERSHIP AND TEAM MATURITY

The design of business ecosystems in the context of design thinking for business growth offers the opportunity to apply completely new ways of working (future of work) and establish them in the organization. By shifting perspectives away from traditional employee development to opportunities to open up the full spectrum to develop entirely new value streams for the business. With increased agility and the ability to share risks, companies can gain new market areas for themselves if they apply this approach.

Successful ecosystem leaders intentionally place the innovation teams close to important market and customer knowledge so that they get to know the context first hand and are able to transfer insights to other teams. By means of rotating teams, a mindful transformation and dialog across the departmental silos are ensured. Software development teams, for example, also need market and customer knowledge to be able to validate MVPs and define use cases.

Technological complexity: **low**
Market complexity: **high**

INNOVATION TEAM MATRIX

high

COMPLEXITY OF THE MARKET AND CUSTOMER KNOWLEDGE

MOVE INFORMATION ABOUT THE TECHNOLOGY TO WHERE MARKET AND CUSTOMER KNOWLEDGE ARE LOCATED.

Move and exchange knowledge through a rotating workforce and temporary co-allocation.

Exchange of information on a higher level is usually sufficient.

Move information about the market and the customers to where the technology is located.

low

low   COMPLEXITY OF KNOWLEDGE ON THE TECHNOLOGY   high

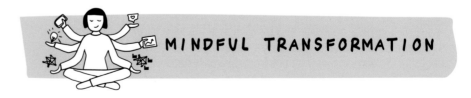

MINDFUL TRANSFORMATION

What Kind of Leadership Is Needed for a Transformation toward an Ecosystem Play?

With regard to design thinking for business growth, we have already adopted various perspectives on mindshifts in this book. To cope successfully with the new models of strategy definition, co-creation, and the paradigm shift in terms of growth and the new business models, additional appropriate leadership profiles are required to launch ecosystem initiatives. From observations of various business ecosystem initiatives, a leadership profile can be derived that is especially good for the implementation of and participation in such business ecosystems.

Six qualities in particular are enablers for successful eco-leadership:

- **Customer centered**
- **Digitally adept**
- **Ambitious**
- **Patient**
- **Open to new relationships**
- **Team oriented**

Autonomy of the implementation teams is needed for the implementation of business ecosystem design. This includes both open talks with various potential actors and a culture of doers that reflects the spirit of an entrepreneurial mindset. Traditional companies often define so-called venture units or dedicated ecosystem units for this that help to increase implementation speed. Leaders who assemble teams for ecosystem initiatives want ecosystem design teams with convincing methodological expertise from the design thinking and systems thinking toolbox. In addition, team members should have big data analytics and UX design skills as well as IT expertise. Enterprise architecture becomes a major issue since in many cases it's necessary to align the interactions from the ecosystem with the existing infrastructure and enable direct or indirect customer contact through increasingly digital—but also analog—interactions, applying multi-channel or opti-channel strategies.

The New Roles of the Ecosystem Leader

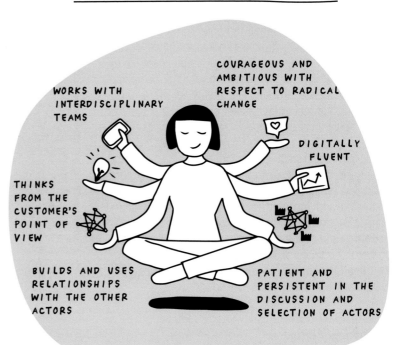

WORKS WITH INTERDISCIPLINARY TEAMS

COURAGEOUS AND AMBITIOUS WITH RESPECT TO RADICAL CHANGE

DIGITALLY FLUENT

THINKS FROM THE CUSTOMER'S POINT OF VIEW

BUILDS AND USES RELATIONSHIPS WITH THE OTHER ACTORS

PATIENT AND PERSISTENT IN THE DISCUSSION AND SELECTION OF ACTORS

Ecosystem leadership is the networking of all actors involved in value creation.

Leadership Role: Transformation of Business Models and Organizations

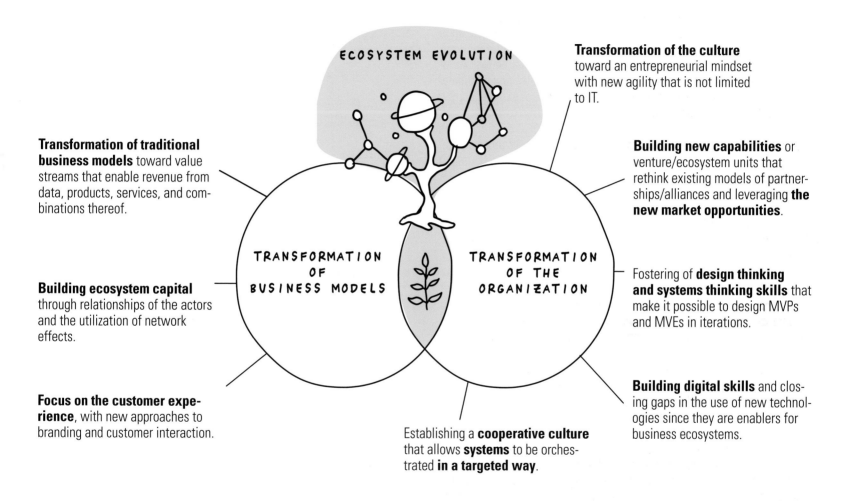

ECOSYSTEM EVOLUTION

TRANSFORMATION OF BUSINESS MODELS

TRANSFORMATION OF THE ORGANIZATION

Transformation of traditional business models toward value streams that enable revenue from data, products, services, and combinations thereof.

Building ecosystem capital through relationships of the actors and the utilization of network effects.

Focus on the customer experience, with new approaches to branding and customer interaction.

Transformation of the culture toward an entrepreneurial mindset with new agility that is not limited to IT.

Building new capabilities or venture/ecosystem units that rethink existing models of partnerships/alliances and leveraging **the new market opportunities**.

Fostering of **design thinking and systems thinking skills** that make it possible to design MVPs and MVEs in iterations.

Building digital skills and closing gaps in the use of new technologies since they are enablers for business ecosystems.

Establishing a **cooperative culture** that allows **systems** to be orchestrated **in a targeted way**.

T-Shaped Ecosystem Design Teams

In design thinking as well as in business ecosystem design, it is particularly important to work with interdisciplinary teams. Preferably with team members who have a strong T shape. The horizontal bar stands for a wide range of knowledge; team members come from many different cultures, disciplines, and systems. The vertical bar represents specialist know-how of the team members, e.g. knowledge of a system, an industry, or a discipline.

Furthermore, qualities such as collaboration capability and interface expertise are extremely important for the design tasks: T-shaped team members are open, interested in other perspectives, and curious about other people, the environment, and other disciplines. Experience shows that the better the understanding of the way others think and work, the faster and greater the common progress and success in the business ecosystem process.

More and more, T-shaped teams are set up for the development of MVPs and in agile software development as well. Such teams cover the need for interdisciplinary software developers and testers in the respective (scrum) teams.

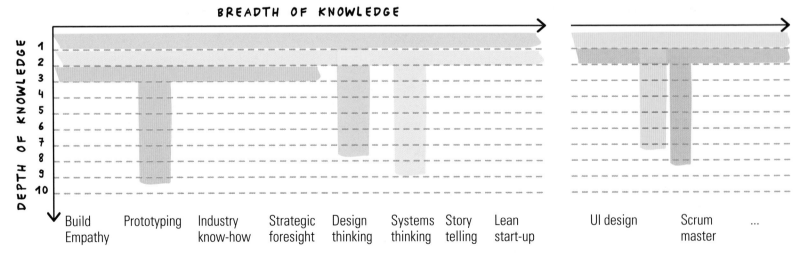

DESIGN THINKING FOR BUSINESS GROWTH TEAMS

SOFTWARE DEVELOPMENT TEAMS

Team-of-Teams Approach

Transforming the team and management structures in one shift from scalable efficiency to scalable adaptability helps to launch business ecosystems successfully and grow exponentially. Traditional organizations are geared to doing things right, while a business ecosystem play requires doing the right things to reach the target image. This rule is particularly important for business ecosystems because the systems are dynamic, and permanent adaptation of the teams to the situation is required. In the case of unpredictable changes, the organization's adaptability is by far the most vital capability. In the team-of-teams approach, the units work in a decentralized way. This type of organizational design allows the unit to act quickly in unknown situations. The required organizational form, governance, and the ecosystem leadership already described are based on the same values and operational principles that make it possible to initialize and simultaneously orchestrate in a targeted manner.

Five crucial values for a team of teams:

1. Confidence in the skills and decisions of the other teams and their members.
2. Transparency of tasks, goals, and results across all teams.
3. Personal relationships in the network structures (at least one team member must know one team member from the other teams).
4. Empowered execution characterizes the decentralization of responsibility and actions.
5. Collective mindset for radical collaboration, flexibility, and adaptability to new situations.

TRADITIONAL ORGANIZATION
SCALABLE EFFICIENCY

TEAM-OF-TEAMS APPROACH
SCALABLE ADAPTABILITY

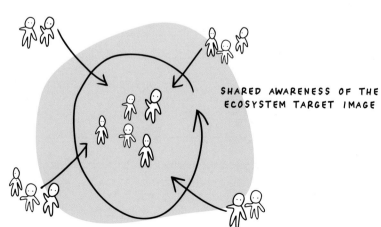

SHARED AWARENESS OF THE
ECOSYSTEM TARGET IMAGE

Communication of the North Star and Objectives, with Specific First Steps

Initialization of a business ecosystem and participation in an existing one both begin with a clear vision. The initiator demonstrates a compelling value proposition that makes it attractive for other companies to participate in the business ecosystem. For an actor who wants to participate in such an ecosystem, the vision must clearly show how the company can benefit in the best possible way from the system (e.g. leverage of skills, positive impact on the core business, or entirely new sources of income) and how it can cash in on the growth in the long term by participating in the business ecosystem.

Target image

Greater ambition, new value streams + digital enablers fully effective
Answering the questions:
• How is the goal to be achieved?
• Who is to be served?
• What is the value proposition?
• Is there a coevolution fit?

MVEs

New actors, testing of new value proposition, design of a functioning system
Answering the questions:
• What capabilities does the system need?
• Which roles can be assumed by which actors?
• Do all actors in the system benefit from participating in the system?
• Is there an actors fit?

MVPs

Improvements without changing the grand vision
Answering the questions:
• What is the customer willing to pay?
• Can we validate the assumptions about customers and functions?
• Is there a market fit?

Prototypes

Get a first idea of potential solutions
Answering the questions:
• What are the customer needs?
• Which customer problem do we want to solve, and how will we solve it?
• Is there a problem/solution fit?

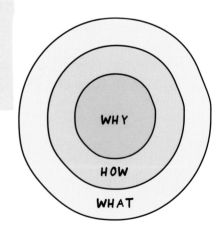

WHY

HOW

WHAT

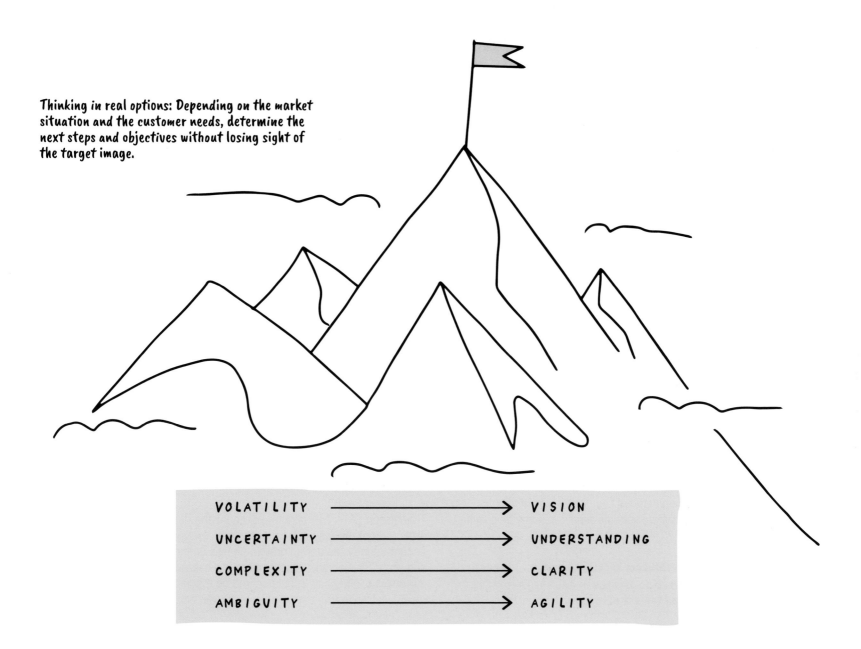

Thinking in real options: Depending on the market situation and the customer needs, determine the next steps and objectives without losing sight of the target image.

VOLATILITY ⟶ VISION

UNCERTAINTY ⟶ UNDERSTANDING

COMPLEXITY ⟶ CLARITY

AMBIGUITY ⟶ AGILITY

Objectives and Key Results

Design thinking for business growth initiatives move incredibly fast, and the latest insights, points of view, prototypes, and tests always deliver new results. The metrics of teams moving in such an environment are often more precise, with the focus on a specific objective and corresponding key results. This is why they can move faster and deliver more specific results. A design thinking for business growth team that is working on something and has no specific objectives or target user benefits needs a lot more time in the respective development steps. The goal of growth takes shape when we learn and execute as quickly as possible. It should be emphasized, though, that it's not about haste but about velocity. Too often, teams hurry and hasten and leave out important steps of the design lenses just to be finished a couple of weeks earlier. In some cases, taking a shortcut may be the right thing to do, but then there is a high risk that the solution isn't radical enough and there is no crisp execution. Taking two steps backward and pondering what would really generate an impact and is desired by the customers is the key to success.

Objectives and key results (OKRs) help with the implementation of a team of teams; moreover, they provide the framework for the individual design thinking for business growth teams for collaboration, expanding capabilities and suitable measuring points that are both transparent and comprehensible. If skills for the initiatives are lacking, it is crucial that the teams be equipped with more team members and resources whose mindset fits into design thinking for business growth. When selecting and hiring such team members, the mindset and the skills are more important than any job titles. Particularly when it comes to the ability to design business ecosystems because there are only a handful of companies with the right mindset and growth background from where suitable candidates may be poached.

> **Business growth and design thinking experts understand the tools that are needed to solve a specific problem — and they are ready to create their own methods and tools if necessary.**

> **For successful design thinking for business growth, you sometimes need a chainsaw, sometimes a chisel. The team should know and sense exactly which tool to use to reach the objectives.**

The right OKRs for successful design thinking for business growth initiatives depend on the maturity of the organization. The extent to which mindshifts have been completed so as to be able to think in business ecosystems can be an indicator of maturity; likewise, another indicator is how much the chosen governance fosters the orchestration of such business ecosystems. Typical questions for design thinking for growth initiatives are:

- How can we change or adjust the mindset?
- How can we bring rigor to the metrics?
- What is important?
- How do we solve user/customer needs? How do we ensure that users/customers continue to get value?

The chosen OKRs can take into account the desired mindset and type of organization, the way in which problems are quickly solved, and customer centeredness across all growth phases within the "problems to growth and scale" framework. Usually, there is a cascade from the strategy to the initiatives to the goals supplemented by the individual objectives and key results, which in turn have a positive impact on the team objectives.

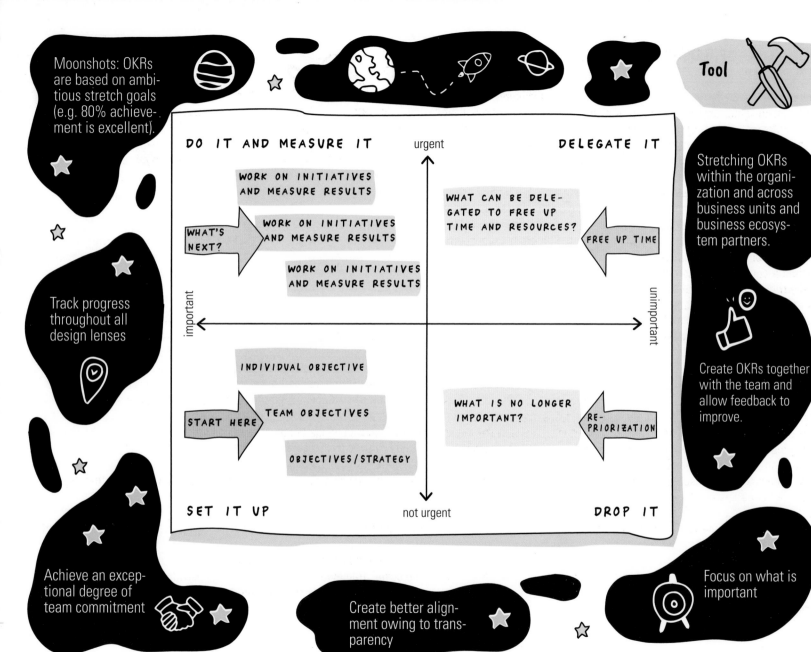

Moonshots: OKRs are based on ambitious stretch goals (e.g. 80% achievement is excellent).

Track progress throughout all design lenses

Achieve an exceptional degree of team commitment

Create better alignment owing to transparency

Tool

DO IT AND MEASURE IT

urgent

DELEGATE IT

WORK ON INITIATIVES AND MEASURE RESULTS

WHAT'S NEXT?

WORK ON INITIATIVES AND MEASURE RESULTS

WORK ON INITIATIVES AND MEASURE RESULTS

WHAT CAN BE DELE-GATED TO FREE UP TIME AND RESOURCES?

FREE UP TIME

important

unimportant

INDIVIDUAL OBJECTIVE

START HERE

TEAM OBJECTIVES

OBJECTIVES / STRATEGY

WHAT IS NO LONGER IMPORTANT?

RE-PRIORIZATION

SET IT UP

not urgent

DROP IT

Stretching OKRs within the organization and across business units and business ecosystem partners.

Create OKRs together with the team and allow feedback to improve.

Focus on what is important

Setting the Appropriate OKRs

There is no carved-in-stone procedure for the definition of OKRs. Each organization should proceed so that the objectives match the context of the goals, the corporate culture, and the growth ambitions. Different recommendations can be derived from the work with OKRs that help with the definition. For one, so-called near-term objectives can be defined, e.g. to be achieved in one quarter, or long-term objectives with a time frame of 12 or more months. A rule of thumb is that a maximum of five objectives per quarter with four key results is a healthy plan. To derive inspired and ambitious objectives constitutes a vital part of the OKR philosophy. Their purpose is to motivate all team members in equal measure, but they may trigger some discomfort as well. After all, it is not about 100% goal attainment. Instead, we want to develop a team of teams that is committed to the objective, able to motivate itself (establishing a bowl of trust), and at the same time can leave its comfort zone. If OKRs are 100% achieved, the objectives were not ambitious enough. This means that an 80% goal attainment can be defined as an outstanding performance.

Cascading strategy with OKRs

VISION
1.–Aligning the vision with the objectives
2.–Deciding which objectives have a high impact/priority

INITIATIVES
3.–Break the team objective down into initiatives and let each team member derive individual objectives

GOALS
4.–Set key results for each initiative and individual objective, and start working on it now!

STRATEGIES
5.–Start to deliver the defined key results

TACTICS
6.–Define tasks

ACTION PLANS
7.–Plan your activities

Compared to traditional goal measurement methods, e.g. management by business objectives (MBOs), OKRs are determined in shorter cycles. They extend to the two to four months mentioned above and are supplemented by measurable key results. These objectives can be adjusted over the year. Following design thinking for business growth and business ecosystem initiatives, new insights are gained after each design lens or design sprint; the new findings in turn influence the individual near-term or long-term objectives. Transparency about the objectives and key results on the team and across team boundaries aims solely at making the company's strategic topics and potential growth initiatives visible at all levels of the organization.

If you want your work to have an impact: Don't start with an action plan. Don't build a kanban board full of tasks. Decide what kind of impact you want to have and then work toward it, performing measurements along the entire way. Use feedback from the real world to make a real difference.

As shown in the simplified example (right), OKRs are used for the implementation of strategic topics of the organization, e.g. the ambition of developing a strategy for a specific business ecosystem topic in the context of participation or initialization. They consist of ambitious objectives that are to be achieved by measurable key results. The concept of OKRs is especially helpful with the transformation of organizations into a team of teams and for establishing a culture of efficient self-organization. OKRs can also help to establish a new design thinking for business growth mindset, new skills, and generally new corporate values such as transparency successfully and incrementally.

Applying design thinking for business growth in combination with team of teams has proven to lead toward breakthrough innovations in many initiatives.

Example: OKRs for a Business Ecosystem Design Initiative

BUSINESS ECOSYSTEM STRATEGY IN A SPECIFIC TOPIC AREA

"Building the umbrella"

TEAM OF TEAMS

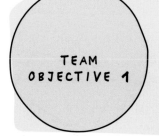

TEAM OBJECTIVE 1

TEAM OBJECTIVE 2

TEAM OBJECTIVE 3

Kick-start radical collaboration

INDIVIDUAL LONG-TERM OBJECTIVES (1-2)

INDIVIDUAL NEAR-TERM OBJECTIVES (2-4)

Establishing a bowl of trust

Explanations of different objectives:

- Creating a team-of-teams culture has been set as a long-term objective for the entire team and constitutes a defined part of the transformation and application of the desired mindshifts.

- The team objectives are aligned to the overall strategy, e.g. the ambition to create or participate in a specific topic area of a business ecosystem based on new or changed customer needs and/or behaviors.

- OKRs are also used to define, for example, 1–2 "individual objectives" and 2–4 "individual near-term objectives." The individual objectives reflect the way in which every team member will contribute individually to the team objectives.

- All objectives are transparent to all team members. In addition, all teams trust in the work and professionalism of the other teams.

To the Point!

Ecosystem leadership is based on the idea of initializing a functioning system and orchestrating it with a clear-cut target image.

Eco-leaders are relationship builders who understand the technologies required for the realization of such ecosystems as well.

From the exploration all the way to scaling, there is a need for inter-disciplinary teams that provide their T-shaped profile to the different phases.

For the development and growth of business ecosystems, it is crucial that all actors in the system can act as innovators and that the team-of-teams idea includes transparency and confidence regarding the activities of the individual decentralized units.

Transparency of the objectives and key results on the team and across team boundaries aims solely at making the company's growth initia-tives visible at all levels of the organization.

NEW WAYS OF WORKING

New Ways of Working and Design Thinking for Business Growth

In addition to the purpose of joint goal attainment, the interaction with the business ecosystem offers other possibilities. Ecosystems provide access to talent and expertise, regardless of whether they are found at a technology supplier, research institution, a start-up, or perceived competitor. The resources of companies are limited, and not all (new) capabilities can be developed within the company. Through participation in business ecosystems, new ways of working policies can be implemented that are designed to generate new knowledge in a cooperative way of working, to obtain problem-solving skills, and to make use of skills in technology.

The decision of a company to enter into a business ecosystem play has a direct impact on the necessary skills of the workforce. Most important is the ability of the team to adapt quickly, to see changes as an opportunity, and to accept the complexity that lies in the design and participation in business ecosystems. As described above, this transformation entails an expansion of tasks not only for the ecosystem leadership team but for all employees involved in such an agile system.

Human beings and technologies work best together when the strengths of both are exploited. And this mutual relationship is needed to ascertain new customer needs with empathy, to use human curiosity and imagination and the technology to boost efficiency, and realize exponential growth. The challenge consists of designing the work in such a way that ensures the success of people and machines.

The future way of working combines traditional roles and functions with technologies to exploit significant gains in productivity and efficiency.

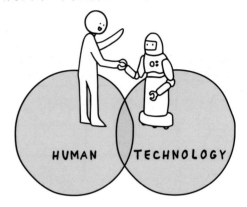

FUTURE:
CLOSE RELATIONSHIP,
HUMAN-TECHNOLOGY AS A TEAM

Intelligent, (semi-)autonomous machine integration with humans and social systems

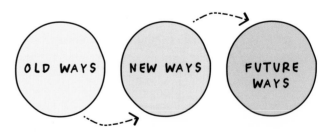

Future ways of working requires a combination of multiple traditional roles with technological capabilities, expertise, and social skills.

Transformation: Future of Work and VUCA

Future of work is a major transformation and takes place at three levels. For one, the work actually carried out is supported by contemporary technology to achieve the desired goals and create value for the business ecosystem initiative to be developed. Then at the level of the staff (workforce), a combination of different skills and talents. Included are not only the permanent employees but also freelancers, gig workers, crowd sourcing teams, and interdisciplinary teams that work together, e.g. in the context of co-creation in the relevant business ecosystem initiatives. The third level is the workplace, i.e. the place where the work is done and teams collaborate. For one, the term refers to the physical location and secondly, to the technologies used for digital collaboration. The location and the way in which collaboration takes place characterize the culture of "future of work." With the increasing use of robotics, cognitive technologies, and AI, new forms of working emerge in which a person acts as a team with the machine. The world today consists of disruption, change, and transformation. The term for this is VUCA (volatility, uncertainty, complexity, ambiguity). In this context, every organization searches for new ways of learning and becomes a learning organization.

The respective design lenses help to get a grip on uncertainty, make complexity tangible and mappable and test assumptions iteratively and with agility.

Key questions about future of work:

- Who can do the work?
- Which work steps can be automated?
- Which technologies help in the collaboration of human beings and machines as a team?
- Where is the work conducted?

Various automation technologies work hand in hand with the teams. Tasks are completed faster this way. The new way human beings and technology work together as a team allows work sequences to be redefined.

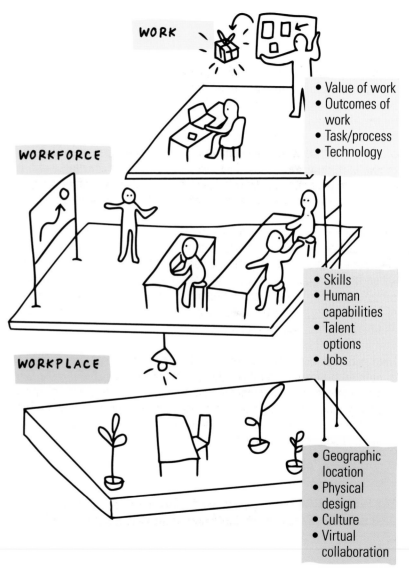

WORK
- Value of work
- Outcomes of work
- Task/process
- Technology

WORKFORCE
- Skills
- Human capabilities
- Talent options
- Jobs

WORKPLACE
- Geographic location
- Physical design
- Culture
- Virtual collaboration

View of VUCA Worlds

VUCA becomes a vital element in the context of design thinking for business growth because the system is rarely static. It is dynamic and changes very quickly and irregularly during particular phases. There is also a certain level of uncertainty about the time during which something is going to take place and what the consequences will be. Since business ecosystems are complex and networked, a complete and static view is not possible. In addition, the situation in a business ecosystem is described and evaluated differently depending on the actor/person, which causes ambiguity.

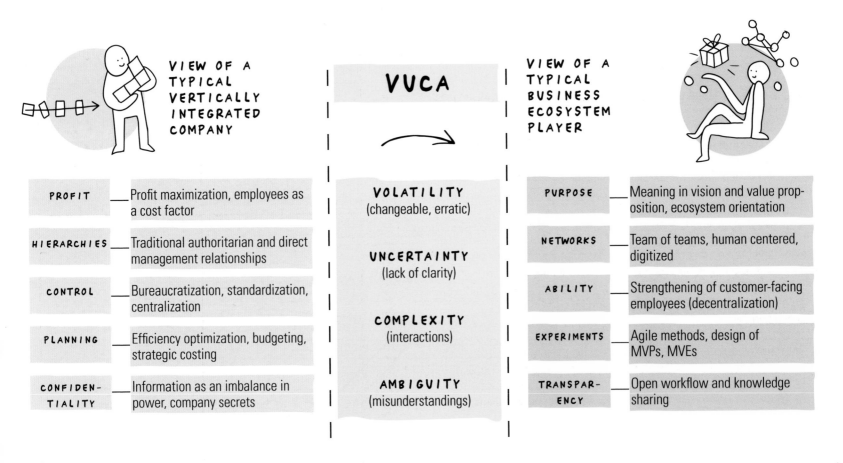

VIEW OF A TYPICAL VERTICALLY INTEGRATED COMPANY		VUCA	VIEW OF A TYPICAL BUSINESS ECOSYSTEM PLAYER	
PROFIT	Profit maximization, employees as a cost factor	VOLATILITY (changeable, erratic)	PURPOSE	Meaning in vision and value proposition, ecosystem orientation
HIERARCHIES	Traditional authoritarian and direct management relationships		NETWORKS	Team of teams, human centered, digitized
CONTROL	Bureaucratization, standardization, centralization	UNCERTAINTY (lack of clarity)	ABILITY	Strengthening of customer-facing employees (decentralization)
PLANNING	Efficiency optimization, budgeting, strategic costing	COMPLEXITY (interactions)	EXPERIMENTS	Agile methods, design of MVPs, MVEs
CONFIDEN-TIALITY	Information as an imbalance in power, company secrets	AMBIGUITY (misunderstandings)	TRANSPAR-ENCY	Open workflow and knowledge sharing

166

Points in Time for Cooperation and Opening Up

Co-creation is a key element in the solution of design challenges, the construction of first prototypes, MVPs, and of course the design of business ecosystems up to scaling since the actors in the system are seen as innovators who are close to the respective customer needs.

As briefly described before, starting points for business ecosystem considerations vary. While some companies are relying on cooperation and openness from the very onset, others are busy discussing the topic amid their ranks and draft first prototypes and MVPs.

Four approaches to opening up can be observed. They all have advantages and disadvantages:

1. **The cooperatives:** Companies that either have an idea to be discussed with other actors at an early stage or rely on the collaboration with others right from the onset to define a shared system.

2. **The exploratives:** These companies not only have a strategy but experiment with various ecosystem approaches and look for opportunities to play an active part in other ecosystems.

3. **The seekers:** Companies with a clear idea of where there are market opportunities for them. They actively seek out other actors to build ecosystems on their own or contribute their capabilities in specific constellations.

4. **The mysterious:** This type of company plays their cards close to the chest. The strategy is discussed at the top management level. Prototypes and MVPs are developed behind locked doors. Only once the business ecosystem has been implemented is information shared with potential actors.

	UNIPOLAR, BIPOLAR	MULTIPOLAR
AUTOCRATIC, HIERARCHICAL	**THE MYSTERIOUS** + Low risk of being copied by other actors − Late value proposition validation	**THE SEEKERS** + Clear vision of the target image and the implementation − Little room for new ideas and changed value propositions at a later stage
EVOLUTIONARY, COOPERATIVE	**THE EXPLORATIVES** + Market opportunities can be exploited ad hoc − High level of effort and expense for the coordination of multiple talks with many actors	**THE COOPERATIVES** + Strong focus on co-creation and development of radically new ecosystems − Collaboration and co-creation are more complex and time consuming

Co-creation Approaches

Different forms of collaboration lead to different goals. The forms of collaboration on the list mirror the mind-set and iterative procedures of the design lenses for an open and radical collaboration. Co-creation can be done with a customer/user and, later, in the context of designing business ecosystems with the other actors in the system.

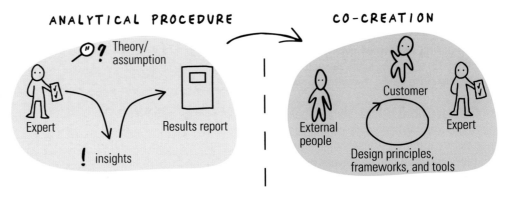

FORM OF COLLABORATION	GOAL	BEHAVIOR
CONDUCT RESEARCH	Learn and understand	Be curious, observe, and understand the needs of customers; explore facts and dig deeper by asking WH questions (referring to Who? What? When? Where? Why? and How?).
OPEN	Develop and grow	Discard assumptions and prejudices; consciously search for other experiences and new perspectives; high level of willingness to change one's opinion due to new insights.
INTEGRATIVE	Be appreciative and act in a solution-oriented way	Avoid any unbalanced compromises when searching for win-win situations for all actors; creative reframing and use of different views of the world as an advantage for dynamics of change.
COLLABORATIVE	Team work and team of teams	Listen actively and build on the ideas from others; collaboration that aims at strengthening social cohesion.
REFLECTIVE	Be prudent and develop spirally	Reflect on actions and effectiveness; view challenges and problems in a wider context; mediate in situations in which different views must be reconciled.

To the Point!

For the design of and participation in business ecosystems, certain values, mindsets, and ideas as well as open and transparent collaboration with other actors are vital.

Traditionally managed companies face the challenge of allowing new collaborative ways of working and simultaneously mapping contextualization in conventional strategy tools.

Employees will remain a decisive factor in work in the future since they take on ever more complex tasks and leave repetitive, mundane tasks to machines and automation.

The use of iterative frameworks in the various design lenses and adapted strategy methods in design thinking for business growth help with the elaboration and contextualization of the ecosystem and growth strategy.

Ecosystem leadership essentially means the task of networking of all actors involved in value creation.

DESIGN LENSES TOOLBOX

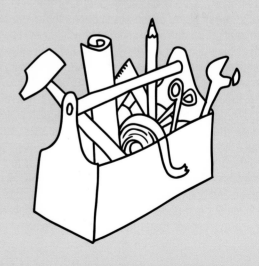

Design Thinking for Business Growth: Project Phases and Planning Horizons

Since every growth initiative is somewhat different and the initiators have different capabilities, it is impossible to define a universal project plan. At best, the research phase comes first in which customer needs are outlined and then in-house capabilities and skills are examined to reach greater certainty and awareness of potential topic areas. In addition, during this phase you can learn about growth and ecosystem initiatives already existing in the market. How long the respective sprint, project, and implementation phases should last depends greatly on the teams, agility — and the budget. In a design thinking sprint, solid results can be achieved in 6 weeks. Usually, it takes longer: several iterations and rounds of customer feedback to create meaningful vision prototypes and prototypes for function and experience. In addition, there are various decision-making bodies that affect the initiatives in the conventional settings with the respective gates at rigid deadlines. Ideally, decision makers release the respective budgets for the next steps immediately after realization, e.g. after the presentation of the final prototype in design thinking. For the lean start-up phase, it is advisable to be aware of the assumptions that need to be checked since without market validation, assumptions will remain just that. Typical examples of assumptions exist with regard to the willingness to pay on the part of customers, which needs to be checked. Depending on the complexity, MVPs are usually ready for testing in 4 to 10 weeks. The MVP becomes a flagship product to persuade potential actors of the value proposition and vision. The design of the business ecosystem also provides information on the value streams, the business model of the ecosystem, and on how individual actors benefit from participating. This design phase is one of the most demanding and lasts from 12 to 16 weeks or more. The MVE shows how the system works in its smallest manifestation. The subsequent implementation and operationalization requires more or less time depending on the complexity and dependencies. Some ecosystems reach the threshold of exponential growth faster than others. While some initiatives reach this threshold as early as after one year, others need several years to get to this milestone. Likewise, there are many ecosystem initiatives that fail to grow through network effects and meaningful expansions of the value proposition. What is important is to adapt the systems constantly and exploit the innovative strength of the other actors to be successful. Governance and orchestration must keep pace with the dynamics of customers and the market. This includes, above all, the expansion of the value proposition to enlarge the market area, stabilize the market position, and address new customer needs.

DESIGN, CONFIGURE, BUILD

Planning Horizons of a Business Ecosystem Initiative

	RESEARCH	DESIGN THINKING	LEAN START-UP	ECOSYSTEM DESIGN	IMPLEMENT AND RUN	SCALE
OUTPUT	• Topic areas/ customer needs • Existing capabilities and skills/ relationships	• Final prototype • Vision prototype • Requirements for MVP	• MVP • Willingness to pay • Validation of assumptions	• MVE • Value streams • Business model • actors in the system	• Realization plan • Product portfolio • Fast learning and adaptation cycles	• Expansion of the value proposition • Innovation by actors • Scaling the IT
DESCRIPTION	• Define features and framework conditions of the solution • Definition of the design principles	• Visualize the prototype and demonstrate the experiences and functions of the product or the service	• Release of the possible functional scope • Focus on critical functions and experiences • Measurement and iterations	• Validation of the value proposition • Definition of the actors and their roles • Definition of value streams	• Implementation of the ecosystem initiative at the level of culture, capabilities, IT, governance, leadership, etc. • Laying down a road map	• Needfinding for value proposition expansion • Adjustment of the ecosystem strategy • Reassessment of IT requirements • Orchestration
TEAM	• Internal team • Strategy experts • Multidisciplinary • Cross-company	• Business ecosystem/design team • Users/test groups • Co-creation with first potential partners/ecosystem actors	• UX designers • Software developers • Potential partners/ ecosystem actors	• Business ecosystem design team • Co-creation with other actors • Testing with customers and potential partners	• Orchestrator • Implementation partners and suppliers • Actors	• Design thinking, ecosystem design, and growth hack teams • IT, software developers • Partners, actors, and suppliers
FUNCTION MARKET MATURITY	Ideas, suggestions, foresight	Vision prototype with critical functions and experiences	MVPs, MMF, backlog	Part of the value proposition	Realization of the value proposition	Expanded value proposition
	~6 weeks	~6–10 weeks	~10–12 weeks	~12–16 weeks	> 16 weeks	Open end

Typical Trajectory of Ecosystem Initiatives

Since business ecosystems undergo constant change, iterative and agile tools are needed that support the design, implementation, and scaling. Unfortunately, an initiator must do without a blueprint for certain topic areas or a specific industry of an initiator, even though decision makers frequently express their wish for such blueprints.

Even an analysis of the past – as conducted by the BCG Henderson Institute on the building of business ecosystems in 2019 – proves to be difficult. This is not least due to the lack of structured data. Not surprisingly, with so little quantitative analysis, it is tempting to look at the best-known current examples (e.g. WeChat, Amazon, Alibaba) and come to believe that business ecosystems are always successful. However, that would mean overlooking the far greater number of initiators, orchestrators and actors who have not prevailed. It's an excellent idea to learn from such companies and initiatives and exploit them for one's own project (see examples of ecosystems, page 298 et seq.).

For this reason, the focus of this section about the four design lenses will be on critical questions and the methods and tools used in the design of business ecosystems. Decision makers need to be aware that, because of their high level of dynamics, even successfully initialized ecosystems are not successful forever if governance and leadership leave much to be desired. In addition, the underlying strategy must be constantly reassessed. During the continuous development of a business ecosystem, new players are constantly being added while others are no longer relevant to the creation of the value proposition. It can also be observed that initiators of business ecosystems over time take a stake financially in other actors or that partners are taken over 100% or by a majority share. Such moves are usually based on the desire to own customer interfaces or data points and use them in the long term.

OPPORTUNITY	PRINCIPLES OF ACTION	SUCCESS RATE
FINAL PROTOTYPE	• Create first prototypes • Create vision prototypes • Describe the potential value proposition based on customer needs	High
MVP	• Use first-mover advantage • Stick to customer-centered approach • Build killer functions or experiences	Medium
MVE	• Invest in building the ecosystem • Choose the right actors • Agree to a shared value system and collaboration model	Medium
IMPLEMENTATION	• Use the capabilities of the actors in the system • Implement in small steps • Act with a team-of-teams approach within the defined governance	Low/medium
SCALE	• Scale quickly • Expand the scope of the ecosystem • Increase commitment	Low

* Success rate following the BCG Henderson Institute (2019)

Business ecosystems are dynamic. Typically, they develop in one of the pathways and branches shown below with regard to their ability to capture and retain market share. In the figure shown as "subway lines," it is important to put in switches at the right points for growth and scaling.

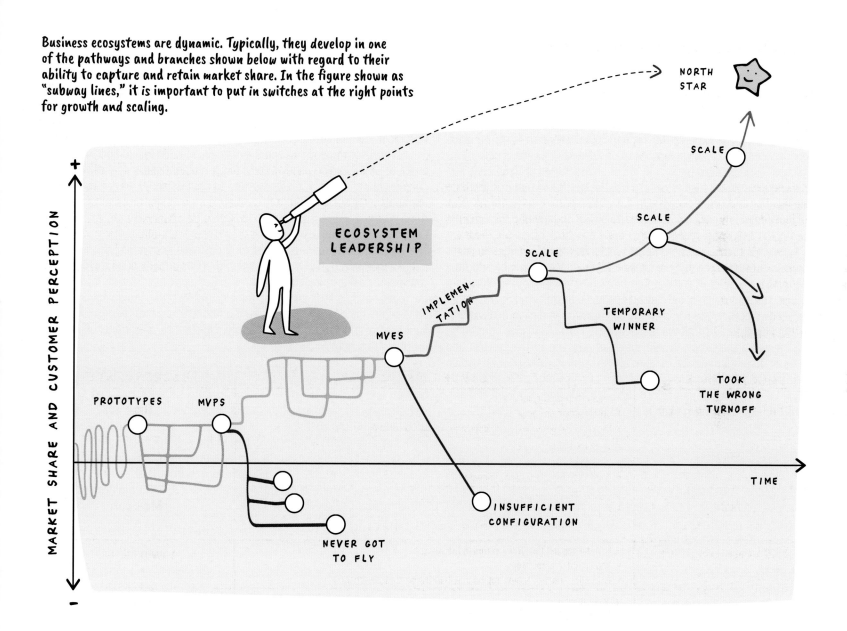

MARKET SHARE AND CUSTOMER PERCEPTION

+

−

ECOSYSTEM LEADERSHIP

NORTH STAR

SCALE

SCALE

SCALE

IMPLEMENTATION

MVES

TEMPORARY WINNER

PROTOTYPES

MVPS

TOOK THE WRONG TURNOFF

TIME

INSUFFICIENT CONFIGURATION

NEVER GOT TO FLY

Simplified "Problem 2 Growth and Scale" Framework

From the bird's-eye view of design thinking for business, the design of business ecosystems often only begins with the realization of the MVP, i.e. with a high level of solution maturity. Frequently, through intense exploration and dealing with the actors in the system, completely new ideas for products or services up to new value propositions evolve in business ecosystem workshops. This can even mean that the original solution is completely discarded and that the findings result in a new, shared value proposition. Thus the application of business ecosystem design can be the trigger for new ideas that bring us right back to the early phase of exploring the problem space. In the following four sections, each of which describes a design lens, the elements and questions necessary for upstream considerations for a business ecosystem design are presented; guidance is provided on how to scale such systems. The presented procedure via the four lenses, as a guided and structured process, may be perceived as quite a rigid approach. But anybody who has already used the combination of design thinking and systems thinking knows that the respective step is more to give orientation to the teams so they know where they currently are in the process and in terms of solution maturity. In general, we work iteratively in all design lenses. The four design lenses help in the co-creation process to establish a common language with other actors and team members, use similar methods and tools, and to reflect upon the joint approach.

Lens #1: Design thinking

Design thinking for business growth gives center stage to the customers and their needs. The design thinking mindset helps bring together different experiences, opinions, and perspectives in terms of a problem statement and create first prototypes, which constitute the basis for an MVP. In the following section, the most important design thinking tools are discussed that have been proven as a useful basis for the next steps in growth initiatives.

Lens #2: Lean start-up

The lean start-up mindset helps with the implementation of first solutions and to focus on the most necessary functions and experiences. First experiences on the market help to improve the MVP iteratively. This procedure has several advantages. For one, time, work, and money can be saved. Secondly, the MVP can be used as the basis for initial talks or co-creation with other potential actors in the ecosystem to validate and – later – realize the formulated value proposition.

Lens #3: Ecosystem design

The starting point for the design of a business ecosystem is usually an initial hypothesis of a value proposition that has already been tested in the context of design thinking and lean start-up activities. During this phase, the focus must be kept on the customer. However, now the selection of the right actors becomes important, taking into account their needs. The configuration of the system with its actors, capabilities, and customer access is critical to success.

Lens #4: Scale

Scaling and exponential growth requires both sophisticated and targeted governance and meaningful elements to expand incrementally the value proposition for the customers. The aim is to optimize customer interaction points and increase frequency. As part of the scaling process, the acquired data becomes another asset of the system. In addition, new versions of business models evolve (e.g. the monetarization of B2B services or data) that are based on the acquired digitization skills and a high-performance infrastructure.

Start ↘

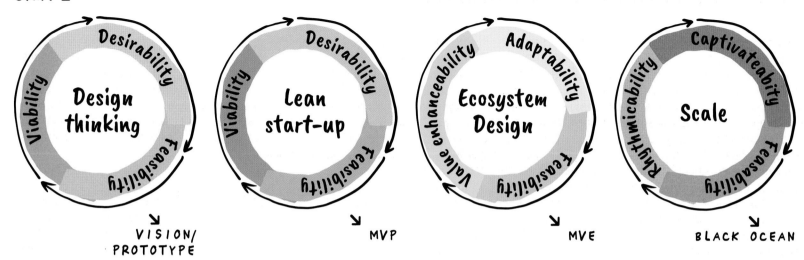

Design thinking
- Desirability
- Viability
- Feasibility

↘ VISION/ PROTOTYPE

Lean start-up
- Desirability
- Viability
- Feasibility

↘ MVP

Ecosystem Design
- Adaptability
- Value enhanceability
- Feasibility

↘ MVE

Scale
- Captivateabity
- Rhythmicability
- Feasibility

↘ BLACK OCEAN

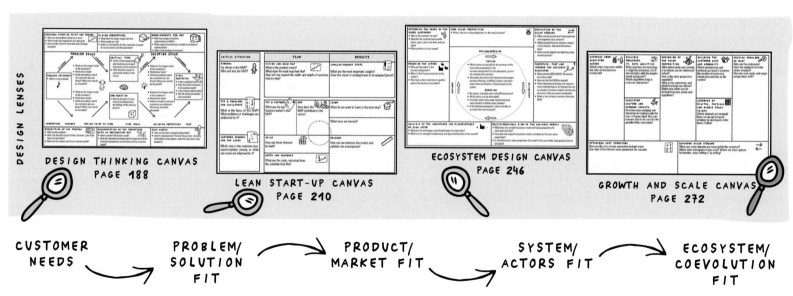

DESIGN LENSES

DESIGN THINKING CANVAS
PAGE 188

LEAN START-UP CANVAS
PAGE 210

ECOSYSTEM DESIGN CANVAS
PAGE 246

GROWTH AND SCALE CANVAS
PAGE 272

CUSTOMER NEEDS → PROBLEM/ SOLUTION FIT → PRODUCT/ MARKET FIT → SYSTEM/ ACTORS FIT → ECOSYSTEM/ COEVOLUTION FIT

Critical vs. Not So Critical Assumptions

In each design lens, different assumptions regarding customers, actors, and individual value streams are questioned and initial findings are validated. It is important and crucial to success to know which assumptions are decisive for future success and which are less significant or negligible. In addition, there will be assumptions that have already been validated and others viewed with some uncertainty.

In some areas, the respective design lens leads to a better understanding, e.g. by using MVPs to validate the problem/solution fit. Over time, the view changes. Naturally, new assumptions are added, in particular

assumptions about actors who might become part of the system or about how actors who might benefit from the ecosystems. The same applies to scaling. Again, assumptions must be tested before making an operational contribution in the ecosystem. The loop starts again with the expansion of the value proposition, where again the assumptions are checked within the framework of design thinking.

A good way of doing this is placing the individual assumptions in a matrix, discussing them on the team and examining those in the top right quadrant.

EXAMINE CRITICAL ASSUMPTIONS

Example

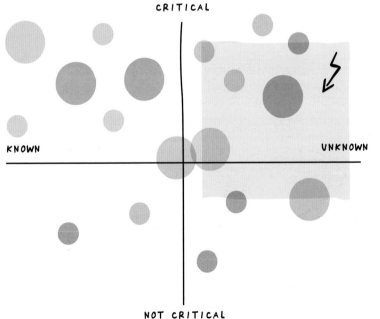

• When was the last time we "walked in our customer's shoes"?
• What triggers a real WOW! effect in customers?
• When and where do customers use an offer?

LEGEND EXAMPLE:

Desirability (e.g. customer wishes and needs)

Viability (e.g. costs of physical and digital touch points)

Feasibility (e.g. standardization in the area of voice interaction all the way to special algorithms for interactions)

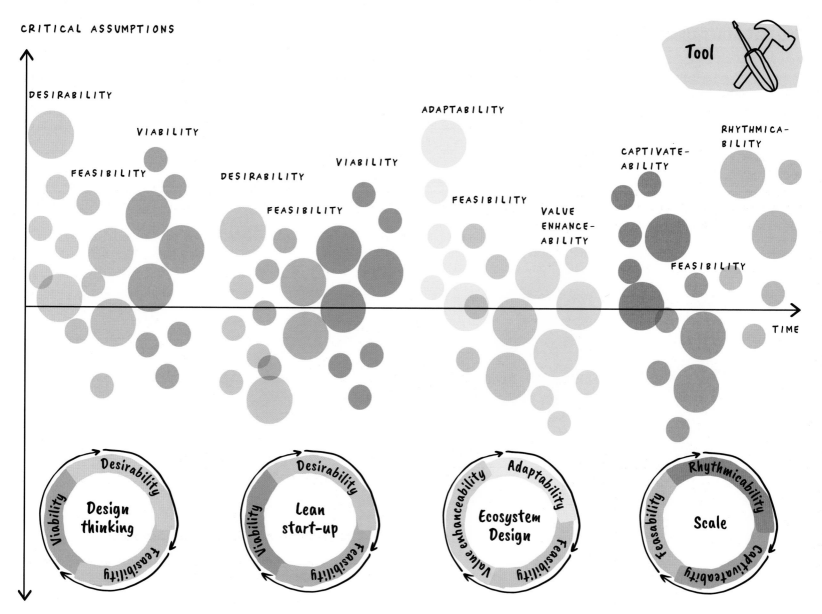

179

Why Not Start Immediately with the Design of the Ecosystem?

From practice we know that in most cases it is necessary to go through the previous design lenses again before the design of the actual ecosystem can be tackled. When the preceding steps have been left out, companies often tend to see customers as actors in the system and not as the absolute center of all activities/value propositions.

For this reason, this section includes the most important tools and techniques from the design thinking toolbox, e.g. persona/user profile, critical items diagram, brainstorming all the way to the final prototype. The lean start-up approach is presented, which helps to validate concepts and check the willingness to pay for selected functions and experiences. Both mindsets support the process of finding a solution. In many cases, they provide the basis for the design of a business ecosystem.

The procedure presented has proven its worth in practice since it puts the customer/user automatically in the center of all considerations. An additional advantage is that, in this way, ecosystem considerations won't focus too much on one's own company, more on explore than on exploit.

Design thinking for business growth teams who already have successfully identified the customer needs and have carried out the required validations by means of an MVP can immediately start with section #3 ecosystem design (page 228 et seq.).

Successful business ecosystem initiatives put the customer and the value proposition in the center of all considerations — not their own company.

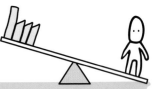

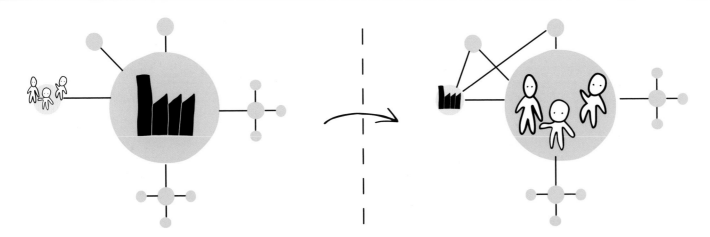

DON'T THINK FROM THE COMPANY'S POINT OF VIEW BUT FROM THE CUSTOMER'S POINT OF VIEW!

Begin with the Customer, Validate the Assumptions, and Build the Ecosystem on This Foundation

As described above, the customer is the central starting point for successful business ecosystems. Through the initial investigation of customer needs and tasks to be performed, selected functions and experiences can be tested with the creation of the MVP. The minimum marketable features (MMF) usually also constitute the test environment for the minimum viable ecosystem (MVE). The aim is to validate the value streams and the interplay among the actors with the creation of a shared value proposition before the business ecosystem is implemented and scaled with the right mechanisms.

DIMENSION	RELEVANT APPROACHES	ACTIONS CRITICAL TO SUCCESS
CUSTOMER NEEDS	Design thinking	• Explore the needs • Derive from it the tasks to be performed • Use critical functions and experiences
PROTOTYPES (MVPs, MMFs, MVEs)	Lean start-up Ecosystem design	• Validate functions, experiences, etc. • Iterative development of target systems • Viewing the business models (multidimensional)
LEADERSHIP	Future ways of working ecosystem Leadership	• Establishing a new mindset • Management of a wide range of interests • Permanent development of differentiating factors (value proposition)
SCALING	Scale Agile development	• Use of the first-mover advantage for radical disruption • Fast scaling • Permanent and sustainable investment in ecosystem building
DYNAMIC DEVELOPMENT	Co-creation	• Expansion of the ecosystem based on customer needs • Increase commitment to the system • Data for innovation and validation

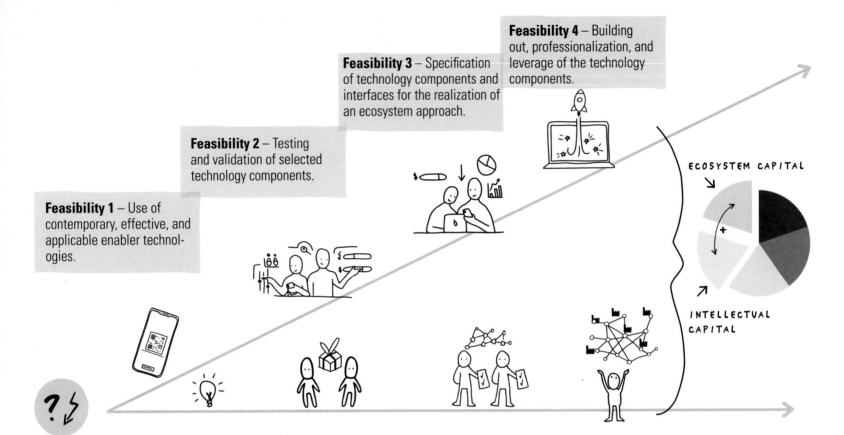

Feasibility 1 – Use of contemporary, effective, and applicable enabler technologies.

Feasibility 2 – Testing and validation of selected technology components.

Feasibility 3 – Specification of technology components and interfaces for the realization of an ecosystem approach.

Feasibility 4 – Building out, professionalization, and leverage of the technology components.

ECOSYSTEM CAPITAL

INTELLECTUAL CAPITAL

- **Desirability** – Focusing on the customers and their needs.
- **Viability** – Creation of an innovative and sustainable business model.

- **Desirability** – Validation of customer needs on the basis of individual functions and experiences.
- **Viability** – Validation of the business model and value of the offering.

- **Adaptability** – Focusing on the needs of the actors and their ability to create a value proposition together.
- **Value enhanceability** – Shaping sustainable value streams and benefits for all actors in the system.

- **Captivateability** – Focus on increasing the frequency of customer interaction, share of wallet, and bond to the system.
- **Rhythmicability** – Exploiting of network effects and scale effects.

To the Point!

From the identification of the customer needs all the way to a solution provided by several actors — most initiatives fail with implementation.

Each of the transitions between the design lenses as well as the mindset and the management of the varied interests of the actors are critical to success.

Many ecosystem initiatives lack the governance and skills needed for the fast scaling of a solution.

The constant adaptation of the system to new and changed customer needs and the development entailed require space for the participating actors and an integrative approach of the orchestrator.

After all, the mindset of all actors that is right for the project is decisive.

LENS #1

DESIGN THINKING

Intro to Design Thinking

The design thinking mindset is a key element and the basis for all reflections in design thinking for business growth. The customers and their needs take center stage in the deliberations. It is essential not to neglect them from the definition of the problem statement to the scaling. In the first two design lenses in particular (design thinking and lean start-up), the focus must be on the customer alone. During these phases, expertise and industry knowledge should be of secondary importance. The thoughts on how to solve the customer problem should be free of prejudice, especially if there are already fairly clear ideas on how it works today or how a solution might work in the future. In both cases, the business design teams should look at everything in an open and unbiased way. It is vital to get to the bottom of things – in design thinking this means that we approach potential customers with a great deal of curiosity and empathy. The interaction and observation of extreme users and lead users can be a source of inspiration or used for the definition of approaches to a solution. Working with personas/user profiles helps in getting away from traditional customer segmentation and exploring the real needs of and tasks to be performed for potential customers. So-called HMW questions help to morph insights from the understand and observe phases into a point of view. Various types of brainstorming work well in the creative part. During an early phase of problem solving, working with the critical items diagram is especially worthwhile. For one, it is a valuable tool for keeping an eye on the most important functions and experiences of the customers; at the same time, it serves as a backlog in the lean start-up phase for further features that expand the MVPs or the entire value proposition for the offer in the ecosystem. The phases of define point of view and ideating, prototyping and testing must be seen as one. In iterations, the prototypes have a ever higher resolution over time. The final prototype is the basis for the specifications of one or more MVPs to be realized within the framework of an MVE and later with the implementation of the ecosystem. Those who want to dive deeper into design thinking with all its tools and methods are well advised to use *The Design Thinking Toolbox*. For Design Thinking professionals and facilitators and all those who want to be inspired beyond that, *The Design Thinking Playbook* is the first choice.

Typical activities

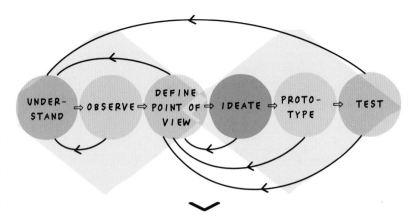

The final prototype excels by the elegance of the thoughts invested in it as well as in its realization. The vision prototype describes a possible future of an entire system, for example.

Preview of the Suitable Methods and Tools for Design Thinking

Key Questions about Design Thinking

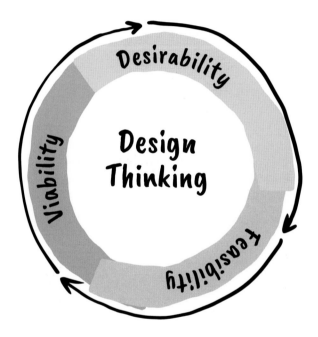

- Who has the problem?
- How is it solved today?
- What tasks of the customer (jobs to be done) are to be solved?
- What pain and gain of the customers are known?
- What customer needs and emotions are relevant?
- What critical functions and experiences for the customer should the solution contain?
- How does the approach to the solution differ from known solutions?
- To what extent does the customer benefit match the values of the service?

FEASIBILITY

- What are important components for implementation?
- What kind of technology is needed?
- What skills are needed for design, building, and operation?
- Which systems are affected?
- What work processes are necessary?
- Which assumptions are the most risky and need to be correspondingly tested?
- How can "fail fast, fail often" be lived without destroying market opportunity?
- How is success defined? How is it measured and communicated to the stakeholders?

VIABILITY

- How to make money with the solution?
- Alternatively: How can costs be saved with the solution?
- Where does added value for the company accrue?
- How can investments be justified?

DESIGN THINKING CANVAS

RESEARCH STARTING POINT AND TRENDS
- How was the problem solved up to now?
- What trends and megatrends are emerging?
- How can the future be described with strategic foresight?

VISION (PROTOTYPE)
- How is the north star described?
- What needs are met?
- What are the benefits for the companies involved (in an ecosystem) and the customers?

REQUIREMENTS FOR MVP

- Which prototypes should be implemented as MVPs?
- What experiences/functions should be tested and validated first?
- What is the backlog of functions?

PROBLEM SPACE

DIVERGE CONVERGE

- What are the deeper needs of the customers?
- What drives them?
- What assumptions about the customers are confirmed? Which ones should be discarded?

PROBLEM STATEMENT
- Where is the problem?

- What are the deeper needs of the customers?
- What drives them?
- What assumptions about the customers are confirmed? Which ones should be discarded?

CRITICAL ITEMS
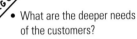
- Which critical experiences and functions are of great importance to the customer?
- What should be a part of a potential solution in the future?

HMW QUESTION
- What is the point of view that can be derived from the findings of the previous phases?

SOLUTION SPACE

DIVERGE CONVERGE

- What are the deeper needs of the customers?
- What drives them?
- What assumptions about the customers are confirmed? Which ones should be discarded?

- What are the deeper needs of the customers?
- What drives them?
- What assumptions about the customers are confirmed? Which ones should be discarded?

FINAL PROTOTYPE

- Is there a problem/solution fit?
- Does the solution correspond to the customer needs?
- Is the solution implementable?
- Will the solution be economically successful?

UNDERSTAND   OBSERVE   DEFINE POINT OF VIEW   FIND IDEAS   BUILDING PROTOTYPES   TEST

DESCRIPTION OF THE PERSONA / USER PROFILE
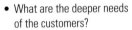
- Who has the problem?
- What are the pains/gains for the customers, jobs to be done, and use cases?
- What are the current and future customer needs?

DOCUMENTATION OF THE PROTOTYPES WITH AN EXPLORATION MAP

- What worked? What didn't work?
- Was the respective prototype able to meet and satisfy individual experiences and functions of the customer needs?

LEAN CANVAS

- How can the short concept be described?
- How do we prepare for the next design lens, including initial ideas on key figures, customer segments, early adopters?

Template download

DESIGN THINKING CANVAS

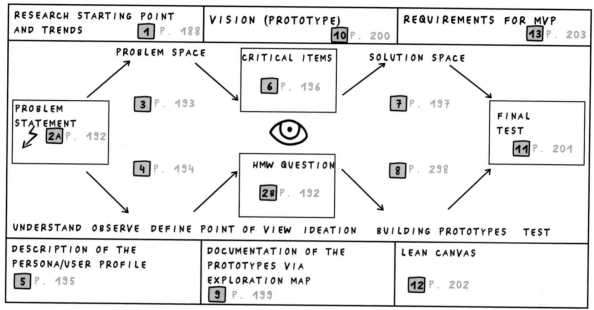

RESEARCH STARTING POINT AND TRENDS **1** P. 188	VISION (PROTOTYPE) **10** P. 200	REQUIREMENTS FOR MVP **13** P. 203

PROBLEM SPACE

CRITICAL ITEMS **6** P. 196

SOLUTION SPACE

PROBLEM STATEMENT ⚡ **2A** P. 192

3 P. 193

7 P. 197

FINAL TEST **11** P. 201

👁

4 P. 194

HMW QUESTION **2B** P. 192

8 P. 298

UNDERSTAND OBSERVE DEFINE POINT OF VIEW IDEATION BUILDING PROTOTYPES TEST

DESCRIPTION OF THE PERSONA/USER PROFILE **5** P. 195	DOCUMENTATION OF THE PROTOTYPES VIA EXPLORATION MAP **9** P. 199	LEAN CANVAS **12** P. 202

METHODS AND TOOLS KEY

1. Research/trends/foresight
2. **a)** Problem statement
   b) HMW question
3. Interview for empathy with journey map
4. Extreme users/lead users
5. Persona/user profile
6. Critical items diagram

7. Brainstorming
8. Prototype to test
9. Documentation of the prototypes via the exploration map
10. Vision prototype
11. Final prototype
12. Lean canvas
13. Requirements for the MVP

The design thinking canvas helps with the documentation of the individual steps and the results from the tools and methods used.

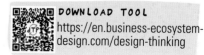

DOWNLOAD TOOL
https://en.business-ecosystem-design.com/design-thinking

Research/Trends/Foresight in the Form of a Progression Curve

A rather general but still helpful approach for a design team is to deal with the relevant trends, demographic changes, and global activities in the context of the problem statement. There are countless methods and tools that can be applied here. One promising way to deal with the future is the application of a "progression curve." At the level of future scenarios, evolutionary thoughts on business models, and so-called innovation accelerators, such a progression curve helps to grasp microtrends, macrotrends, and megatrends.

A progression curve helps the design thinking for business growth team:
- to put events, life cycles, and other developments in the right context;
- at a later time, with the validation of a vision prototype or the corresponding future target image of a business ecosystem;
- to give the vision and the future customer needs a sharper contour;
- with the design and selection (filtering) of important topics across the entire design cycle;
- to find out how to solve problems in the future.

Procedure and template:
1. Different but related topics can be clustered together on the progression curve (see page 191).
2. For a given theme, the combination of strategic foresight, the identified trends, and design thinking can create a theme map (see "The future of mobility").
3. The respective trends can be brought to different levels, which helps to discuss and assess their impact and relevance to the project.
4. The basis for the visualization of the progression curves is provided by corresponding reports from future observatories and trend researchers.

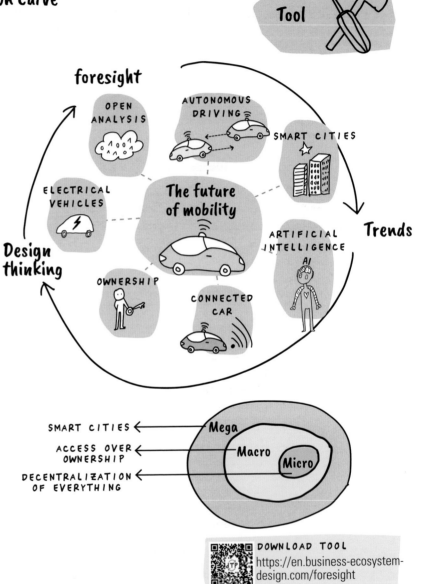

DOWNLOAD TOOL
https://en.business-ecosystem-design.com/foresight

PROGRESSION CURVE

Below are some examples of scenarios revolving around digitization, technologies, and business models. Through the combination of several trends in the progression curve, new, innovative ideas can be constructed.

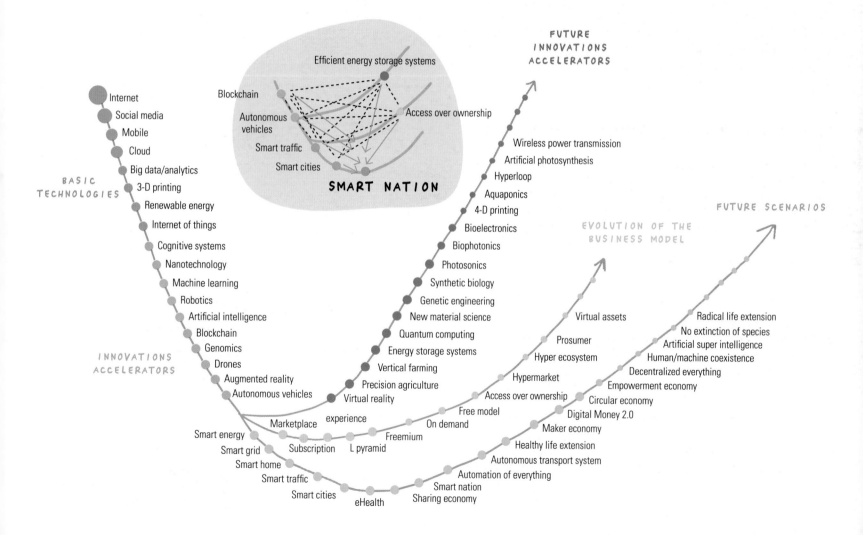

FUTURE INNOVATIONS ACCELERATORS

Efficient energy storage systems

Blockchain

Autonomous vehicles

Access over ownership

Smart traffic

Smart cities

SMART NATION

BASIC TECHNOLOGIES

- Internet
- Social media
- Mobile
- Cloud
- Big data/analytics
- 3-D printing
- Renewable energy
- Internet of things
- Cognitive systems
- Nanotechnology
- Machine learning
- Robotics
- Artificial intelligence
- Blockchain
- Genomics
- Drones
- Augmented reality
- Autonomous vehicles

INNOVATIONS ACCELERATORS

- Smart energy
- Smart grid
- Smart home
- Smart traffic
- Smart cities

- Marketplace
- Subscription
- L pyramid
- experience
- Freemium
- On demand
- eHealth
- Sharing economy
- Smart nation
- Automation of everything
- Autonomous transport system
- Healthy life extension

- Wireless power transmission
- Artificial photosynthesis
- Hyperloop
- Aquaponics
- 4-D printing
- Bioelectronics
- Biophotonics
- Photosonics
- Synthetic biology
- Genetic engineering
- New material science
- Quantum computing
- Energy storage systems
- Vertical farming
- Precision agriculture
- Virtual reality
- Free model

EVOLUTION OF THE BUSINESS MODEL

- Virtual assets
- Prosumer
- Hyper ecosystem
- Hypermarket
- Access over ownership
- Maker economy
- Digital Money 2.0
- Circular economy

FUTURE SCENARIOS

- Radical life extension
- No extinction of species
- Artificial super intelligence
- Human/machine coexistence
- Decentralized everything
- Empowerment economy

191

Problem Statement/HMW Question

Too often, people think in solutions. This is why the first step in design thinking is to develop awareness of the customer's problem. The problem statement allows the problem to be formulated succinctly in one sentence. The problem statement and the HMW question introduced later are thus the starting point and the end of the problem space in design thinking.

A problem statement helps the design thinking for business growth team to:
- develop a shared understanding of a problem;
- formulate the collected findings from the problem analysis in one statement;
- outline the direction and the framework for ideation;
- create a basis for the formulation of targeted "how might we..." questions (HMW questions);
- develop a reference value for the subsequent measurement of success.

2a.) Problem statement:

1. In the beginning, various WH questions can be asked about the problem, such as: Why is it a problem?
   This helps the team to come to a shared understanding of the problem space.
2. Based on the answers, the problem statement is developed iteratively on the team. The problem statement has the form: "How might we redesign… (what?) (for whom)…so that…(his/her need)…is satisfied?"

2b.) Procedure for HMW question:

The HMW question results from the collected findings and is based on a point of view. In other words, the HMW question is a substantiation of the problem statement.

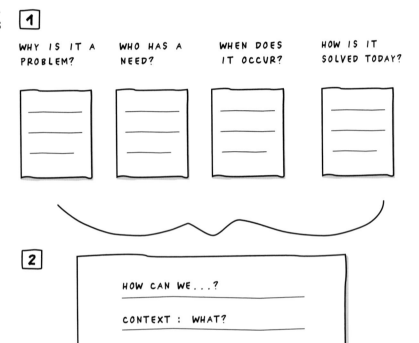

1

WHY IS IT A PROBLEM? WHO HAS A NEED? WHEN DOES IT OCCUR? HOW IS IT SOLVED TODAY?

2

HOW CAN WE...?

CONTEXT : WHAT?

ACTOR : FOR WHOM?

PROBLEM : WHICH PROBLEM IS TO BE SOLVED?

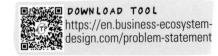

DOWNLOAD TOOL
https://en.business-ecosystem-design.com/problem-statement

Interview for Empathy

Tool

With the interview for empathy, the problem outlined beforehand is looked at from the user's point of view. Particularly in one of the early phases, the interviews help to understand the context in which a potential user or customer acts. For the business ecosystem design team, it is especially helpful to break out of previous thought patterns and transform the mindset from a product-centered or company-centered to a customer-centered attitude.

An interview for empathy helps the design thinking for business growth team to:
- build a solid understanding of the needs, emotions, motivations, and ways of thinking of a potential customer;
- gain insights that would have remained hidden in a superficial consideration, e.g. frustration and deeper motives of a potential customer;
- find out which task flow the customer prefers and on what mental model it is based.

Procedure and template:
1. Initially, a question map can be created. This has the advantage that not only these are queried in the interview for empathy but WH questions are raised to examine initial statements.
2. In addition to the question map, so-called journey stages can help to recognize patterns early on. For example, prompt the interviewee to present or deepen a topic in the form of a sketch or a chronological sequence. This offers the opportunity to explore the causes and reasons for a particular action by asking more in-depth questions. In this way, you can find out:
   - all the places where a user had gathered information before;
   - what information was valuable;
   - when he made the decision to purchase;
   - how easy the payment was.

Empathy is about listening to the echo of another person in yourself and drawing conclusions about their needs.

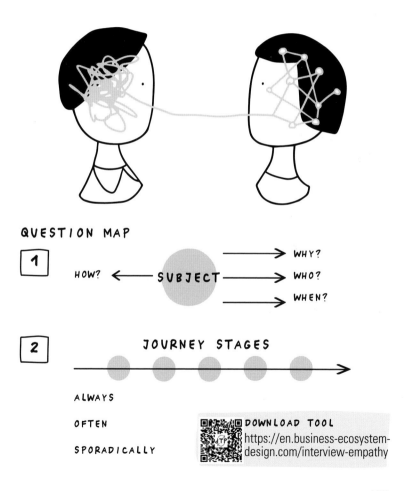

QUESTION MAP

1 HOW? ← SUBJECT → WHY?
→ WHO?
→ WHEN?

2 JOURNEY STAGES

ALWAYS

OFTEN

SPORADICALLY

DOWNLOAD TOOL
https://en.business-ecosystem-design.com/interview-empathy

Extreme Users / Lead Users

The interaction with extreme/lead users helps to find innovative ideas and identify needs that are not yet known to the average customer. Lead users often act as innovators. They satisfy their requirements that have not been known to the mass market up till now. Extreme users normally exceed the normal use limits of a product, service, or system. Both concepts help to gain knowledge about the leading edge of new market areas as yet not addressed. For business ecosystems, people's ordinary needs and dreams are of particular importance.

The extreme/lead user concept helps the design thinking for business growth team to:
- explore customer needs that average users and customers are not able to articulate;
- find new innovative ideas;
- identify early trends in user behavior or needs;
- ideate for a more integrative design.

Procedure and template:
- For example, dimensions that have relevance in the context of the problem can be defined first (in the case of extreme users), or lead users who have become innovative for their cause can be identified through social media posts.
- In both cases, new insights can be gained through interviews and observation. The findings can then be used to create personas and validate existing assumptions; they may also contain initial solution ideas.
- The findings of the lead and extreme users can be documented in the form of a video presentation or in illustrated storytelling and shared with internal and external teams.

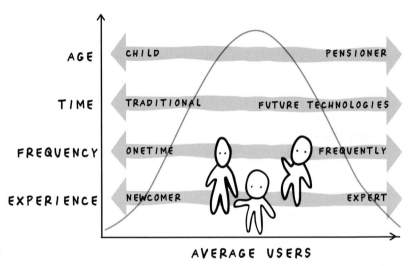

Successful business for growth initiators do not simply create new products in a fishing expedition. They think, very specifically, about which value proposition will trigger a great response from customers.

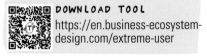

DOWNLOAD TOOL
https://en.business-ecosystem-design.com/extreme-user

Persona/User Profile

The concept of personas helps to present the findings from the in-depth interviews, interviews for empathy, or even the interactions with lead/extreme users as a profile of a possible customer group with the explored needs. One or several fictitious characters are created to represent a type of user or customer type. A persona should be described as accurately as possible. This means it has a name, gender, and basic demographic data, e.g. age, profession, hobbies.

A persona helps the design thinking for business growth team to:
- create a fictional character who is a potential customer of a solution;
- create a picture of the potential customer that is shared by everybody on the team;
- visualize the goals, desires, and needs of a typical customer and share them with the design team;
- come to a consistent understanding of a target group.

Procedure and template:
The user profile canvas encompasses eight areas. The division helps to find the right questions when creating a persona.

1. Describe the persona as exactly as possible (name, age, gender, etc.).
2. Explain the persona's task to be performed.
3. Describe use cases in the context of the problem statement.
   Typical questions: Where? What? How?
4. Description of pains, i.e. challenges, or existing problems.
5. Description of gains, i.e. opportunities or benefits that exist, e.g. due to life situations or social status.
6. Creation of a sketch, or a picture of the persona.
7. Exploring the persona's surroundings. Typical question here: Who influences the persona?
8. Which trends exist that might affect the persona?

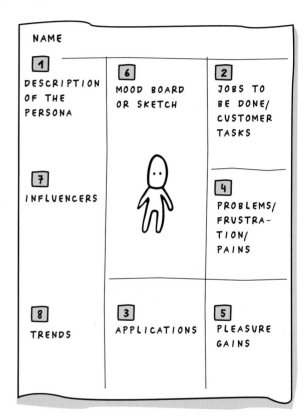

DOWNLOAD TOOL
https://en.business-ecosystem-design.com/persona

Critical Items Diagram

The critical items diagram helps the team to agree on the critical success elements for the target group based on the initial findings, the definition of a POV, or building a persona. These elements must be solved later with the final prototype and often enter the MVP development phase. The described elements in the critical items diagram can either describe the experience a user expects the solution to provide or present an expected function. The elements of the diagram should be questioned after each iteration. However, some will necessarily have relevance to a critical experience or critical function all the way to the final prototype/MVP.

A critical items diagram helps the design thinking for business growth team to:
- appraise the results from the understand and observe phases and filter out the crucial elements;
- prepare the ideate and prototype phases and later the realize MVP phase, to establish a good starting position;
- figure out the things that are essential to the project and agree on what might be important to success.

Procedure and template:
1. At the beginning of this step, ponder the question: "What is crucial for a successful solution to the problem?" This is based on the findings from the understand and observe phases.
2. Sketch a critical items diagram on the whiteboard or a large sheet of paper and discuss on the team which experiences the user must have / which functions are crucial for the user.
3. Each team member writes the eight elements that are crucial for them on Post-its.
4. Each member names four experiences and four functions, one of which focuses on completely new or future expectations.
5. Consolidate the results and agree on the team about eight crucial elements. On this basis, define "How might we..." questions that are interesting enough to launch the ideate phase successfully.

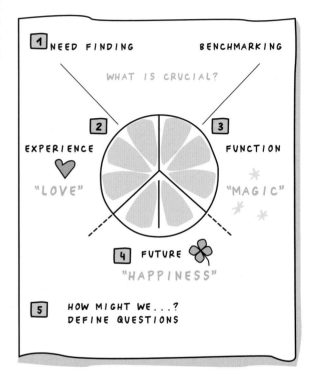

The contents from the critical items diagram are highly relevant to the creation of prototypes, MVPs all the way to the realization of MVEs.

DOWNLOAD TOOL
https://en.business-ecosystem-design.com/critical-items

Brainstorming

Brainstorming is an ideation technique in which all participants can contribute their knowledge. A brainstorming session helps to find a great number of ideas for the problem statement or to develop a point of view. Good brainstorming sessions stimulate creativity and allow all participants, regardless of their hierarchical level, to contribute their ideas. Brainstorming has no limits — all ideas are welcome. Various questions related to brainstorming help to boost creativity. From the tool set of special forms of brainstorming, super heroes (e.g. How would Steve Jobs solve the problem?) or analogies/benchmarks (e.g. How would Amazon solve the problem?) can be used here.

Brainstorming helps the design thinking for business growth team to:
- generate many ideas that the team spontaneously comes up with;
- exploit the entire creative potential of the team;
- have a high number of variants at hand in a short period of time;
- obtain an interdisciplinary perspective on a problem that represents different skills and knowledge;
- collect ideas and viewpoints from a heterogeneous group.

Procedure and template:
1. Prepare a clear HMW question for the brainstorming session, e.g. in the form of "How might we..." or "What possibilities are there..." (see page 192).
2. Repeat the brainstorming rules before the brainstorming session. Try to motivate the group to provide more ideas during the session and to build upon the ideas of others. Make sure that all are heard and all ideas are written down. Point out that only one idea is to be written per Post-it and that they should write clearly and legibly. Instead of words, small sketches may be drawn on the Post-its.
3. Cluster and assess the ideas together with the team at regular intervals.
4. Make a judgment as to whether even more creativity is needed, e.g. to obtain even wilder ideas, or start a brainstorming session in areas where more ideas are sought in general.

Creativity is a team sport. In a session of free association of thoughts and the brainstorming of many people, a random thought may lead to the best solution ideas.

Tool

BRAINSTORMING RULES

CREATIVE CONFIDENCE

QUANTITY BEFORE QUALITY

VISUAL IDEAS

USE GESTURES

BUILDING ON THE IDEAS OF OTHERS

ALWAYS, ONLY ONE PERSON SPEAKS AT A TIME

NO PREJUDICES

CONTINUE WITH THE BRAINSTORMING

FAIL OFTEN AND EARLY ON

DOWNLOAD TOOL
https://en.business-ecosystem-design.com/brainstorming

Prototype to Test

Tool

The work with prototypes is a fundamental concept of design thinking. This procedure helps with direct customer interaction to receive feedback, e.g. on the experience or the function. After various ideation phases and the application of different creativity techniques, the ideas are implemented in prototypes and tested with the potential customers. The procedure is primarily about designing an experiment for the user to learn something from the interaction for improving the prototype. It is best when the potential customer interacts with the prototype and experiences the prototype in this way.

The prototype to test helps the design thinking for business growth team to:

- make ideas tangible and observe how the potential customer interacts with the prototype;
- deepen the understanding of the potential customer;
- validate needs and review assumptions;
- acquire feedback on various dimensions of feasibility, desirability, and viability.

Procedure and template:

1. Before prototyping, we should ask ourselves what type of insights we want to gain and why we want to do an experiment. Therefore, it is necessary to formulate assumptions to be tested and decide how the experiment is to be carried out.
2. Think about how interacting with the prototype will become an exciting experience for the user (test person) and how the test will result in new insights.
3. Determine the level of resolution and what exactly is to be done. Define different prototypes to be built. Frequently, it makes sense to think of alternatives.
4. Choose a variant and outline the experiment, if necessary. Low-resolution prototypes focus on the insights with respect to needs, practicality, and functionality and are mostly used in the divergent phase. High-resolution prototypes concentrate on feasibility and profitability.

PROTOTYPE TO TEST – PREPARATION

WHY? WHAT ASSUMPTIONS DO WE WANT TO VERIFY?

1 _____

HOW MIGHT WE MAKE IT TANGIBLE AND PRECEPTIBLE FOR THE USER?

2 _____

WHAT SHOULD WE DO? OUTLINE POSSIBLE VARIANTS

3

CHOOSE THE BEST IDEA AND OUTLINE THE EXPERIMENT

4

DOWNLOAD TOOL
https://en.business-ecosystem-design.com/prototype-to-test

Documentation of the Prototypes via the Exploration Map

Tool

The exploration map helps to keep track of all the experiments and prototypes already carried out. It normally has an experience and a function axis. The two axes symbolize known or existing and new or unexpected behaviors and functions, respectively. In addition, the feedback of the users/customers with respect to the experiments can be entered on the exploration map. This way, it can be determined whether the expected user behavior conforms to real-life experience. The exploration map shows – at the end of the entire design cycle – the path the team took to reach the ultimate solution.

An exploration map helps the design thinking for business growth team to:

- make visible the types of experiments that were carried out and the prototypes that were realized;
- get a quick overview of the experiments or prototypes that can still be performed;
- record the difference between the expected and actual outcome of an experiment;
- come to a shared understanding of the experiments carried out so far.

Procedure and template:

The exploration map gives the team an overview of the experiments carried out and shows the areas in which experiments can still be done. It provides information on the expectations regarding an experiment and its effect on the target group.

1. Enter the experiments that have already been performed. They might have to be repositioned. Each experiment is recorded on the exploration map – it is best to do so with a name and an image, e.g. of the prototype and the testing.
2. Discuss the positioning of the experiment on the team. Have we really left our comfort zone? Based on the previous exploration and the previous experiments, the goal for a new experiment, for instance, can be defined.

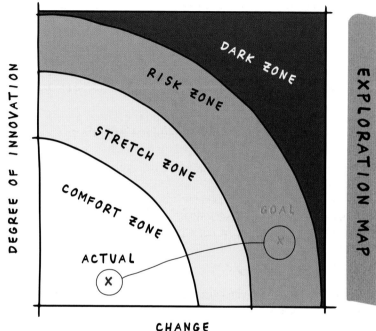

EXPLORATION MAP

3. After the prototype has been built and the expectation regarding the result has been formulated, they are also entered on the exploration map and correspondingly positioned.
4. After the tests, the reaction of the users and the findings of the tests can also be captured. The critical discussion of the feedback may correspondingly change the position of the experiment on the exploration map.

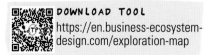

DOWNLOAD TOOL
https://en.business-ecosystem-design.com/exploration-map

199

Vision Prototype

The vision prototype is the first concept that attempts to solve all identified needs and problems of the user. The sketched vision usually has a rather distant time horizon that can be reached through a series of solutions in the form of products and/or services. This concept must also be tested and verified with the users. In this step, it is quite common that new insights about the user and their behavior emerge. The vision prototype is designed to help the team overcome the "groan zone" better – the transition of the divergent phase of problem exploration to the convergent phase of problem solution.

Tool

NORTH STAR

A vision prototype helps the design thinking for business growth team to:
- develop a first vision on how the problem can be solved;
- create a vision of what is to be marketed in the future;
- make sure that the vision solves the needs and problems of the user;
- design the transition from problem exploration to problem solution.

Procedure and template:
1. Describe the target group: The target is once again described in specific terms for the vision prototype. The insights gained through personas and other segmentation techniques are of help here.
2. Describe the needs: In addition, the specific needs are described for which a solution is developed.
3. Description of the product/service: What matters a great deal here is how the problem/solution fit is achieved and what the customer gets to satisfy their needs or solve their problem.
4. Benefits for customers and the actors involved: The benefits for the customer are described. Anybody already thinking of ecosystems at this point can integrate the benefits for the system or the individual actors.
5. Describe the vision: Steps 1–4 are a guide to describe the actual vision statement. Good vision statements are ambitious and include the information about who the solution is created for and what benefits the defined target segment brings.

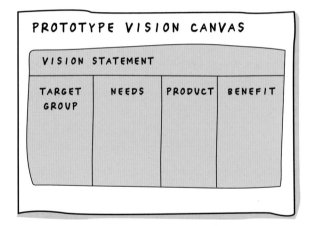

PROTOTYPE VISION CANVAS

VISION STATEMENT

TARGET GROUP	NEEDS	PRODUCT	BENEFIT

Ideas must be turned into stories that are important to the customers and to potential partners in the business ecosystem.

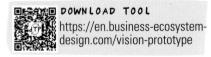

DOWNLOAD TOOL
https://en.business-ecosystem-design.com/vision-prototype

Final Prototype

An iterative procedure ensures that the prototypes become more and more high-resolution over time. The final prototype concludes the phase of problem solving. The final prototype should be elegant and simple at the same time. Before we begin to formulate specifications for an MVP, it is vital to check once more whether the solution still fits the needs originally identified and fits the problem of the target group. In this step at the latest, all criteria for one or more minimum viable product(s) should have been met.
.

The final prototype helps the design thinking for business growth team to:

- exit the prototype phase and thus the early innovation phase;
- avoid any overfulfillment of needs;
- reduce all required elements to what is essential;
- map intelligent combinations of sub-functions;
- create an elegant ultimate solution for the needs and problems;
- get closer to the lean start-up phase and thus to a marketable step toward realizing the vision and having initial assumptions about the business model verified.

Procedure and template

While many previous prototypes were rather low-resolution, when creating the final prototype, it is important to make sure that it contains elements from the critical items diagram since they are usually critical to success. Implementation should be well planned. One thing that has passed the test is to get all the help we can, e.g. from user interface designers or other service providers. One principle for the final prototype is: The simpler the functionality, the better. When implementing the final prototype, elegance will show up on its own – in thought and in its realization. Ultimately, only reality will produce the truth. The customer will either love the solution or else lose interest fast.

Tool

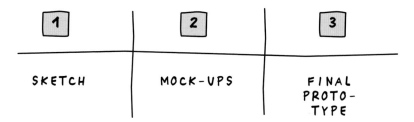

1	2	3
SKETCH	MOCK-UPS	FINAL PROTO-TYPE

DOWNLOAD TOOL
https://en.business-ecosystem-design.com/final-prototype

Lean Canvas

Tool

The canvas supports us with structuring and visualizing the project. The completed lean canvas documents the final problem/solution fit. The blocks of the lean canvas lead through a logical sequence from customer issues all the way to unfair advantage. The canvas provides a good basis for the transition to the next design lens. The business model canvas can be used as an alternative. The lean canvas is far more suitable for the transition toward the minimum viable product, however, because it is relatively less inside-oriented than the business model canvas.

The lean canvas helps the design thinking for business growth team:

- summarize the results from the design thinking iterations and thus get a clear picture of the requirements for the MVP/MVE;
- visualize and structure the hypotheses to review them afterward and capture the findings in an overview;
- think and make observations about the implementation or the business model to identify risks entailed in the implementation;
- compare different variants and business models.

Procedure and template:

1. Fill in the lean canvas incrementally and supplement it with new findings. In the early phases, the focus is on fields I through V to review the problem/solution fit (problem, customer segments, value proposition, solution, and existing alternatives). **Tip:** First, iterate in these five fields until a stable image has emerged.
2. Complete the other fields in any order. **Tip:** Depending on preferences, use Post-its of different colors for different customer segments or according to risks (e.g. pink = high risk, must be tested quickly; yellow = medium risk; green = already tested or low risk).
3. Identify the most risky hypotheses and test them in experiments.

TITLE

PROBLEM [I]	SOLUTION [IV]	UNIQUE VALUE OFFER [III]	UNFAIR ADVANTAGE	CUSTOMER SEGMENTS [II]
EXISTING ALTERNATIVES [V]	KEY FIGURES	HIGH-LEVEL CONCEPT	CHANNELS	EARLY ADOPTER
COSTS STRUCTURE		REVENUE STREAMS		

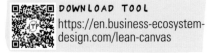
DOWNLOAD TOOL
https://en.business-ecosystem-design.com/lean-canvas

Requirements for MVP

Tool

The final prototype may contain the requirements for one or more MVPs. Together with the prioritized elements from the critical items diagram and the vision prototype, a backlog can be defined that will form the basis for the next steps in the lean start-up lens #2.

The list of requirements helps the design thinking for business growth team:
• to bring all relevant information for the validations in a topical and chronological order;
• alongside the features, functions and experiences, elements dealing with the integration of third-party systems should be included;
• begin with initial deliberations about how the future of the overall enterprise architecture and the system architecture might look, including the relevant components, products, and interfaces in a future business ecosystem.

Procedure:
• The requirements for the MVP are usually based on the final prototype from the design thinking phase. The final prototype frequently leads to various MVPs or approaches that can be traced back to the vision prototype.
• The requirements can be itemized on lists; they can be described or laid down in initial sketches and wireframes. It is crucial that the teams will have a clear picture in the next phase of WHAT is to be implemented. Taking the larger target image with its dependencies into the next phase is helpful as well.
• The core team should accompany the next phase so no losses in knowledge transfer are incurred.
• Based on the MVP, in design lens #3: business ecosystem, the so-called MMFs (minimum marketable features) as part of the MVE (minimum viable ecosystem) can be fitted into the market and tested in interaction with the actors. Once the MVE phase has been successfully completed, the other features, functions, and experiences can be managed and evaluated in a product backlog.

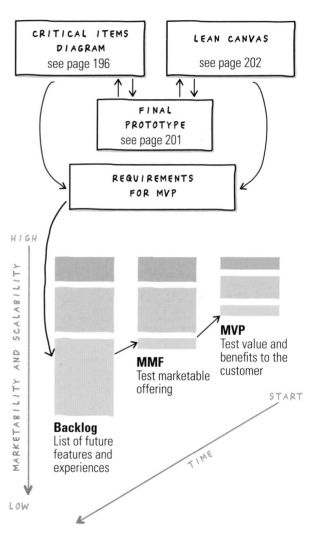

To the Point!

Design thinking in its pristine form provides the right mindset, procedural model, and methods to start a business ecosystem initiative. It helps to adopt a customer-centered mindset, to question assumptions critically and redefine problem statements.

Working with iterations, the collaboration of interdisciplinary teams all the way to co-creation with other companies prepares the organization so that this work attitude will be applied across company and industry boundaries.

In design thinking for business growth, the goal of this lenses is to develop solutions that meet the needs of the customers. The final prototype and elements from the critical items diagram constitute the basis for the specifications regarding the implementation of one or more MVPs.

Transition from Design Thinking to Lean Start-Up

DIMENSION	OUTPUT: #1 DESIGN THINKING FINAL PROTOTYPE	ACTIONS: #2 LEAN START-UP MINIMUM VIABLE PRODUCT
PURPOSE	Mainly, the testing of feasibility and desirability of the prototype of a solution that is to be integrated in an ecosystem	Validation at all levels of the design lenses (feasibility, desirability, and viability) with as little effort as possible and a maximum of learning
FOCUS	Presentation to decision-making bodies and stakeholders, e.g. for the funding of the next phase	Good enough for market launch and the interaction with real (test) customers
FEATURES	Various; among other things, they are rejected via MVP as part of the validation	Basic functions, functional elements, and experiences
TARGET GROUP	Small audience of stakeholders and decision makers	Larger group of initial (test) customers and potential actors in the ecosystem to realize the overriding value proposition
LEGACY	Is discarded after the final presentation and definition of MVP requirements	First version of a marketable solution
TYPE OF FEEDBACK	Feedback of the concept, the idea and the experience for the customer	Feedback on individual functions and experiences or a chain of experiences from different MVPs
DESIGN	Mock-ups, wireframes	Product functionality, features, and experiences
CUSTOMER BENEFIT	Shows a potential value proposition	Delivers a true/validated value proposition
CREATION TIME OF THE ENTIRE DESIGN CYCLE	Business case and product untested; low funds; future risks unknown; current risk low	Business case and product/features validated; sufficient financing; moderate risks
TESTS	Customer and market needs	Test of the solution and the relevant functions; checking the willingness of customers to spend money on the service or product
REVENUE	Normally, no revenue from the prototype	Possible initial income from the interaction with early adopters as (test) customers

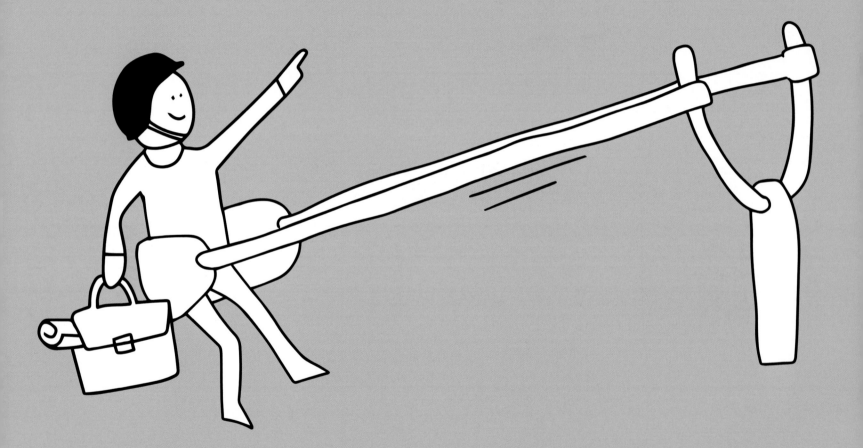

LENS #2

LEAN
START-UP

Intro to Lean Start-Up

The lean start-up methods and the associated procedural model help gain initial experience with a product or service on the market. The primary goal is to draw conclusions from customer feedback, which in turn helps to advance the MVP. This is done by iteratively testing the most key experiences and functions. In addition, the MVP allows for performing initial tests in terms of pricing. The iterative procedure is repeated until the MVP covers the customer needs. The mindset of lean thinking and the work with iterations pervades all stages: from design thinking to the MVP all the way to the MVE, which will be described in greater detail in the context of the design of business ecosystems (page 243 et seq.). "Minimum viable" describes the approach to the implementation of products and services, in which all processes and development steps are kept as lean as possible. Such a pragmatic procedure to risk minimization has become an effective method for all radical changes in existing companies and is used today from digital transformation all the way to the exploration of new growth fields. The models presented in this section follow the conceptual ideas of Eric Ries, Steve Blank, and Ash Maurya. Several MVPs are needed in preparation for the MVE; often various options are implemented simultaneously so that appropriate conclusions can be drawn for the next steps. The results from the lean start-up cycle validate and focus strategic considerations. Especially in the application of design thinking for business growth it is important to leave the decades-old formula in the definition of growth topics, moving away from a linear approach with its analyses of competitors, addressable markets, and market segments to finally write a business plan and sell it to the decision makers (see page 35) to an approach where agile development works hand in hand with customer development to prove the benefit and value to the potential customer/user from the beginning. The validated value proposition is also the starting point for following considerations on a functioning business ecosystem. The lean start-up canvas helps with the description of the starting point, the planning, and documentation of the results of one or more MVPs.

Typical Activities

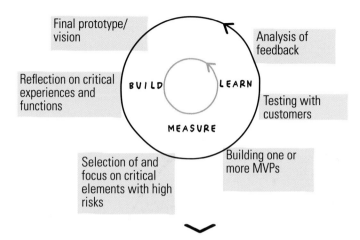

Final prototype/ vision

Analysis of feedback

Reflection on critical experiences and functions

BUILD LEARN

Testing with customers

MEASURE

Selection of and focus on critical elements with high risks

Building one or more MVPs

Ideas for a sustainable business model based on experiments with MVPs for new functions, experiences, and features that contribute to the overriding value proposition of an ecosystem.

Preview of the Suitable Methods and Tools for the Lean Start-Up

Key Questions Lean Start-Up

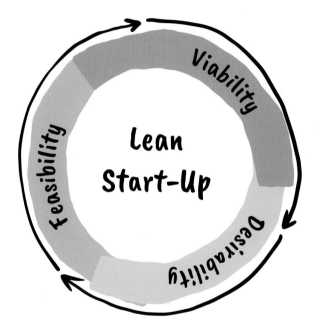

VIABILITY

- Which problem is to be solved with the business model?
- Where do fixed and variable costs arise?
- What value streams yield income?
- Are both the commercial model and the price attractive to the customer?
- Does the MVP have the potential to grow exponentially in an ecosystem later?
- How can the concept be implemented and financed?

DESIRABILITY

- Who are the most important customers?
- Which customers are potential early adapters?
- What additional needs should be taken in consideration (e.g. partners, suppliers, external influencers, decision makers)?
- Who are the most important stakeholders and interest groups?
- Does the value proposition match the customer profile?
- Do customers come back again and again (stickiness)?
- What channels are most effective for customer cultivation?
- What sets us apart from the competition?

FEASIBILITY

- What's the short concept?
- How should success be measured?
- Which functions are to be built and tested?
- Which experiences and functions are absolutely necessary?
- Which user stories are part of the MVP?
- To what extent should existing systems be integrated?
- What does the product/solution/service system look like?

LEAN START-UP MVP CANVAS

INITIAL SITUATION

PERSONA
For whom is this MVP?
Who will test the MVP?

TOP 3 PROBLEMS AND CHALLENGES
What is the focus of this MVP?
What problems or challenges are addressed by it?

CUSTOMER JOURNEY AND USE CASES
Which step in the customer journey / ecosystem journey or what use cases are improved by it?

PLAN

VISION AND ROAD MAP
What is the product vision?
What does the road map look like?
How will we expand the width and depth of functions step by step?

TOP 3 FEATURES
What are the top features tested in this MVP?

MVP
How does the MVP contribute to the vision?

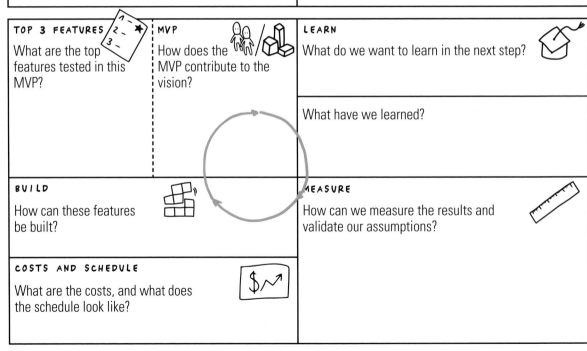

BUILD
How can these features be built?

COSTS AND SCHEDULE
What are the costs, and what does the schedule look like?

RESULTS

CONCLUSION/NEXT STEPS
What are the most important insights?
Does this vision or strategy have to be adapted (pivot)?

LEARN
What do we want to learn in the next step?

What have we learned?

MEASURE
How can we measure the results and validate our assumptions?

LEAN START-UP MVP CANVAS

Template download

INITIAL SITUATION	PLAN		RESULTS
PERSONA	**8** P. 221 VISION AND ROAD MAP		CONCLUSION INCLUDING PORTFOLIO **9** P. 223
TOP 3 PROBLEMS/ CHALLENGES **6** P. 218	TOP 3 FEATURES P. 218	MVP **1** P. 212 **2** P. 213	LEARN **5** P. 218
4 P. 216 USE CASES CUSTOMER JOURNEY	BUILD COSTS AND SCHEDULE, INCLUDING INNOVATION ACCOUNTING **3** P. 218		MEASURE **7** P. 220

INPUTS FROM LENS 1

The lean start MVP canvas helps to transfer insights from the design thinking phase to a documentation of MVP validations.

METHODS AND TOOLS KEY

1. Minimum viable product (MVP)
2. Build – measure – learn
3. Innovation accounting
4. User stories / user story map / acceptance tests
5. The pivot
6. Usability tests
7. Willingness-to-pay analysis
8. MVP portfolio and MVP portfolio planning
9. Transition of MVPs into MMFs for MVE

DOWNLOAD TOOL
https://en.business-ecosystem-design.com/lean-startup

Minimum Viable Product (MVP)

Unlike conventional product development, the MVP aims at testing individual experiences and functions with potential customers and finally making the value tangible for the customer. The MVP runs through an iterative feedback loop (see "Build – Measure – Learn" on page 213). The focus here is on building an MVP, which, in the procedural model presented here, is more high-resolution than the prototypes that were realized in design thinking all the way to the final prototype. The word "product" in MVP is in many cases a combination of a product or a service with a function and/or experience.

The MVP helps the design thinking for business growth team to:
- enable quick learning and minimize the costs of a later failure;
- obtain direct feedback from potential customers;
- minimize the risk of building products, solutions, or services that no one wants to use later;
- develop the value proposition based on customer feedback;
- carry out many iterations until the product, service, or experience meets the customer needs.

Procedure and template:
1. **Building on existing findings:** For one, include all activities that were already relevant in design thinking help. The critical items diagram is especially useful for defining the functions and experiences for an MVP. It is also advisable to develop several MVPs in tandem, test them all, and learn from it.
2. **Prioritization of functions, experiences, and MVPs:** The individual elements can be entered into a matrix that reflects the impact on the added value for the customer as well as the urgency for testing. Not least, the MVP is used to test assumptions that have not yet been confirmed and are highly uncertain with respect to the acceptance and willingness to pay on the part of the customers (see "Willingness-to-Pay Analysis" on page 220).

Tool

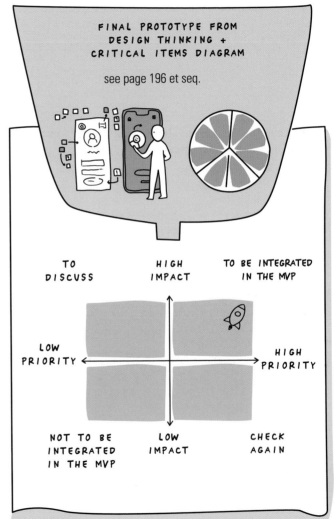

INPUTS:

FINAL PROTOTYPE FROM DESIGN THINKING + CRITICAL ITEMS DIAGRAM

see page 196 et seq.

TO DISCUSS — HIGH IMPACT — TO BE INTEGRATED IN THE MVP

LOW PRIORITY ← → HIGH PRIORITY

NOT TO BE INTEGRATED IN THE MVP — LOW IMPACT — CHECK AGAIN

Build – Measure – Learn

Build – measure – learn is an iterative feedback loop that is applied until the product or service has reached the desired market maturity or marketability. This procedure saves time and money. The procedure is similar to the one used when developing prototypes in design thinking. The MVP, for instance, is also used for questions in relation to pricing. This certainly doesn't mean that a limited version of a future solution is to be realized. Instead, the aim is achieving a maximum gain in knowledge with the least effort. After all, it is crucial to find out what customers really want and not to rely on pure, unvalidated assumptions that usually turn out to be false.

Build – measure – learn helps the design thinking for business growth team to:
- obtain inferences for the development or radical transformation of the MVPs at the earliest possible time;
- find out which (functional) design properties or features are accepted by potential customers;
- perform initial testing of digital and physical channels;
- exploit customer feedback on pricing opportunities.

Procedure and template:
1. **Build:** After the MVP has been built with a real added value for the customer (value proposition) and made available to potential customers, it's time to measure the effects.
2. **Measure:** The measurement is based on two key questions: How do potential customers accept the MVP? What improvements are desired? From these insights, a learning process is set in motion to improve the MVP or adapt it to customer requirements.
3. **Learn:** Iterative feedback loops enable learning based on the feedback from customers. The build – measure – learn cycle has the main advantage that it allows for a fast response to changes on the market so the MVP can be improved based on customer feedback.

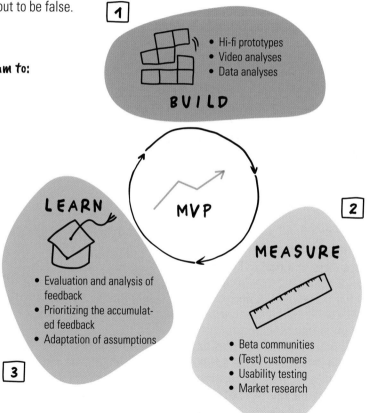

1 **BUILD**
- Hi-fi prototypes
- Video analyses
- Data analyses

MVP

2 **MEASURE**
- Beta communities
- (Test) customers
- Usability testing
- Market research

3 **LEARN**
- Evaluation and analysis of feedback
- Prioritizing the accumulated feedback
- Adaptation of assumptions

Innovation Accounting

Measuring innovation success is an integral part of the lean start-up method. It allows the business ecosystem team to prove objectively that the right conclusions are drawn from the experiments with the MVPs and then used for the improvement of the MVP. One specific or several MVPs constitute the later basis for the design of a business ecosystem, in which several actors generate a shared value proposition. In general, innovation accounting is different from the KPIs normally used in companies. Early simulations of sales figures can be performed with so-called driver trees (see the example on page 215). This view helps later during the design lens #4, scale.

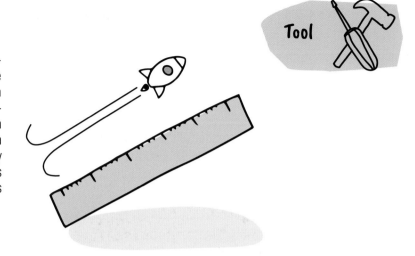

Tool

Innovation accounting helps the design thinking for business growth team to:
- determine the starting point as to which MVP with its associated functions and experience should run through the build – measure – learn cycle;
- carry out fine-tuning by testing the relevant hypotheses;
- decide whether something should be discarded (pivot) or retained (preserve).

The aim of innovation accounting is to verify the most risky business model assumptions by way of empirical testing with customers.

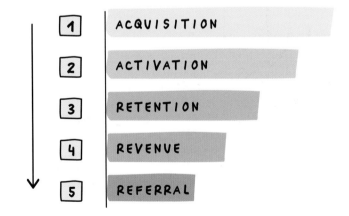

Sample questions:
1. **Acquisition:** How do customers find us?
2. **Activation:** Do the customers have a first positive experience?
3. **Retention:** Are the customers coming back?
4. **Revenue:** How does the offer or function make money?
5. **Referral:** Do the customers recommend the offer to other people?

DRIVER TREE

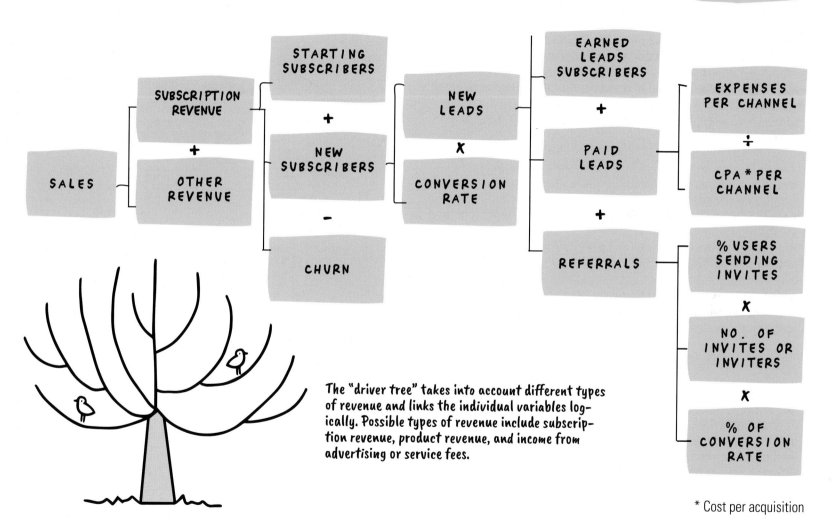

SALES

SUBSCRIPTION REVENUE
+
OTHER REVENUE

STARTING SUBSCRIBERS
+
NEW SUBSCRIBERS
-
CHURN

NEW LEADS
x
CONVERSION RATE

EARNED LEADS SUBSCRIBERS
+
PAID LEADS
+
REFERRALS

EXPENSES PER CHANNEL
÷
CPA * PER CHANNEL

% USERS SENDING INVITES
x
NO. OF INVITES OR INVITERS
x
% OF CONVERSION RATE

The "driver tree" takes into account different types of revenue and links the individual variables logically. Possible types of revenue include subscription revenue, product revenue, and income from advertising or service fees.

* Cost per acquisition

215

User Stories / User Story Map / Acceptance Criteria

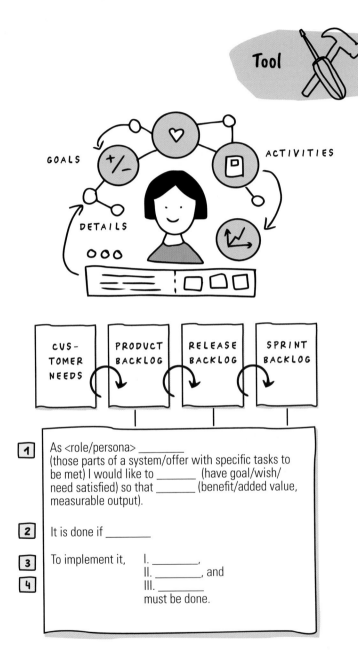

User stories provide the basis for an agile development. They help to look at needs satisfaction holistically while simultaneously mapping specific elements, e.g. the ones that are necessary in an acceptance test. Typical user stories have three elements. For one, they describe the role/persona (i.e. for whom something is to be developed, namely in the system in which the persona has the application); secondly, the wish/goal is included (i.e. which needs are to be satisfied) so that a measurable result is achieved in the end (benefits).

The user stories help the design thinking for business growth team:
- not lose sight of the higher-level goals and customer requirements;
- to plan and carry out the MVP backlog, release backlog, and sprint backlog;
- to automate elements such as the acceptance test;
- to divide the individual work cycles for the development teams into tasks.

Procedure and template:

1. A first assessment about the feasibility and viability from the design thinking phase is on hand that shows whether something is realistic and achievable. A common way of starting is to formulate the intention of the user in one sentence:

As <role/persona>_____ I want to _____ so that_____.

2. Special acceptance criteria can be defined for a detailed assessment of the test goal. User stories that are not yet completely convincing can be implemented or tested again as a prototype, or they can be spruced up.

3. The acceptance tests can be automated in later phases.

4. The development teams have the opportunity to break down the individual packages of the implementation process and thus perform the tests one by one and pass them or, if necessary, have the individual steps honed and improved again by the design team.

Tool

TEMPLATE USER STORY AND ACCEPTANCE CRITERIA CANVAS

TITLE	PRIORITY	COST ESTIMATE
WHO WHAT WHY	AS... ...I WOULD LIKE... ...TO...	ROLE GOAL WISH BENEFIT

ACCEPTANCE CRITERIA

Every user story should have at least one acceptance criterion that:
- is identified before implementation;
- is testable;
- has a clear result (e.g. passed/failed);
- contains functional and nonfunctional criteria;

Additionally, members of the business ecosystem should be able to describe all criteria, and all criteria is normally verified by the product owner.

Specified.. (how things begin)

Is carried out........ .... (action taken)

Then the result is.................................... (result of action)

DOWNLOAD TOOL
https://en.business-ecosystem-design.com/user-story

The Pivot

In the context of lean start-up, pivot means a radically modified version of the entire MVP or a part of it. The change of direction is crucial if experiments have shown that the originally intended solution does not work. The right time for a radical change is decisive. Frequently, it's the gut feeling that decides when this change of direction is due.

A playing field of pivots helps the design thinking for business growth team:

Zoom-out pivot:
The MVP becomes an integral part of a new, much larger product or offer.

Zoom-in pivot:
A single component of the MVP becomes the new product or service.

Platform pivot:
App with function turns into a business ecosystem or a transaction platform.

Channel pivot:
The physical or digital channels are changing.

Value capture pivot:
The value creation and the business areas involved in it are changing.

Customer need pivot:
The customer needs are changing or have been misjudged.

Customer segment pivot:
The customer target group or segment for the MVP is changing.

Business architecture pivot:
Reversal – high margin, low volume with low margin, high volume.

Engine of growth pivot:
Change of the growth model from linear to exponential.

Technology pivot:
New technology for improved performance, cost savings, or data models.

Procedure and template:
The individual pivots can be documented in a matrix in which, in addition to the actual customer hypothesis, the problem hypothesis and finally the solution hypothesis are documented. The experiment is conducted based on the respective assumptions. With regard to the assumptions, it is sensible to prioritize the assumption with the greatest risk and test it first.

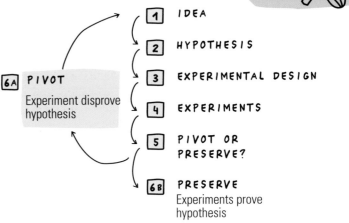

Minor adaptations and features of customer needs or of the functions/features are not pivots but part of the MVP process.

TRACK PIVOTS	START	1ST	2ND	3RD	4TH
CUSTOMER HYPOTHESIS					
PROBLEM HYPOTHESIS					
SOLUTION HYPOTHESIS					

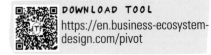

DOWNLOAD TOOL
https://en.business-ecosystem-design.com/pivot

Usability Tests

Tool

A key element in the building and validation of MVPs is to involve potential customers in a user-centered development process to create maximum user experience with the function, experience, or individual features. There's a whole box of usability tools that generate both quantitative and qualitative results. Offering a single feature is not enough to be successful on the market. Rather, the point is to make a proposition to future customers with the offer, to provide a solution to their problem, and ultimately to deliver on the value proposition. Customers are happy, for instance, if they are willing to use an offer repeatedly or recommend it to others.

The usability tests help the design thinking for business growth team to:
- check functionality at a very early stage;
- explore whether the potential customers actually understand the offer;
- determine whether the offer or one function requires prior knowledge on the part of the customer or explanations;
- recognize reactions and emotions that the offer triggers in customers.

Procedure:
One way to record the feedback from the usability tests consists of entering it in a four-quadrant matrix.
1. Write down what the potential customers do.
2. Document the key statements from test customers.
3. Find out why customers behave in a certain way and how they have chosen workarounds or solved the problem up till now.
4. Record everything that is countable and measurable, e.g. how many clicks were needed or when a process was aborted, and information on how much the customers would have paid.

TOOLBOX USABILITY TOOLS	What is to be tested?		What results are wanted?	
	Formatively	Summative	Quantitatively	Qualitatively
A/B testing		X	X	
Field studies		X		X
Hallway testing	X	X		X
Heuristic evaluation	X	X		X
Hypothesis testing		X	X	
Interviews	X	X		X
Log analysis		X	X	
Remote testing		X	X	X
Surveys	X	X	X	
Think aloud	X	X		X
Wizard of Oz	X			X

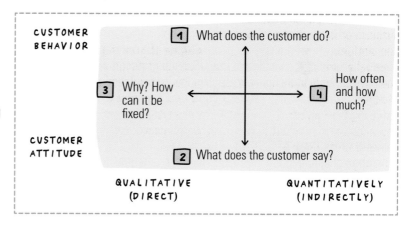

Usability is about the question of how the customer/user understands, perceives, and uses something; it is not about the technology used for it.

Willingness-to-Pay (WTP) Analysis

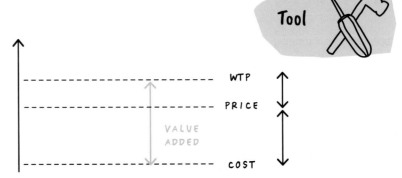

For certain offers, pricing can be tested in an early phase and be validated as part of an MVP. Well-known models for pricing are cost plus pricing, comparison pricing, or the willingness-to-pay analysis described here. There are different ways to determine the willingness to pay. One option is discreet choice analysis, either based on actual purchase data or on asking the customers for their preference among alternatives with different sets of attributes. In most cases, the potential customers are not able to articulate the value they place on a feature directly; what they can do is compare two alternatives in an A/B test and express their preference. Given a sufficiently large number of votes, this method (conjoint analysis) can be an implicit evaluation of each feature by the customers.

The willingness-to-pay analysis helps the design thinking for business growth team to:
- obtain an initial idea about the willingness to pay for products and services on the part of certain customers and segments;
- establish an estimate of demand that can serve as a basis for predicting the overall size of the market or segment for the nascent ecosystem;
- generally develop an assessment on whether the costs are in a healthy relationship with the validation from the willingness-to-pay analysis;
- begin with tactical thoughts on pricing, business model, and ecosystem design and evaluate individual functions and experiences.

Procedure and template:
1. An open question in the interaction with the potential customer and the MVP may mark the starting point: What is the attribute/feature worth to you?
2. Or is there already an indication of what it may cost, of what is the initial situation for the willingness-to-pay analysis.
3. As part of A/B tests, questions about various pricing aspects can be asked.
4. The analysis may relate to the overall offer, individual features, or specific services, e.g. neutral consultancy.

It is unlikely that each customer has the same willingness to pay for a particular product or service, and it is recommended to create a market demand curve that shows how many customers will buy at a given price; from this, the market price elasticity can be calculated.

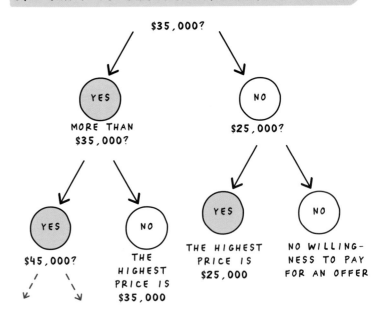

MVP Portfolio and MVP Portfolio Planning

Successful design thinking for business growth leaders think in terms of opportunities and understand that, beyond the initial MVP, they need to reach new target customers continually with their offers. Target portfolios, defined and implemented incrementally, are good for this. At the beginning, an Ansoff matrix can be used. The original matrix shows four portfolio fields and contains the dimensions of market penetration, product development, market development, and diversification. This matrix can be adjusted to the development of MVPs in potential business ecosystems, where it helps to evaluate the projects. Products in the form of existing offers and existing markets normally don't require lean start-up considerations. The focus in design thinking for business growth is on innovative customer development (new markets/new offers = potential black ocean offer).

ANSOFF MATRIX

	EXISTING OFFERS	NEW OFFERS
EXISTING MARKETS	USUALLY NO MVP NEEDED FOR THE REALIZATION OF A UNIQUE VALUE PROPOSITION	INNOVATIVE OFFER DEVELOPMENT
NEW MARKETS	FIRST-MOVER ADVANTAGE (TIME TO MARKET)	INNOVATIVE CUSTOMER DE-VELOPMENT

In the mindset of integrated and rather traditionally managed companies, "innovative customer development" is seen as risky because there is often little room for the exploitation of existing know-how or for achieving economies of scale.

MVP Portfolio Planning

Ecosystems and business growth initiatives need a comprehensive combination of functions, experiences, and features that are explored, developed, and provided by the actors. There are various options for portfolio planning and portfolio presentation. The individual MVPs alternate between discovery and delivery. Individual functions should be validated and introduced to the market as quickly as possible, for instance. Projects with a high risk in terms of time to market usually require additional resources, implementation know-how, or are dependent on new technologies.

Portfolio planning helps the design thinking for business growth team to:
- prioritize individual MVPs and align them with the strategic goals;
- align future functions and experiences with the business goals, e.g. run, grow, or change the business;
- get an overview of the status of the individual portfolio elements;
- coordinate the respective project phases, e.g. planning, implementation, project management;
- carry out adequate resource planning and allocate the respective roles and resources accordingly.

Procedure and template:
- The individual projects are entered on the portfolio grid; their progress is reflected upon every four weeks or at shorter intervals.
- The size of the bubble per initiative indicates the value added. Depending on the project, you can work with net present value (NPV), internal rate of return (IRR) revenue, or other figures.
- The four phases show where the initiatives are in terms of implementation. A rough classification is discovery and deliver.
- The arrows indicate whether there are any shifts regarding the next phase or whether some initiatives go back to the discovery phase since the first usability test yielded new insights, for instance.

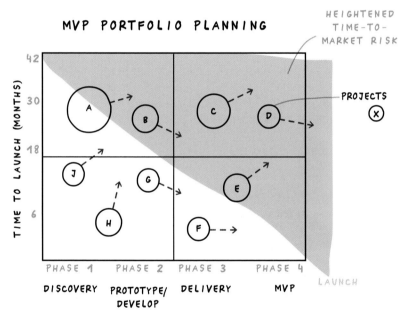

Transition of MVPs to MMFs for MVE

Tool

In many ways, the MVPs delivered validation of the relevant functions, experiences, and features, so the whole attains true added value for the customer. To move from the MVP phase to the design of business ecosystems, something like an MMF (minimum marketable feature) is needed that, in the prototype of a business ecosystem, is used to establish the MVE, test it, and gradually improve it. Here a feature and a part of a value proposition/offer should be chosen that has the greatest benefits for the customer – a sort of killer function or experience that brings the ecosystem to life, engenders enthusiasm in the customer, and convinces potential actors of the overall system. Depending on the level of complexity, an MVP can also be used directly for the development and testing of the MVE.

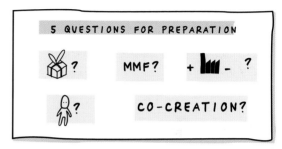

THE TRANSITION FROM THE MVP TO THE DESIGN OF AN MVE

Various questions help the design thinking for business growth team:
- with the reflection upon whether this is actually the right way to implement the project;
- to find out which killer function and experience the focus should be on so as to make the ecosystem intriguing for other actors;
- to perform a gap analysis with regard to the skills existing and the skills needed to realize the system and/or parts of it.

Five questions related to the transition to the MVE:
1. Is a business ecosystem needed for the realization of the overriding value proposition, or does a normal partnership suffice?
2. What is the experience, function, or feature (MMF) to start the minimum viable variant of the ecosystem?
3. What skills are needed by the other actors? What does your own company bring to the table?
4. For which persona/target group is the first function and experience?
5. Have potential business ecosystem partners been involved in the preliminary deliberations? Should they also be a part of the co-creation for the business ecosystem? Are there any other actors who should be a part of the process of finding a solution as early as in the design phase?

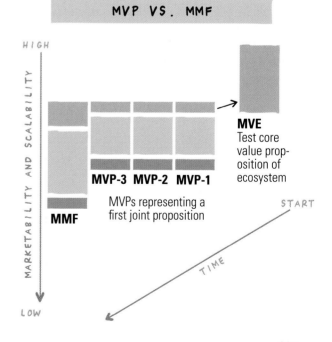

MVP VS. MMF

MVE
Test core value proposition of ecosystem

MVP-3 MVP-2 MVP-1

MVPs representing a first joint proposition

MMF

The lean start-up design lens is mainly about reflecting upon initial validations of the value proposition and the added value for the customer on the basis of an MVP.

A good MVP aims at the value and benefit to the customer. The validation of individual features alone usually does not make a good MVP.

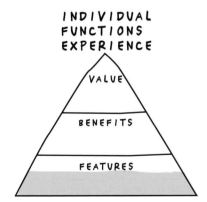

INDIVIDUAL FUNCTIONS EXPERIENCE

Which function can be built?

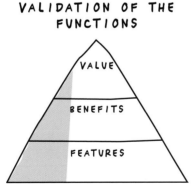

VALIDATION OF THE FUNCTIONS

Which function is capable of offering a benefit to the customer?

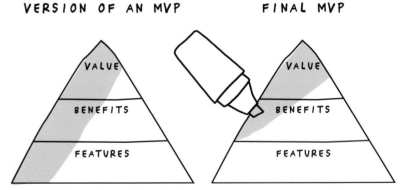

VERSION OF AN MVP

Which version of an MVP can yield the greatest measurable added value?

FINAL MVP

How can the value proposition be validated?

Transition from Lean Start-Up to Ecosystem Design

OUTPUT: 2 LEAN START-UP **ACTIONS: #3 ECOSYSTEM DESIGN**

DIMENSION	MINIMUM VIABLE PRODUCT	MINIMUM VIABLE ECOSYSTEM
PURPOSE	Validation at all levels of the design lenses (feasibility, desirability, and viability) Principle: Achieving maximum learning with as little effort as possible	Validation at all levels of the design lenses (feasibility, adaptability, and value enhanceability) Principle: Achieving maximum learning with the smallest number of actors per role in the system
FOCUS	Good enough for market launch and the interaction with real (test) customers	Use of the MVP as the basis for testing a functioning business ecosystem with the involvement of all actors and (test) customers
FEATURES	Basic functions, functional elements, and experiences	All necessary experience and functions for at least one key experience for the customer in terms of the defined value proposition
TARGET GROUP	Larger group of initial (test) customers and basis for talks with potential actors in the ecosystem to realize the overriding value proposition	Interaction and co-creation with actors in the system for the building and validation of the business ecosystem
LEGACY	First version of a marketable solution	First validation of a functioning business ecosystem
TYPE OF FEEDBACK	Feedback on individual functions and experiences or a chain of experiences from different MVPs	Feedback on value streams, customer interfaces, data, algorithms within the scope of the MVE
DESIGN	Product functionality, features, and experiences	Interaction of components for the design of the value proposition or parts of it in the form of experiences or functions
CUSTOMER BENEFIT	Delivers a validated value proposition within the scope of one or more MVPs	Delivers a validated value proposition from actors in an MVE
CREATION TIME OF THE ENTIRE DESIGN CYCLE	Business case and product/features validated; sufficient financing; moderate risks	Interplay of actors and value streams validated; multidimensional view of the business models carried out; business model of the business ecosystem is known; financing by the initiator or by other actors in the system; increased risk
TESTS	Test of the solution and the relevant functions; checking the customers' willingness to spend money on the service/product	Test of the value proposition and the associated services, value streams, and interactions of the actors; checking the customer interfaces
REVENUE	Possible initial income from the interaction with early adopters as (test) customers	Possible initial income from functioning ecosystem with (test) customers

LENS #3

ECOSYSTEM DESIGN

Procedural Model Intro

This section begins with explanations about a generic procedural model for the design of business ecosystems. Then, analogous to the other design lenses, the individual tools and methods, key questions, and the corresponding canvas are described. Business ecosystem design aims to develop a minimum viable ecosystem (MVE), so in the end the potential target system of an ecosystem and its value streams can be validated. What is important here is to combine different mindsets across the entire design cycle. In many cases, the foundation for the design of an MVE is the first prototype of an idea or by following the proposed structure in this book a set of MVPs. The prototype is presented to other potential ecosystem partners, or it is created in the co-creation mode. Since even simple ecosystems can be very complex, it is advisable to break down the overall system into subsystems and to map the relationships between the actors. This procedure allows a shared value proposition to be created, tested, measured, and improved iteratively with a minimum number of necessary actors. The basic thoughts in this procedure are similar to those in the lean start-up approach where validation is done via an MVP. This pragmatic method to minimize risks quickly shows which actors fit the target system, which value streams are sustainable, and whether the desired benefits per actor and for the entire system go well together. The procedural model presented here has been applied in various ecosystem challenges and was gradually improved. Business ecosystem design as an independent discipline was presented for the first time in the *Design Thinking Playbook* (2018) in the discussion of future factors for a successful digital transformation. This section deals with the individual steps in the four loops of the procedural model. The tools and methods for the design of business ecosystems are elucidated on pages 244 to 267. Both the loop model and the associated tools help to intuitively understand ecosystems, define clear strategies, and design strong core value propositions to grow the business. From identifying the appropriate ecosystem actors, with complementary skills, data, products, services, and customer access, to their role in the system and the multidimensional design of business model opportunities, the key steps are covered in ecosystem design to help shaping systems that can later be successfully scaled.

Typical Activities

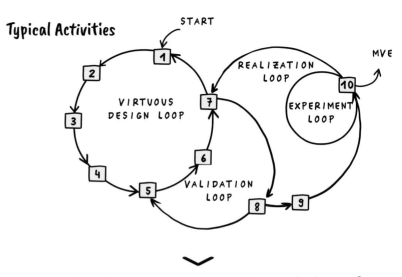

Starting with a value proposition and initial MVPs, the design of the business ecosystem embarks on its journey with four loops. After several iterations, validations, and initial implementations, the MVE is the first functioning system that provides an offer on the market in its smallest manifestation.

You can find the steps in the four loops for ecosystem design in the following sections:

The Virtuous Loop, Validation Loop, Realization Loop and Experiment Loop: 10 Steps in the (Re)design of a Business Ecosystem

The starting point in business ecosystem design are the customers/users and their needs. In the best-case scenario, the customer needs and the value proposition have already been validated through design thinking and the lean start-up tools. This is done either in the co-creation mode with potential ecosystem partners or in a narrower sphere of activity by ecosystem initiators.

The design of the business ecosystem usually takes place on three levels: customers, business and technology. The procedure for the design of an ecosystem model shown below comprises a total of 10 steps distributed across the **virtuous design loop, validation loop, realization loop,** and the **experiment loop.** It is not meant to be a blueprint for a procedure. Instead, it is a suggestion to map the most important elements for achieving an MVE. The final MVE constitutes the first functioning system in its most efficient manifestation.

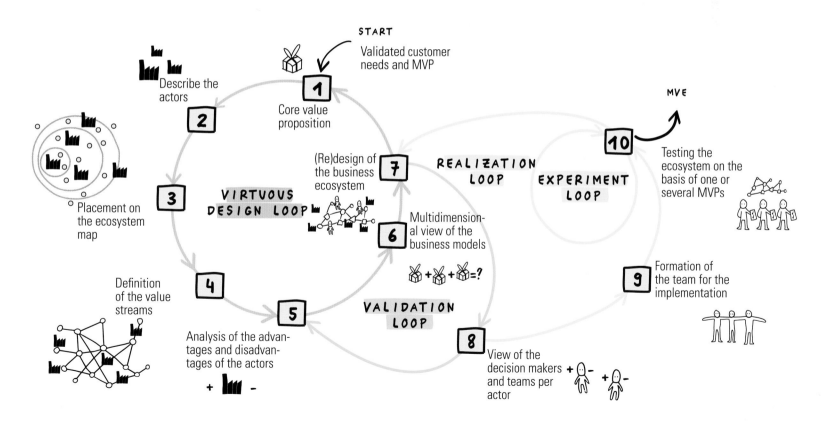

START
Validated customer needs and MVP

1 Core value proposition

2 Describe the actors

3 Placement on the ecosystem map

4 Definition of the value streams

5 Analysis of the advantages and disadvantages of the actors
+ ■ -

VIRTUOUS DESIGN LOOP

6 Multidimensional view of the business models
▨ + ▨ + ▨ =?

7 (Re)design of the business ecosystem

VALIDATION LOOP

REALIZATION LOOP

8 View of the decision makers and teams per actor

9 Formation of the team for the implementation

EXPERIMENT LOOP

10 Testing the ecosystem on the basis of one or several MVPs

MVE

Shift from a Customer Journey to an Ecosystem Journey

Although such a notion can be observed in actual practice, creating customer experience chains is not enough for the design of business ecosystems. An expanded view of things should be taken to work out a holistic ecosystem journey that takes the actors and customers on board. This view helps to define radically new approaches, which provide an optimal integration of the offers and services of all actors and, secondly, define the optimal provision of touch points with the customer/user. Thus the focus is on all customer groups and customer segments as well as on actors, suppliers, and other players who are active in the business ecosystem.

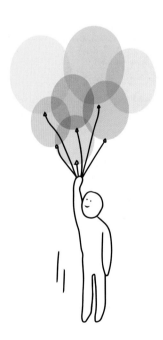

Traditional Design Thinking View vs. Expanded Ecosystem Design View

DIMENSION	CUSTOMER JOURNEY	ECOSYSTEM CUSTOMER ACTORS JOURNEY
TOUCH POINTS	Customer touch points with a company	Mapping all connections and interactions in an ecosystem
PURPOSE	Improvement of existing interactions with the customer/user via different touch points, e.g. inform, order, pay, deliver, install, handle warranty, and dispose of	Design of a holistic experience for all actors in the system who together provide a unique value proposition for the customer/user
TOUCH POINTS	Interaction of the customer/user with a company and its offer via different channels	Interaction of the customer/user with the business ecosystem via different channels and in different configurations of the customer interfaces across the ecosystem
APPLICA- TION	Optimization of existing customer interactions by means of data analytics, observation, and A/B testing for new forms of interaction	Radically new approaches to customer interaction, usually with a high degree of automation and elements of mass customization for recurring interaction with customers; easy integration of the offerings from the actors to provide the value proposition
ROLES	Focus on specific customer groups and customer segments and their needs in terms of the customer experience chain	Focus on the customer groups and customer segments as well as on actors, suppliers and other players who are active in the business ecosystem

What Are the Core Elements in the Virtuous Design Loop?

1) Formulation of the Key Value Proposition

The value proposition for the customer – or for the business ecosystem to be designed – can be inferred from the customer needs and the validations carried out later through the testing of prototypes and the MVP. The core value proposition for the overall system may very well differ from the individual considerations carried out in design thinking and lean start-up since oftentimes two, three, or more MVPs merge into a more comprehensive ecosystem approach. A valuable help for the formulation of the core value proposition is the use of tried-and-tested tools, e.g. the value proposition canvas of Osterwalder (page 248) or the user profile canvas that was presented on page 195 in the context of the design thinking lenses. The core value proposition canvas listed as one of the tools (page 249) brings together the value propositions for the customers/users and for each individual actor/role.

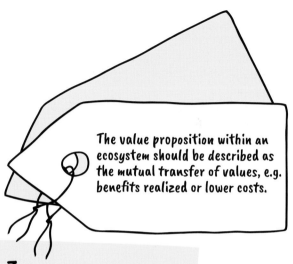

The value proposition within an ecosystem should be described as the mutual transfer of values, e.g. benefits realized or lower costs.

WE HELP X DO Y DOING Z.

→ THE TAGLINE IS THE BIG IDEA.

→ THE VALUE PROPOSITION IS WHAT SUPPORTS THE BIG IDEA.

→ THE "BRAND MESSAGING PILLARS" ARE THE STORIES TOLD TO THE VARIOUS ACTORS IN THE SYSTEM TO WIN THEM OVER SO THEY PARTICIPATE IN THE BUSINESS ECOSYSTEM AND SUPPORT THE VALUE PROPOSITION.

A core value proposition is a concise explanation of the functional and emotional benefits offered by the ecosystem as a whole. The focus is clearly on solving a customer problem or satisfying a customer need. It is **not** a positioning in the form of self-presentation and underscoring distinguishing features.

2) Brainstorming to Select and Describe the Actors in the Business Ecosystem

Considering first which actors might have relevance in the ecosystem has been proven to be a good starting point. The insights from the internal analysis, e.g. the work results from the cooperation/industry matrix (page 114) can be used for this purpose. There are also a number of generic market roles in systems that can be defined in advance. For the analysis, well-known strategic and systemic analysis methods, e.g. PESTLE analysis (page 120), can be used. Corresponding questions are formulated that match the target image definition of the ecosystem. Brief descriptions of the actors are used to summarize the findings. The descriptions include the function and role in the system, the primary motivation and the compatibility with the value proposition (page 248). The intensity of current relationships as well as the current business model of each actor can also be determined at this point.

It is important to know all the potential players who can contribute to the provision of the current and future value proposition when choosing the right actors.

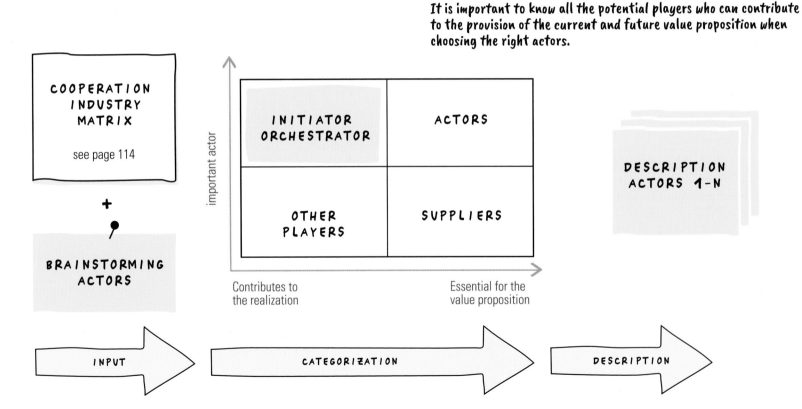

3) Allocation of the Actors on the Ecosystem Map

In step 3, the actors are entered on an ecosystem map (page 254). For the business ecosystem map, you can work with a three- or four-part division, for instance; depending on the sector and use case, other ways of structuring are possible. The customer with the expected value proposition is best positioned in the center. The expanded complementary offers and the enabling networks with their actors (and depending on the specific ecosystem with their customers) can be placed on the outer circles. The boundaries between the individual areas are usually blurred. The ecosystem map establishes an understanding for the interaction of all actors and suppliers for the delivery of the value proposition. Only with a comprehensive overview can the system be gradually optimized and the value streams and business activities be mapped in the subsequent steps.

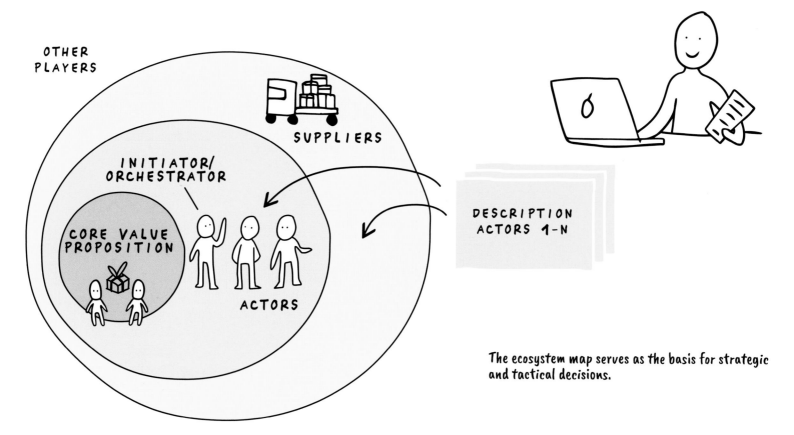

OTHER PLAYERS

SUPPLIERS

INITIATOR/ ORCHESTRATOR

CORE VALUE PROPOSITION

ACTORS

DESCRIPTION ACTORS 1-N

The ecosystem map serves as the basis for strategic and tactical decisions.

4) Definition of the Value Streams and Links between Actors

A core element in the business ecosystem design is the shaping of current and future value streams (page 255). Simple ecosystems in traditional businesses are fine with physical product/service flows, money/credit flows, and information. For digital and digitized value streams, intangible values are highly relevant. Intangible values can be knowledge, software, data, design, music, media, addresses, virtual environments, cryptocurrencies, tokens, or access and transfer of ownership and possession. These value streams are increasingly decentralized and are exchanged directly between the actors. In addition, it should be borne in mind that there are negative value streams in the system, which emerge, for example, through a transfer of risk.

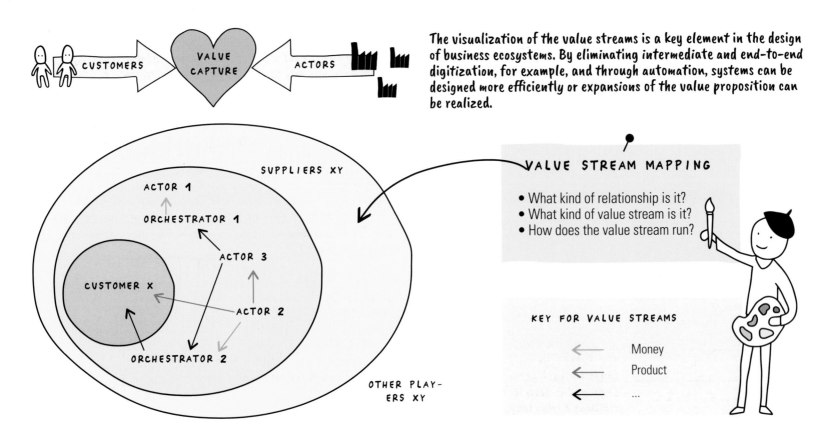

The visualization of the value streams is a key element in the design of business ecosystems. By eliminating intermediate and end-to-end digitization, for example, and through automation, systems can be designed more efficiently or expansions of the value proposition can be realized.

VALUE STREAM MAPPING

- What kind of relationship is it?
- What kind of value stream is it?
- How does the value stream run?

KEY FOR VALUE STREAMS

← Money
← Product
← ...

234

The combination of different value streams in a business ecosystem allows for mapping value creation as a dynamic and networked exchange in which, theoretically, every actor maintains a connection with one another. In this way, well-thought-out ecosystems can generate more value than the sum of the individual actors acting independently of one another. This wealth of relationships is the ecosystem capital.

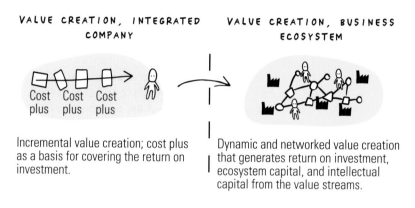

VALUE CREATION, INTEGRATED COMPANY

VALUE CREATION, BUSINESS ECOSYSTEM

Incremental value creation; cost plus as a basis for covering the return on investment.

Dynamic and networked value creation that generates return on investment, ecosystem capital, and intellectual capital from the value streams.

5) Elaboration of the Benefits and Disadvantages for Each Individual Actor

After the actors are positioned in the ecosystem and clarity exists about the value streams, the effects can be analyzed for the individual actors. In this phase, it is advisable to focus on the advantages and disadvantages that each actor has through the collaboration in the system. Without clear advantages, it is impossible to engender enthusiasm for the ecosystem in the actors (page 250).

	PRO	CON
ACTOR 1		
ACTOR 2		
ACTOR 3		

The advantages and disadvantages for each actor should be discussed in each iteration of the virtuous design loop.

6) Multidimensional View of the Business Models of all Actors in the Target Business Ecosystem / Business Model of the Ecosystem

The analyses from the previous phases help with a multidimensional view of the business models. The contribution to the value proposition for the customers that each individual actor makes and ultimately the contribution the actor might make to the overall value proposition of the business ecosystem currently under consideration are decisive. It must be ensured that the (partial) offers of the individual actors are optimally matched to the values and goals of the business ecosystem. In the end, all actors should perceive the distribution of opportunities and risks in the system as fair and have understood the value streams resulting directly or indirectly from the system. For many companies, the interaction with a business ecosystem is part of a growth strategy or a strategic option to leverage existing capabilities or participate in existing market areas for the realization of growth opportunities. The task of a multidimensional view of the business models is complex and asks too much of many business ecosystem design teams. This knowledge is nonetheless highly relevant to later considerations and the interaction with potential actors who are to participate in the system. The type of business model also varies according to the role each actor chooses or that is made available through participation. Most actors will make the decision based on their skills, risk appetite, and growth ambitions. In any case, it is crucial that the choice of role and the type of participation be a conscious decision based on the strategy chosen by each individual actor (page 259).

The more options there are for all actors and the better thought-out the options are for extracting added value from the business system through positive value streams, the more attractive the ecosystem is for all those involved.

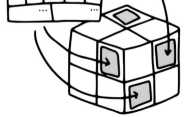

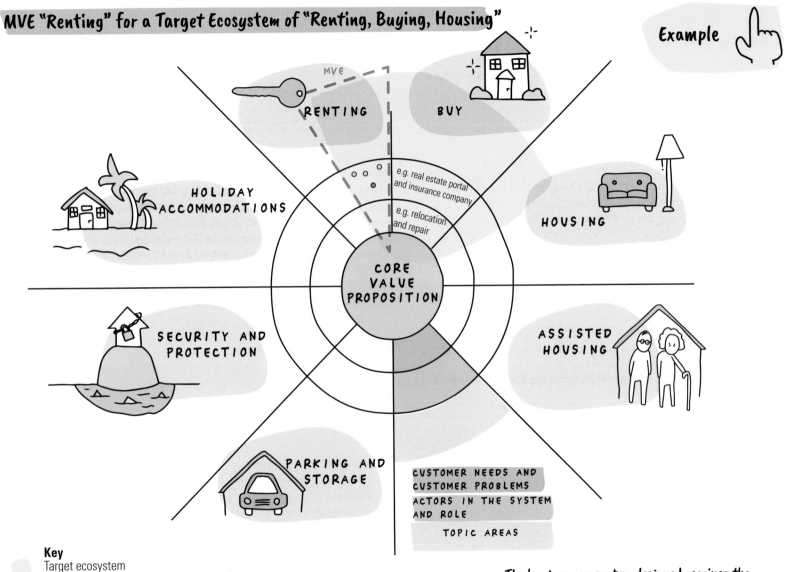

Example

Key
- Target ecosystem
- Actors and roles in the system (minimal)
- Possible orchestrator/initiator
- ----- MVE

The business ecosystem designed receives the validation of the system/actors fit through the realization of an MVE

7) (Re)design of the Business Ecosystem

In this phase, the business ecosystem is iteratively improved. Actors are added in the iterations or are eliminated. For example, platform providers, hardware vendors, or value-added services can be added that change and improve the existing system. The impact on the individual actors and value streams should be determined for each variant or idea of the new or adapted ecosystem. Most of all, it is important to prove the robustness of the scenarios by means of iterations and experiments. The design and redesign of different ecosystem maps with partly changing actors and value streams yields the greatest added value, since in this way different scenarios can be played through before any realization (page 254). Dealing with different constellations in the virtuous loop brings new ideas and business model approaches that help to amplify the uniqueness or find new pathways for expanding the value proposition. The new findings in turn can be tested as MVP within the framework of an initial MVE or be parked in the backlog for future growth and expansion possibilities.

The redesign and the discussion of value streams, roles, and actors hones the view of the target system and the subsystems to be realized, e.g. they are potentially validated in an MVE and are later implemented.

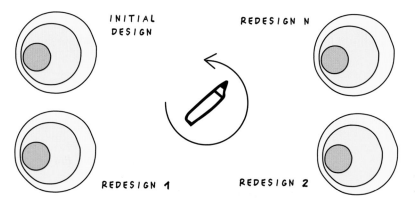

INITIAL DESIGN

REDESIGN N

REDESIGN 1

REDESIGN 2

What Happens in the Validation Loop?

8) Looking at the Collaboration between the Actors

In phases 1 to 7, the ecosystem was designed. But only reality shows whether ideas are really viable. In the validation loop, the business ecosystem design team usually considers with which specific actors the envisioned system will be initially validated and, if necessary, developed. The so-called inter-specific relationship between participating individuals and teams ensures the existence of a business ecosystem. This involves understanding the personal interests, needs, and motivations of those involved. Especially in a symbiosis (in the wider sense) in which all individuals (alongside the companies as such) benefit from the interaction, positive effects are generated, which lead to the growth of the system. Alongside the rational decision to be part of the ecosystem, personal motivation (e.g. of a decision maker) is at least as relevant.

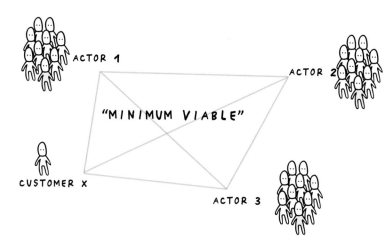

ACTOR 1

ACTOR 2

"MINIMUM VIABLE"

CUSTOMER X

ACTOR 3

Companies acting in a business ecosystem know the benefits and the target image. They know that coordination among them all is needed to create value.

237

What Happens in the Experiment and Realization Loop?

9) Formation of a Team to Implement the MVE

The needs of potential customers and actors in the system have already been taken into account in the design of business ecosystems. For a successful implementation, people, teams, and decision makers who create the business ecosystem are also needed.

The decision makers set the framework conditions, such as range of the MVE, budget, time frame, and so forth. They are the enablers of the projects. The teams are the actual doers who bring their skills to the table. Personal relationships and trust among the decision makers, who work for the different actors in a potential ecosystem, are one decisive factor in the realization of business ecosystems. This kind of trust is initially needed in the beginning for opening up to the outside and the first steps of co-creation. The upper tier of teams and decision makers determines to a great extent the implementation of an MVE and later the forms of collaboration. The tiers below it reflect the contextualization of the results via the respective design lenses (see play, configure, win on page 105 et seq.). The associated digital enablers complement the strategy and business view. As part of an initial MVE, individual aspects of the overall system are carried out manually or, if feasible, with the first digital components. In many digital ecosystems, the validation of the technology is crucial. The corresponding components must function accordingly. For MVE considerations, elements and procedures from lean start-up can be adapted to reflect on the ecosystem and improve it. Applying the same principles of build, measure, and learn as in the realization of an MVP and to complete preparations for the MVE before realization has proven to be a good thing.

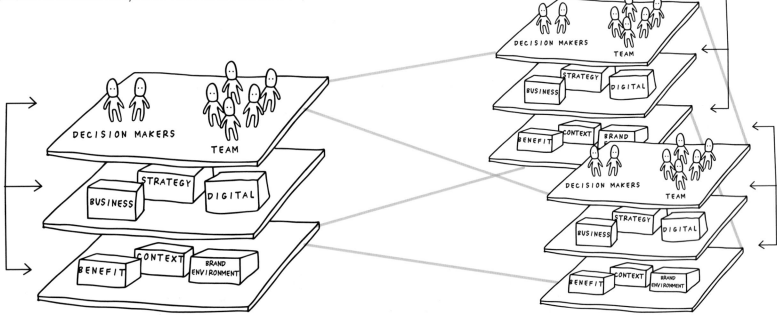

10) Implementation of the Final MVE

Governance structures and ecosystem leadership are needed for the implementation of the MVE. While the initiator moves more and more to the background of the activities, responsibility is increasingly passed on to the orchestrator. The final MVE is the first functioning system with a high level of efficiency owing to its minimum number of actors; simultaneously, it is an initial service offering that is part of the core value proposition. The orchestrator needs to be aware of the risks during implementation and subsequent orchestration. This primarily relates to implementation risks that are inherent in any complex project or innovation plan. The coevolution of the actors entail opportunities and risks, which often occur in tandem and have great dynamism. It must be defined and regulated how the actors in the system are to act and what they should do. The list ranges from dealing with touch points and customer interfaces all the way to the manner in which the individual components work together to provide the value proposition, e.g. at the levels of technology and business. Ecosystems usually only develop positively if they allow for continuous adaptation and work

being done to expand the value proposition. In many cases, this is the greatest challenge for the value streams and defines the right to be in the business ecosystem for each actor.

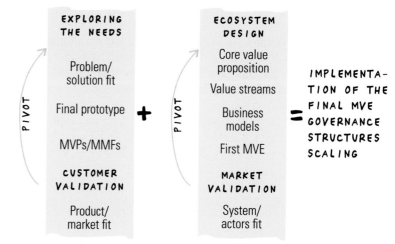

DIMENSION	CHALLENGES FOR THE INITIATOR AND THE ORCHESTRATOR	CHALLENGES FOR THE ENTIRE ECOSYSTEM
FIRST MVE	• Find the right actors for the roles • Create transparency and trust • Define degrees of leeway and appropriate rules	• Establishing a shared culture of collaboration • Recognize the strengths and weaknesses of the system • Continuous improvement and optimization
IMPLEMENTATION OF MVE	• Mastering complexity • Managing uncertainty • Establishing governance	• Establishing high entry barriers for competitors • Allowing co-competition (where it makes sense)
LEADERSHIP	• Communicate the vision clearly • Respond dynamically to change • Expansion and adaptation of the value proposition	• Harmonization of one's own vision with the target image of the ecosystem • Constant reflection upon success, new requirements and dynamics in the system
SCALE	• Collaboration with the other actors • Driving innovation and growth together • Expand the value proposition and retain market share	• Exploitation of lock-in effects • Scaling through network effects • Keep focus on exponential growth

Choice of the Right Governance Structures

Various models exist for the choice of ecosystem governance, including operating model and associated structures. Some companies drive the business ecosystem from the venturing portfolio; other initiators rely on vehicles such as associations and cooperatives. The approach presented here is particularly suitable for an early implementation phase and for initial scaling measures of the final MVE. Governance can be organized from one department up to the establishment of a new venture in which several actors are involved. In many cases, the structures develop over time. See options and paths from 1 to 5 in the figure below.

Example

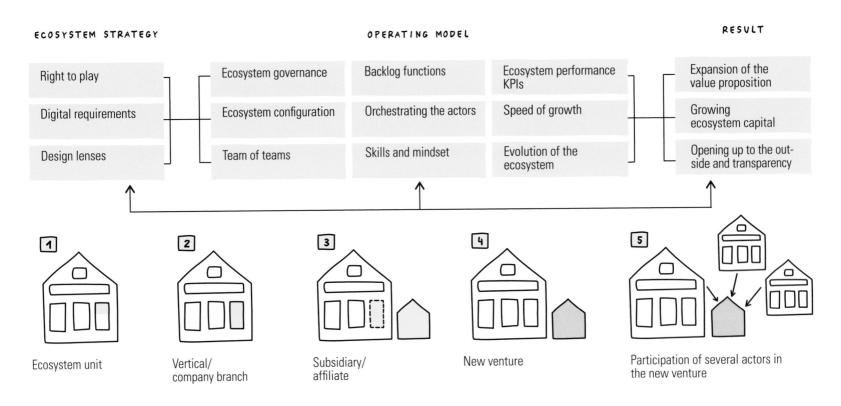

ECOSYSTEM STRATEGY

Right to play	Ecosystem governance	Backlog functions	Ecosystem performance KPIs
Digital requirements	Ecosystem configuration	Orchestrating the actors	Speed of growth
Design lenses	Team of teams	Skills and mindset	Evolution of the ecosystem

OPERATING MODEL

RESULT

| Expansion of the value proposition |
| Growing ecosystem capital |
| Opening up to the outside and transparency |

1 — Ecosystem unit

2 — Vertical/ company branch

3 — Subsidiary/ affiliate

4 — New venture

5 — Participation of several actors in the new venture

Success Factors in Dealing with Business Ecosystems

To apply a paradigm based on business ecosystem / design ecosystems successfully, it is imperative to keep five factors of success in mind:

1. Ecosystem awareness

Each company should see itself as part of the ecosystem and develop the ability to recognize its roles and behaviors in the ecosystem through the eyes of other actors as well as from different angles.

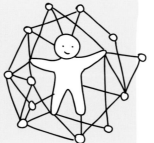

4. Sustainable ecosystem intelligence

Companies should establish the ability to promote and improve long-term systems thinking and design thinking and to develop strategies and techniques for the agile advancement of the ecosystem.

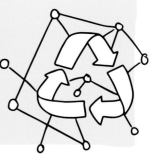

2. Understanding systemic possibilities

Companies should consciously reflect on ecosystems and possess the ability to imagine what productive behaviors are possible for themselves and for the whole ecosystem so as to change the value streams in a targeted way.

5. Leadership with business ecosystem design

Companies should build out the ability to integrate systems design in the culture of the organization and to break out of existing rules consciously (black ocean).

3. Governance of ecosystems

Companies should have the ability to work on and in the system, integrate partners (co-creation), and generate benefits for all actors.

To the Point!

The design of a business ecosystem can be done in several loops. The goal is to create an MVE that makes it possible to position the ecosystem in its minimal manifestation efficiently on the market. There should be transparency in the ecosystem as to whom the values accrue in a fair value exchange.

Over time, an initial value proposition that is part of the overall core value proposition is enriched with additional value-added services, which in turn are provided by existing or new actors in the system.

Alongside the skills, products, and services contributed by the actors, the mindset and ability to think in ecosystems is a crucial factor of success.

The relationship to the other actors is based on trust and long-term collaboration across company boundaries.

ECOSYSTEM DESIGN TOOLS

Ecosystem Design

Business ecosystem design has become a discipline in itself. The demands of the digital world in particular, with its various interconnected dependencies for the delivery of a unique value proposition, require a new mindset, methods, and tools. With the iterative development of an MVE, the understanding of the participating actors in the system is heightened; the fluent transitions are designed and correspondingly mapped. The development of a MVE keeps expenses low and increases the chances of success. The iterations and loops shown in the procedural model deliver the appropriate methods and tools for this crucial phase in design thinking for business growth. The ecosystem design canvas in turn is used to represent all essential steps and record the key findings from the loops and redesign phases. The work status should be documented after every major redesign to be able to understand, at a later time, the thoughts that went into it. If different teams work on subsystems, it is important to keep in mind that the systems need to work together in the end. In general, new systems (greenfield approach) or existing ecosystems can be improved with the business ecosystem design procedural model. When designing radically new ecosystems, certain actors in the business ecosystem can be eliminated as early as in the run-up. Another practical approach is first to create the business ecosystem predominant today and optimize it in a iteration (redesign). Especially if existing business ecosystems are to be radically restructured, the second approach makes sense since processes, procedures, information, and value streams can be redefined in this line of thought so as not to lose sight of the customer needs and the desired value proposition. To this end, these elements are included in the canvas again. During the design of an ecosystem, new ideas or altered value propositions frequently crop up, which can be adapted to the original needs; if necessary, these ideas should be verified and tested again with the potential customers. The final documentation of the blueprint in the ecosystem design canvas and ecosystem strategy canvas (page 106) provides the basis for the definition of suitable governance (page 240) and the possibility of an expanded view of data ecosystems as a subsystem in the definition of the value streams (see example on page 257).

Typical Activities

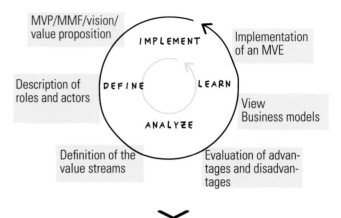

MVP/MMF/vision/value proposition

IMPLEMENT

Implementation of an MVE

Description of roles and actors

DEFINE

LEARN

View Business models

ANALYZE

Definition of the value streams

Evaluation of advantages and disadvantages

The MVE that has been realized is the least complex ecosystem that enables the participating actors to establish first parts of the core value proposition on the market at small expense.

Suitable Methods and Tools

Key Questions about Ecosystem Design

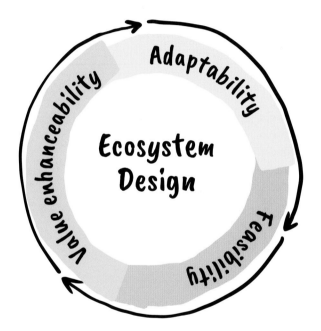

ADAPTABILITY

- How can it be ensured that the other actors in the system support the solution?
- How can lasting value be created (e.g. first-mover, lock-in, exclusiveness)?
- How can the other actors develop innovations and integrate them in the ecosystem?
- How are the actors involved selected, and what are the requirements in terms of skills, quality, technology, and handling the customer interface?
- How is the data on customers and offerings shared with the other actors?

FEASIBILITY

- Which additional technologies are needed for the integration of and interaction with other actors in the system?
- Which system architecture will support digital interaction?
- Which partnerships and suppliers should be built out and exploited?
- Are the necessary skills and assets available or can they be provided by other actors/suppliers, e.g. to develop, launch, and scale a technology platform?

VALUE ENHANCEABILITY

- What is one's own business model and that of the other actors in the system?
- Which downstream value streams exist?
- How can values be created together in the ecosystem?
- What does the ecosystem economy look like?
- How can compliance with provisions and rules be ensured?
- How can network and ecosystem effects be used for exponential growth?

ECOSYSTEM DESIGN CANVAS

DETERMINE THE NEEDS OF THE USERS/CUSTOMERS

- Who is the customer or user?
- Describe the customer/user profile (pains, gains, jobs to be done, and use case)
- What problem is to be solved?

CORE VALUE PROPOSITION
- What is the core value proposition for the user/customer?

DEFINITION OF THE VALUE STREAMS
- What are the current and future (positive and negative) value streams?
- Which product/service streams, money/credit streams, data and information flow?
- What are the digital and digitizing value streams/assets?

DESCRIBE THE ACTORS

- Who are the actors in the business ecosystem?
- What is their function and role in the system?
- How high is their motivation to participate in the business ecosystem?

DESIGN/REDESIGN

DESIGN
- Which actors are pivotal for the provision of the core value proposition in the business ecosystem? (For the placement, go from the inside to the outside.)
- Also place the actors with advanced and complementary offerings, enabling functions and other actors who are directly or indirectly part of the system.

REDESIGN
- Do various scenarios exist with different actors?
- Which actors can be eliminated?
- Are there actors who scale multidimensional value streams or better value streams?
- Is the business ecosystem robust and able to survive in the new scenario?

EXPLORE

BUILD/TEST

PROTOTYPE, TEST, AND IMPROVE THE BUSINESS ECOSYSTEM
- What are the MMFs/MVPs the ecosystem starts with?
- How can the first MVE be tested?
- What interactions/testing and measurement methods help us to improve the value streams, business models, and the role of actors in the ecosystem iteratively?
- What is the minimum version of the first MVE?

ANALYSIS OF THE ADVANTAGES AND DISADVANTAGES OF EACH ACTOR

- What are the advantages and disadvantages for each actor?
- What are their strengths/weaknesses and opportunities/risks in the system?

MULTIDIMENSIONAL VIEW OF THE BUSINESS MODELS

- What does the resultant business model and value proposition for each actor look like?
- How does the respective business model contribute to the core value proposition?
- Is the defined core value proposition the result of the sum of the value propositions of all actors?

ECOSYSTEM DESIGN CANVAS

Template download

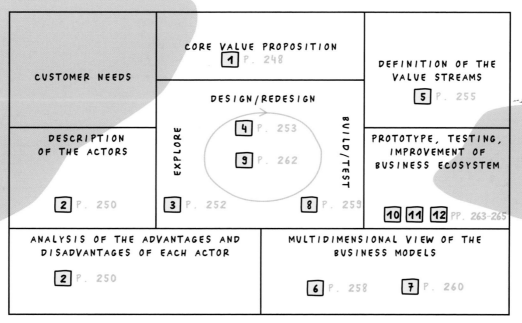

INPUTS FROM LENS #3

CUSTOMER NEEDS

CORE VALUE PROPOSITION
1 P. 248

DEFINITION OF THE VALUE STREAMS
5 P. 255

DESCRIPTION OF THE ACTORS

DESIGN/REDESIGN

EXPLORE

4 P. 253

9 P. 262

BUILD/TEST

PROTOTYPE, TESTING, IMPROVEMENT OF BUSINESS ECOSYSTEM

2 P. 250

3 P. 252

8 P. 259

10 11 12 PP. 263-265

ANALYSIS OF THE ADVANTAGES AND DISADVANTAGES OF EACH ACTOR
2 P. 250

MULTIDIMENSIONAL VIEW OF THE BUSINESS MODELS
6 P. 258   7 P. 260

METHODS AND TOOLS KEY

1. Value proposition statement
2. Identification and description of actors
3. Role playing: actors in the system
4. Variations in ecosystem maps
5. Definition of value streams
6. Exploration of revenue models
7. Multidimensional view of business models
8. Co-creation as part of (re)designs
9. Prototyping, testing, and improvement of the MVE
10. Final MVE
11. Design error in implementation
12. Embedding the MVE in the ecosystem strategy

The ecosystem design canvas helps with the documentation of the individual steps and the results from the tools and methods used.

DOWNLOAD TOOL
https://en.business-ecosystem-design.com/ecosystems

Value Proposition Statement for MVE

For the development of the core value proposition statement, either validated personas can be used that were defined with the aid of the user profile canvas or else the value proposition canvas of Osterwalder that consists of two areas: On the right side, the selected customer segments for the ecosystem currently under consideration are described. On the left side, the envisioned core value proposition for the ecosystem is juxtaposed. After all, the performance promise of the ecosystem must be consistent with the needs of the potential customers. The core value proposition canvas documents all views of the value proposition.

The value proposition helps the design thinking for business growth team to:

- initiate a shared starting point for the design of the ecosystem;
- discuss the value proposition statement with other actors in the system or to share the value proposition with partners before co-creation activities;
- grasp the higher-level needs, customer segments, and the solution for the entire system of the MVE.

Procedure and template in the core value proposition canvas:

1. Work out together on the business ecosystem design team the elements in the core value proposition canvas (page 249) for each individual customer segment and the respective actors in the system. Make use of the value proposition canvas for the customer side and consolidate the already validated user profiles from the previous design phases.
2. For the formulation of the value proposition, the two sample formulations can be used. It is vital to emphasize the uniqueness when formulating the core value proposition. Both sides, the customers/users and the potential actors, must see that there is a difference regarding the satisfaction of customer needs in the system, and it must be clear that the desired value proposition can be presented successfully only in the network.

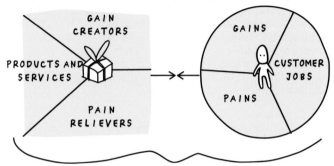

PROBLEM SOLUTION FIT FROM PROTOTYPES MVPS

SAMPLE PHRASES FOR THE FORMULATION OF VALUE PROPOSITION STATEMENTS FOR CUSTOMERS USERS

FORMULATION I:
For _____ (target customer),
who _____ (problem statement, need), our product
delivers _____ (solution) with the
promise that _____ (unfair advantage, outcome)

FORMULATION II:
We help _____ (target customer)
to solve _____ (problem)
by _____ (solution).

The "ecosystem core value proposition" is like a contract between the customer and all actors in the business ecosystem. The customer has a unique experience that no single company can provide for itself.

CORE VALUE PROPOSITION CANVAS

Template download

CUSTOMERS/USERS	ORCHESTRATOR/INITIATOR		ACTOR/ROLE
NEEDS Which customers should be addressed? What is the main customer need? What does the customer have problems with? Where are opportunities for improvement? Where does an opportunity offer itself for the ecosystem? What are the main problems?	**NEEDS** Where are opportunities for the initiator/orchestrator?		**NEEDS** Which actors should be addressed? What is the main need of the respective actors? Where does an opportunity offer itself for the individual actors? What might be their concerns?
ACTIVITIES What are the tasks to be performed by the customers? How do the customers purchase services? How does the customer interact with the business ecosystem?	**ACTIVITIES** What activities are carried out by the initiator/orchestrator?		**ACTIVITIES** What activities should be performed by the individual actors/roles for the business ecosystem?
BENEFITS What are the benefits for the customer? What are qualitative and quantitative benefits for the customer? What is the best way to communicate with the customer/user as part of storytelling?	**APPROACH (SOLUTION)** What is the approach to a solution or the performance promise? What is the proposal for the product, service, or process? How will the product or service be developed and launched on the market? How does the ecosystem make money with it? (business model) What technology drivers affect the business model?		**BENEFITS** What are the benefits for each actor? What are qualitative and quantitative benefits for the actor? What is the best way to communicate with the actor through storytelling?
COMPETITION (EXISTING ALTERNATIVES) What alternatives exist today and will exist in the future? What is the risk? How were the problems solved up to now?	**UNIQUENESS** In what dimensions is the offer unique for the customer?	**VALUE STREAMS** What incentives/value streams make the ecosystem interesting for the actors?	**COMPETITION (EXISTING ALTERNATIVES)** What alternatives exist today and will exist in the future? What is the risk? What other options do the actors have for realizing growth?
VALUE PROPOSITION What is the value proposition for the customer/user, a particular target group, a segment?	**CORE VALUE PROPOSITION** What is the value proposition for the ecosystem?		**VALUE PROPOSITION** What is the value proposition for the participating actors, particular roles, or individual actors in the system?

DOWNLOAD TOOL
https://en.business-ecosystem-design.com/value-proposition

Identification and Description of the Relevant Actors

The description of all actors in an existing or future business ecosystem helps in the configuration of the system to understand the capabilities better and to assess whether the respective actors and roles are right for the realization of the desired value proposition. It is also important to analyze how high the motivation is for the actor to participate in the planned ecosystem. If known, companies may be mentioned in this phase that might take on this role.

The description of relevant actors helps the design thinking for business growth team to:

- get an overview of potential actors for the ecosystem and their capabilities;
- find out whether existing partnerships can be used to provide quick access to skills, offerings, and other assets;
- carry out an initial assessment with regard to the fit of the actors with the defined core value proposition;
- evaluate the impact the actors might have on the ecosystem.

Procedure and template:

Begin with a brainstorming session about all current roles in an existent ecosystem or the roles relevant to the building of a new ecosystem. Describe the relevant actors with the information at hand. Missing information can be supplemented bit by bit later. Use the template for the description or answer on a DIN A4 sheet for each actor/role the following question: "What are the advantages and disadvantages for the actor of participating in the defined ecosystem?" Further questions help to assess the actor's motivation to get involved in the system or to find out how much influence the respective actor might have in different roles. Use tools such as role playing with potential actors in the system (see page 252) for honing statements to be checked with the actors later.

A simple rule in business ecosystem design: Without an advantage or a corresponding financial incentive, actors will not be enthused about the system! Examples of other possible benefits for actors in a business ecosystem:

Benefiting from innovation

Heightened efficiency

Better analytics and data quality

Quicker scaling

Part of a new value proposition

Utilization of new technologies

Access to data and intellectual property (IP)

Better access to resources and talent

New touch points and new customer access

Access to existing key customers

...

...

TEMPLATE: DESCRIPTION OF ACTOR ROLE

Template download

FUNCTION ROLE OF THE ACTOR
Which role or function does the actor assume?

EXAMPLES
What company could assume such a role?

MOTIVATION FOR PARTICIPATION
How high is the primary motivation for the actor to participate in the defined ecosystem?

=?

TIME HORIZON
From what point in time will the actor be needed? For which part of the value proposition?

MVP   MVE   Expansion stage 1   ...

DEGREE OF COMPATIBILITY WITH THE VALUE PROPOSITION
(strong, neutral, weak)
What is the degree of compatibility of the actor with the value proposition and the achievement of the target image?

| + | 0 | − |

MARKET DOMINANCE (strong, neutral, weak)
How much influence would the actor have on the ecosystem?

| + | 0 | − |

ANALYSIS OF THE ADVANTAGES AND DISADVANTAGES OF EACH ACTOR
What are the advantages and disadvantages for the actor to participate in the defined ecosystem?

+	−

VALUE CONTRIBUTION OF THE ACTOR
What kind of value contribution can the actor make?

CURRENT BUSINESS MODEL OF THE ACTOR
What is the current/primary business model of the actor?
How does the actor make money today?

DOWNLOAD TOOL
https://en.business-ecosystem-design.com/value-proposition

Role Playing Based on the Potential Actors in the System

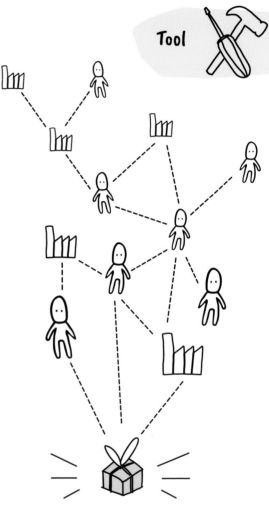

Tool

Role playing based on the description of the actors helps to understand other views better and to place them in the context of the value proposition or the overall target image of a business ecosystem. The distance of actors to the delivery of the value proposition and to other actors reveals how systemically relevant they are in each case. Each team member can present one or two actors in the role-playing game and take on their view.

Role playing helps the design thinking for business growth team to:
- listen to all actors (played by team members) with the assumptions or validated statements about their position;
- share knowledge about the actors with team members and launch a discussion;
- question whether the respective actor fits the ecosystem;
- find out how close to or distant from the value proposition actors are;
- identify missing skills or actors.

Procedure:
1. Each team member takes on the role of one of the defined actors (assign a maximum of 12 roles in the first phase). The value proposition is written down in the middle of the room. The actors are grouped according to importance or to the direct or indirect relation they have with other actors in the room and with the value proposition.
2. Each team member (= actor) is asked to explain their role, advantages, and disadvantages and why they have taken this position. As a result of the discussion, the positions of the actors toward the value proposition can be changed; new actors can be added or the distance changed.
3. The findings are integrated in the description of the respective actors and help with the creation or iterative advancement of the ecosystem in the following step.

VALUE PROPOSITION

Design Variations in Ecosystem Maps

The descriptions of current and potential actors and role-playing sessions held by the ecosystem design team make it easier to place the actors on the business ecosystem map. For most business ecosystem initiatives, consistent thinking from the customer's point of view and the associated value proposition is the right approach. The customer takes center stage. The respective circles show the distance of the actors to the customer and the importance of making a direct contribution to the creation of the value proposition. The number of circles depends on the complexity of the system. For initial considerations, two or three circles suffice, allowing for a quick placement of actors, orchestrators, and suppliers.

The creation of design variations on ecosystem maps helps the design thinking for business growth team to:
- place existing findings, actors, and roles;
- establish a dynamic and agile way of working for the creation of a new map or the adaptation of existing ecosystems;
- visualize, discuss, and evaluate multiple variants and scenarios;
- gain an overall view of the system, its actors, and potential suppliers, e.g. for technology components.

Procedure and template:
1. Cover a large table with paper so that all team members can see the ecosystem map well.
2. Divide the space (according to closeness to the core value proposition). This can be done with circles that are drawn on the paper and correspondingly arranged.
3. Place the individual actors on the ecosystem map.
4. Discussion with the business ecosystem team or as part of co-creation about the actors in the presented variation of a business ecosystem.

Tool

CURRENT ECOSYSTEM

ITERATION TO GET TO NEW ECOSYSTEM

OR

GREENFIELD APPROACH

CURRENT SYSTEM (ACTUAL STATE) OR GREENFIELD APPROACH

Example

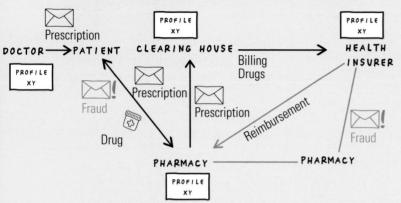

(RE)DESIGN OF ECOSYSTEMS

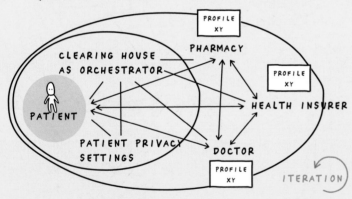

ITERATION

VARIANTS OF NEW OPTIMIZED ECOSYSTEMS

PROTOTYPE 1	PROTOTYPE 2	PROTOTYPE 3
+ PRO − CON	+ PRO − CON	+ PRO − CON

TEMPLATE, ECOSYSTEM MAP

Description of the actor/role
(see worksheet on page 251)

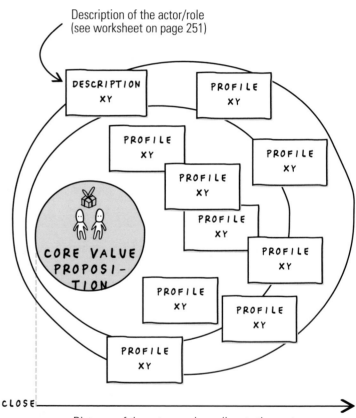

CLOSE

Distance of the actors and suppliers to the customer
regarding the fulfillment of the value proposition

Definition of the Value Streams

Tool

When defining the value streams, the basic idea is that – owing to their nature and lasting existence – business ecosystems as a whole generate more value than the sum of the individual actors who do business independently of one another. In a conventional view of value streams, value creation is incremental, i.e. the respective actors cover a certain return on investment, usually on the basis of cost plus. In business ecosystems, the actors generate value through their involvement in the system as a whole. The customer/user interacts with the ecosystem or with individual actors in the system (depending on the configuration).

The definition of the value streams helps the design thinking for business growth team to:

- design a functioning system that generates a higher return on investment than the sum of the ROIs made by all the actors individually.
- design a network of relationships that enables the generation of ecosystem capital;
- have systems come into being that go beyond the mere exchange of products, services, and money;
- configure the interaction of value streams in such a way that the system is viable.

Procedure and template:

For an initial discussion of the value streams, the existing business ecosystem map can be used; as an alternative, subsystems can be outlined (see value streams data on page 257). The value streams can be sketched in both versions and then be discussed.

With the "value streams mapping" template, a stocktaking can be conducted to describe the most important value streams and to demonstrate the interactions between the actors in which the value streams come to fruition.

For complex projects and major ecosystem initiatives, digital tools should be used, e.g. the software from trdent.com (www.tr3dent.com). Such programs allow for the mapping of a large number of actors and value streams.

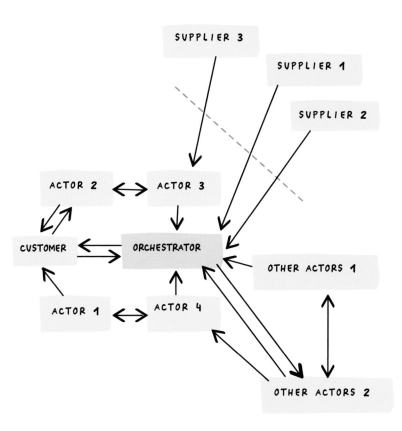

TEMPLATE: VALUE STREAMS MAPPING

VALUE STREAM TYPES

What types of value streams
are relevant to the ecosystem?
For example: services, money, information, data,
innovation/IP, intangible assets.

MANIFESTATION

In what way do the value
streams flow?

TYPICAL VALUE STREAM

What does a typical value stream
(of a specific kind) look like – between the actors,
with the orchestrator, or directly with a customer?

VISUALIZATION OF INDIVIDUAL VALUE STREAM OF SUBSYSTEMS OR FOR THE ENTIRE ECOSYSTEM MAP

Mark on the ecosystem map how values streams flow between the actors

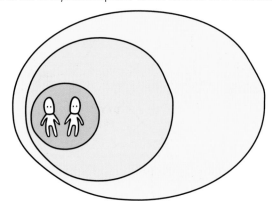

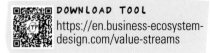

DOWNLOAD TOOL
https://en.business-ecosystem-design.com/value-streams

Expanded View of Data Ecosystems as a Subsystem in the Definition of the Value Streams

In many business ecosystems, data is the lubricant to ensure fast and agile innovation. From this, subsystems in the form of data ecosystems may arise that comprise value streams with the business ecosystem and its actors and allow for further monetization.

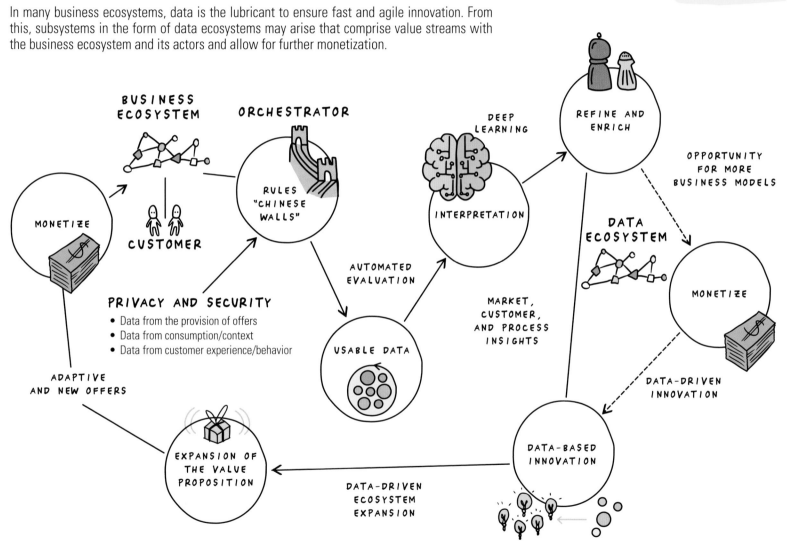

BUSINESS ECOSYSTEM

ORCHESTRATOR

DEEP LEARNING

REFINE AND ENRICH

OPPORTUNITY FOR MORE BUSINESS MODELS

MONETIZE

CUSTOMER

RULES "CHINESE WALLS"

INTERPRETATION

DATA ECOSYSTEM

PRIVACY AND SECURITY
- Data from the provision of offers
- Data from consumption/context
- Data from customer experience/behavior

AUTOMATED EVALUATION

MARKET, CUSTOMER, AND PROCESS INSIGHTS

MONETIZE

ADAPTIVE AND NEW OFFERS

USABLE DATA

DATA-DRIVEN INNOVATION

EXPANSION OF THE VALUE PROPOSITION

DATA-DRIVEN ECOSYSTEM EXPANSION

DATA-BASED INNOVATION

257

Exploration of Revenue Models for the Ecosystem

There are various approaches to the design of revenue models for the offer of the actual business ecosystem. Many newer models bank on a unique customer experience, the collaboration of various market actors and a continuous cycle of innovations in response to new or changing customer needs. Digital platforms such as Uber, Lyft, and Airbnb use on-demand models; Salesforce and Netflix primarily offer subscription models. Facebook and Google rely on advertising and ad-supported models, while Alibaba and Amazon have moved from 100% e-commerce models to new digital models in evolutionary steps. Beside 100% digital models, hybrid models are used in business ecosystems, Tencent, for instance. Alongside many other models, the ecosystem orchestrator has combined forms of a transaction facilitator in the payments area (WeChat Pay), online-to-offline (O2O) business with physical and digital services, and online shopping offerings integrated with Tencent's partners in the ecosystem (JD.com). Monetization ranges from technology fees, premium service fees, third-party access fees, data fees, to established revenue models.

Tool

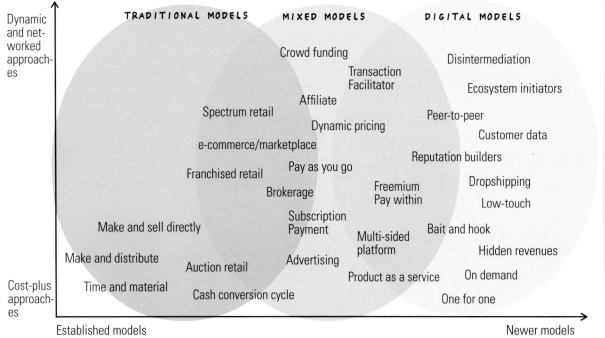

The properties of the newer models

- Lower and more flexible cost base
- Utilization of automation to attain superior operational excellence
- Competitive edge through the connection of offers and the undercutting of prices through cross-subsidization
- Rapid learning in a trial-and-error culture
- Focus on customer experiences and a unique value proposition
- Dynamic and networked collaboration among the actors
- Proactive elimination of intermediaries
- Provision of value-added digital elements of the ecosystem

258

Expanded View of Business Models in Business Ecosystem Design

In addition to defining the business model for actual business ecosystems, leading ecosystem initiators and orchestrators design possible business models for the actors involved in the system. After all, business ecosystem capital can only be generated through the connection with the actors and their value-adding activities. It is therefore advisable to expand traditional business model considerations and to include an ecosystem view along with purpose, skills, leadership, strategic foresight, and market dynamics. The ecosystem view primarily means generating a win-win situation for all actors involved.

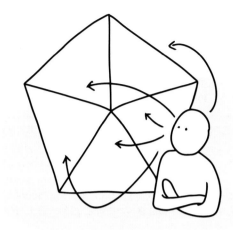

Ecosystem Business Model (initiator/orchestrator)   **Multidimensional View of the Business Models (actors)**

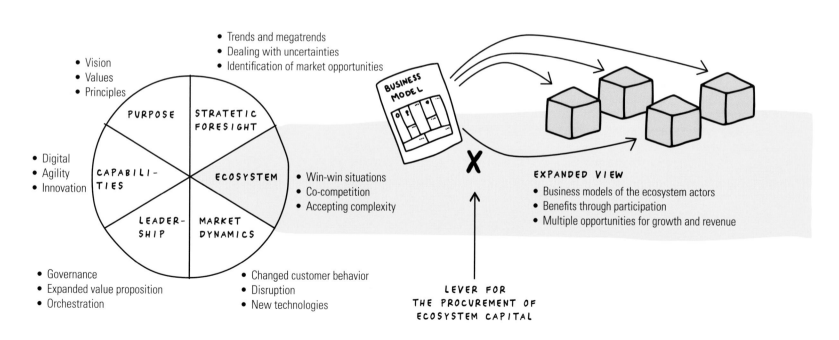

- Vision
- Values
- Principles

- Trends and megatrends
- Dealing with uncertainties
- Identification of market opportunities

- Digital
- Agility
- Innovation

PURPOSE **STRATETIC FORESIGHT**
CAPABILI-TIES **ECOSYSTEM**
LEADER-SHIP **MARKET DYNAMICS**

- Win-win situations
- Co-competition
- Accepting complexity

- Governance
- Expanded value proposition
- Orchestration

- Changed customer behavior
- Disruption
- New technologies

X

LEVER FOR THE PROCUREMENT OF ECOSYSTEM CAPITAL

BUSINESS MODEL

EXPANDED VIEW

- Business models of the ecosystem actors
- Benefits through participation
- Multiple opportunities for growth and revenue

Multidimensional View of the Business Models

Tool

It is a key task of the initiator/orchestrator of a business ecosystem to design the business model of the business ecosystem as described in the tool above. However, it is equally as important to think about how each and every actor in the ecosystem can make money. A well-thought-out business ecosystem not only gives each individual actor the opportunity of positive participation; they also point out how other possibilities can be tapped to generate revenue. If it is the purpose of the ecosystem to open up a larger market that is not controlled by the orchestrator, such considerations are all the more important. Thus the initiator/orchestrator has the task of identifying more with the whole (ambition of the entire ecosystem). The multidimensional view of the business models helps to develop strategies and business models that define opportunities for the whole and not only for oneself as the initiator/orchestrator.

A multidimensional view of the business models helps the design thinking for business growth team:

- not to lose sight of the big picture and not primarily take care of the design of one's own business model;
- to find more arguments to convince potential actors to become part of a business ecosystem;
- to check whether existing value streams suffice for more comprehensive considerations;
- to create an all-around view of the potential ecosystem capital;
- to explore further ideas and possibilities to expand the value proposition.

Procedure:

For a multidimensional view of business models, it makes sense to proceed in two steps.

1. Think about the business model with which an actor can make money on the basis of the defined value streams. The lean canvas (page 210) with the corresponding expansions helps with the definition.
2. Assume the view of the respective actor/role. Ask yourself how the actor can make additional money on the basis of services from the ecosystem; e.g. particular skills and capabilities, customer access, regional presence, physical locations, or know-how in certain key technologies. After all, the initial business model and the expanded business models present the total of opportunities for a specific role, a specific actor, and for the orchestrator/initiator.

Example

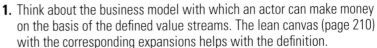

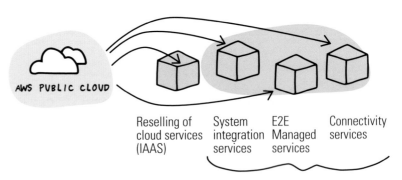

Reselling of cloud services (IAAS) System integration services E2E Managed services Connectivity services

Multiple possibilities for further business models (cumulative levers with a factor of 5 to 10, depending on the business model)

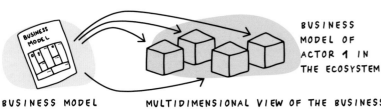

BUSINESS MODEL ECOSYSTEM

MULTIDIMENSIONAL VIEW OF THE BUSINESS MODEL OF ACTOR 1 IN THE ECOSYSTEM

BUSINESS MODEL OF ACTOR 1 IN THE ECOSYSTEM

Co-creation as Part of the Ecosystem (Re)design

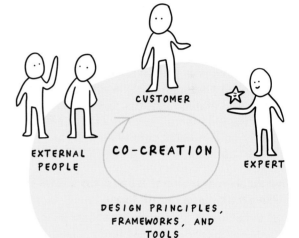

Tool

Co-creation in the system helps to structure a complex problem statement and develop adaptable and feasible changes in a business ecosystem in which different actors work together to deliver a value proposition. Co-creation helps when dealing with different perspectives on a business ecosystem and is suitable for the initial design of a business ecosystem as well as for the redesign of such a system with different actors.

Co-creation helps the design thinking for business growth team to:
- discuss the system with different actors of the ecosystem map;
- discuss the impact of changes directly;
- ensure transparency in the design of business ecosystems;
- understand the needs of individual actors better;
- recognize the impact of changes on the value proposition and the value streams.

Co-creation Procedure:
Starting with a first target image of a business ecosystem map, find possible improvements of the situation of everybody in the system. The improvements can be put down in a sentence: "A system of activities results in...", followed by the idea, e.g. formulated as the input/output of a targeted transformation of the effect. The sentence specifies what is transformed, by whom, and for what purpose. Different questions and a change of perspective support the process:

DEFINITION: DESIGN PRINCIPLES, MINDSET, PURPOSE	QUESTIONS AND POINTS OF VIEW	CLARIFICATION ROLES AND RESPONSIBILITIES	COLLABORATION	REALIZATION
• What is to be worked on together? • What is the ambition?	• What are the questions to be answered to fulfill the purpose of the ecosystem? • What information and insights are necessary?	• Who is to contribute what? • Who will assume what tasks?	• What scenarios are there? • What benefits exist? • Are there any other options or better ideas? • Is there a similar mindset?	• How can a first MVE be realized together? • How can the value proposition be realized? • What are the requirements?

Prototype, Testing, and Improvement of an MVE

The MVE unites initial technology components with the value proposition and the designed value streams. It is far more complex than a product or service provided to the customers. Several actors are needed for the MVE, who together deliver the added value to the customers. "Viable" means that there is an actor for each role in the system so the system can be tested. The validation shows that it works technically and that the actors and the customers obtain the promised benefits. The MVE is proof that the system is viable, it can correspondingly grow, and in the best-case scenario, can be scaled over time.

The MVE helps the design thinking for business growth team to:
- validate the core value proposition of the ecosystem and individual value propositions for specific actors/roles;
- test whether the defined value streams will generate the desired offer;
- test assumptions regarding the skills, benefits, and willingness to cooperate on the part of the participating roles/actors;
- test multiple scenarios and manifestations of MVPs or combinations of MVPs to create an initial holistic ecosystem offering;
- test, measure, and improve the business model of the ecosystem and the assumptions on the multidimensional view of business models.

Procedure:
The realization of an MVE requires the relevant MVPs/MMFs (usually a selection of necessary individual components for an initial overall offer). At least one actor and a defined number of customers should participate for each role in the system.

The goals of the MVE and the underlying assumptions must be communicated in a transparent way. The actors are encouraged to contribute their improvements and ideas at an early stage. The customers should be closely accompanied and involved in the respective improvement loops.

THE 8 GOLDEN RULES FOR AN MVE

1. Combine design thinking and systems thinking.
2. Think not only of transformation but also how the system evolves.
3. Find inspiration in the working of biological ecosystems.
4. Think at all levels: customer, relationships among actors, and technology.
5. Begin with considerations about the benefits for each individual actor, and use the value streams to show the actor's viability.
6. Accept the complexity of multiple business model considerations and assume the perspective of the other actors.
7. Start with the implementation of the ecosystem on the basis of the virtuous loop, validation loop, realization, and experiment loop.
8. Adapt the system if it doesn't work in its minimal version.

Final MVE

The final MVE is much more than a prototype or an experiment. It is actually the minimal implementation of a system, which then will be gradually expanded and scaled. This blueprint is proof that business ecosystem design has yielded a relevant system that is viable and generates value. On the basis of the final MVE, further actors for specific roles can be added, or the core value proposition can be completed and expanded incrementally.

The final MVE helps the design thinking for business growth team to:

- get a blueprint of a functioning system;
- use efficient configuration to create initial values and provide the customer with a first partial offer;
- lay the foundation for the step-by-step expansion of the value proposition;
- choose an alternative and agile path in contrast to a traditional approach; first all functions and experiences are built and piloted, and the rollout is planned based on that.

Procedure:

1. Launch the MVE on the market Make sure that the selected features and experiences have a WOW! effect on the customer from the very onset. Adjust the collaboration of the actors for the delivery of the offer in an early phase.

2. Utilize the momentum on the market to continue an alternative development path in the gradual expansion of the ecosystem. Make use of the methods and tools for the scaling of the ecosystem (page 270 et seq.)

3. Exploit the full potential of all actors for further innovation and network effects and to realize exponential growth. Adjust and expand the offer constantly and respond quickly and specifically to new or emerging customer needs.

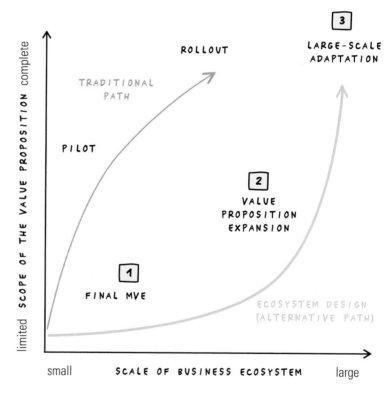

The Most Common Design Errors in Realization

The final MVE constitutes the basis for further growth steps. Well-designed business ecosystems are attractive and win over new actors, who in turn increase the ecosystem capital. Ambitious ecosystem initiatives aim at a "black ocean" strategy right from the outset; they give the right impetus with the core value proposition and have governance structures that make it possible to initialize the market launch of the MVE quickly and effectively. Often, similar ecosystem initiatives emerge in a region or a country for certain topic areas. A detailed analysis of the individual initiatives reveals that in most cases, no well-thought-out business ecosystem design was applied, thus decreasing any chances of success.

The most common design errors in the initialization of business ecosystems are:
- Insufficient focus on new or changed customer needs;
- Weak core value proposition;
- Wrong configuration of the business ecosystem;
- Lack of governance structures and skills in orchestrating business ecosystems;
- Wrong business model for the objectives of the business ecosystem;
- Too little commitment in the multidimensional view of business models;
- Sluggish implementation of the ecosystem initiative and wrong leadership approaches in the implementation of the scale-up phase.

According to a survey conducted by the Henderson Institute (2020), the main cause for the failure of business ecosystems (85%) is a weak business ecosystem design; only 15% of the initiatives examined came to naught due to implementation errors. In the area of governance, existing ways of thinking must be overcome, which is why traditional companies find it difficult to open up to the outside and to accept the transparency entailed in it.

You avoid the most frequent design errors, if you:
- start with design thinking and a customer problem;
- realize initial MVPs and create compelling value propositions;
- design the business ecosystem through various loops up to the realization of an MVE;
- pay attention to a form of governance that fits the system and to adequate ecosystem leadership approaches.

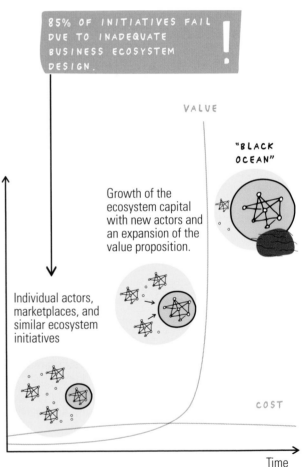

85% OF INITIATIVES FAIL DUE TO INADEQUATE BUSINESS ECOSYSTEM DESIGN.

VALUE

"BLACK OCEAN"

Growth of the ecosystem capital with new actors and an expansion of the value proposition.

Individual actors, marketplaces, and similar ecosystem initiatives

COST

Time

Embedding Value Creation, Delivery, and Capture Approaches as the Basis of the Ecosystem Strategy and Business Model Considerations

The activities related to the configuration of the business ecosystem are crucial to the definition of "where to play" and "how to win." Only a functioning system, consisting of value creation, delivery, and capture, can be sustainably successful.

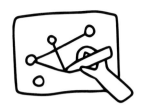

WHY IS A BUSINESS ECOSYSTEM NEEDED?

VALUE CREATION

HOW SHOULD THE BUSINESS ECOSYSTEM BE CONFIGURED?

VALUE DELIVERY

WHAT DOES THE BUSINESS ECOSYSTEM NEED TO GROW?

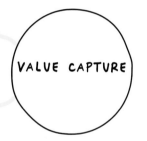

VALUE CAPTURE

Step 1: Design thinking and lean start-up
- Create awareness of market opportunities arising from the design or initialization of business ecosystems or participation in them.
- Use foresight, future persona concepts, and successful blueprints of networked and dynamic approaches.
- Redefine the customer experience and create unique value propositions.

Step 2: Configure
- Make use of digital enabler technologies for value delivery.
- Expand activities to include cognitive technology and data platforms.
- Apply the team-of-teams idea for agile and networked organizational development.
- Use hybrid models in business model considerations.
- Should the focus be more on EXPLOIT or more on EXPLORE?

Step 3: Scale
- Orchestrate exponential growth.
- Figure out possible levers for profitable growth.
- Demonstrate the opportunities for actors/shareholders to obtain sustainable returns.
- Establish structures, governance, and freedoms for the agile adjustment of the value streams, customer experiences, and the expansion of the core value proposition.

Ecosystem design helps with the validation of the shared value proposition, the value streams, the benefits for the various actors in the system, and not least, with honing the vision and the roles individual actors assume.

The iterative procedure up to the final MVE helps to test the feasibility of the new system with little effort and expenditure. With each design loop, the system and the interaction of the respective actors gets better.

The findings are used to carry out adaptations to the final MVE as well as all business model considerations and to define the implementation plan and scaling activities of the solution and the system.

The final MVE aims at achieving maximum efficiency with the smallest number of actors per role in the system.

Transition from Ecosystem Design to Scaling

DIMENSION	OUTPUT: # 3 ECOSYSTEM DESIGN MINIMUM VIABLE ECOSYSTEM	ACTIONS: # 4 SCALE IMPLEMENTATION AND GROWTH
PURPOSE	Validation at all levels of the design lenses (feasibility, adaptability, and value enhanceability) Principle: Achieving maximum efficiency with the smallest number of actors per role in the system	Validation of the system at all levels of the design lenses (feasibility, captivateability and rhythmicability) Principle: Leverage of network and lock-in effects for rapid and efficient growth
FOCUS	Use of the MVPs as the basis for testing a functioning business ecosystem with the involvement of all actors and (test) customers	Focus on the use of state-of-the-art technology, end-to-end automation, and mechanisms to retain new customers quickly
FEATURES	All necessary experience and functions for at least one key experience for the customer in terms of the defined value proposition	Gradual build-out of functions and experiences based on customer needs, coevolution, and innovation with/through other actors in the system
TARGET GROUP	Interaction and co-creation with actors in the system for building and validation of the business ecosystem	Interaction and data of customers for the improvement and expansion of the value proposition; co-creation with other actors in the system for optimizing the overall ecosystem
LEGACY	First validation of a functioning business ecosystem	Validation of growth drivers, measures, and different customer channels
TYPE OF FEEDBACK	Feedback on value streams, customer interfaces, data, and algorithms within the scope of the MVE	Feedback from customers and defined KPIs for performance in the overall system
POSSIBLE DESIGN	Interaction of components for the design of the value proposition or parts of it in the form of experiences or functions	Utilization of all capabilities of the four design lenses; use of state-of-the-art information technology and scalable infrastructure; end-to-end automation
CUSTOMER BENEFIT	Delivers a validated value proposition from actors in an MVE	Incremental expansion of customer benefits in line with new needs
CREATION TIME OF THE ENTIRE DESIGN CYCLE	Interaction of the actors and value streams validated; multidimensional view of the business models carried out; business model of the business ecosystem is known; financing by the initiator or by other actors in the system; increased risk	Initial experiences, functions, and features established in the market; value proposition known in the market and unique; innovations of other participants in the market realized through new customer needs
TEST	Test of the value proposition and the associated services, value streams, and interactions of the actors; checking the customer interfaces	Testing the new features, channels, and the expanded value proposition; tests with lead users and extreme users
REVENUE	Possible initial income from the functioning ecosystem with (test) customers	Well-though-out business models with lock-in effects and a clear added value for the customer

LENS #4
SCALE

Intro to Scale

After the MVE has been implemented, ecosystems need different amounts of time to scale. Depending on the value proposition and market area, it may take a few months or many years. In some cases, dependencies exist that can be affected by the ecosystem only to a limited extent but that are necessary for scaling. The scaling of the business ecosystem is one of the greatest challenges. To think exponentially means ensuring growth (e.g. doubling of the customer base every six months). However, it also includes deliberations about how one's own business model could be disrupted to attain greater leverage from existing components, capabilities, and network connections. The size of exponential growth depends on the type of business ecosystem, the regional reach, and the target group for which a value proposition was defined. Thinking exponentially requires adapted questions and goals that are radically different from those known from more familiar business model considerations. Most business models are linear and designed to boost profit or to reduce costs, e.g. by 15% within one year. To scale successfully, you must have the courage to think exponentially, i.e. to deal with levers greater than 5, 8, and 10 of the current value. The term "10x" is often used for exponential growth. Business ecosystems that successfully exploit an exponential growth strategy usually have undergone a paradigm shift in terms of business models and growth. The mindset is aligned to learn quickly as an organization and achieve the greatest customer benefit. Further development and disruption is done on agile teams that work together across company boundaries. Responsibilities are clearly defined, but roles and job names are constantly changing. Governance consists more of a playbook for exponential growth than of rigid rules. The individual management tasks are carried out in a multifunctional way.

Thinking for business growth initiatives that scale up have built multidimensional business models and embrace a design thinking for business growth mindset that is structured around a value creation strategy that has been iteratively developed over interlocked and at the same time agile design lenses.

Typical Activities

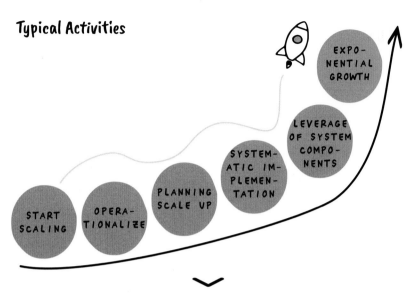

Alongside a scalable business model, exponential growth needs adequate forms of governance and a scalable IT.

Suitable methods and tools

Key Questions about Scale

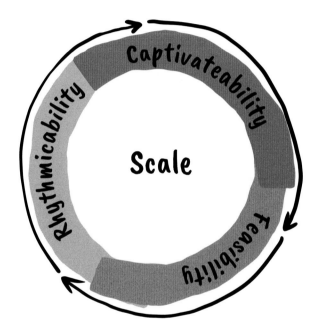

CAPTIVATEABILITY

- What basic needs are addressed?
- How can customers be retained in the ecosystem?
- How can the frequency of transactions be increased?
- Which experiences and functions favor daily, monthly, annual interaction with the customer?
- Which data points of customers and segments bring the highest added value for the development of new offers?
- How can the value proposition be augmented and communicated in a meaningful way?

RHYTHMICABILITY

- What activities are necessary to align the processes, the IT, and analytics with the requirements and growth?
- Which algorithms help in customer interaction?
- What skills are needed to develop, implement, and scale digital initiatives in coordination with other actors in the system?
- How can the heartbeat be doubled to deliver new products, services, and experiences to many customers, with the focus on the respective minimum viability?

FEASIBILITY

- Are the technologies used future-proof?
- Can automation be improved by using enabler technologies?
- Can functions be provided to a large number of customers with artificial intelligence, machine learning, and deep learning?
- Can technology components, algorithms, or the entire infrastructure be used for additional B2C and B2B services?
- Are the right capabilities and technology expertise being built up for the dynamic changes?

EXPONENTIAL GROWTH AND SCALE CANVAS

LEVERAGE FROM ECOSYSTEM ACTORS

Which actors innovate within the rules of the business ecosystem?

SCALABLE PROCESSES, IT, DATA ANALYTICS

What activities are necessary to align the processes, the IT, and analytics with the requirements and growth?
Which algorithms help with customer interaction?

ECOSYSTEM CULTURE AND NETWORK EFFECTS

How can cross-company collaboration be realized with the team of teams idea? How can network effects be used for the growth of the ecosystem?

EXPANSION OF THE VALUE PROPOSITION

What other needs and customer problems can be addressed/solved?
How is the value proposition expanded?
What is the experience, and which functions are offered?
Which new offers can be derived from data points and algorithms?

BUILDING THE CUSTOMER BASE AND COMMUNITY

Which mechanisms and methods are used to increase the number of customers, interactions and ties to the system?

LEVERAGE OF DIGITAL, PHYSICAL AND HYBRID TOUCH POINTS

Which channels are needed?
How can an opti-channel strategy be developed on the basis of data?

SOLVING PROBLEMS OF MANY

Who are the customers?
Have the segment considerations changed?
How are new needs and target groups dealt with?

OPTIMIZED COST STRUCTURE

How can the cost of user acquisition be kept lower than that of the lifetime value generated, for example.

EXPANDED VALUE STREAMS

What new value streams are rewarded by the customer?
Where is there a willingness to pay? Where are there options for bundles, cross-selling, or up-selling?

EXPONENTIAL GROWTH AND SCALE CANVAS

Template download

INPUT FROM LENS #3

LEVERAGE FROM ECOSYSTEM ACTORS	SCALABLE PROCESSES, IT DATA ANALYTICS	EXPANSION OF THE VALUE PROPOSITION	BUILDING THE CUSTOMER BASE AND COMMUNITY	SOLVING PROBLEMS OF MANY
7 P. 281	**5** P. 279	**2** P. 275	**3** P. 276	**1** P. 274
	ECOSYSTEM CULTURE AND NETWORK EFFECTS **6** P. 280		LEVERAGE FROM DIGITAL, PHYSICAL, AND HYBRID TOUCH POINTS **4** P. 277	

OPTIMIZED COST STRUCTURE **8** P. 282 EXPANDED VALUE STREAMS

The exponential growth canvas helps with the documentation of the individual steps and the results from the tools and methods used.

METHODS AND TOOLS KEY

1. Solve the problem of many
2. Expansion of the value proposition
3. Scaling processes and IT
4. Building a customer community
5. Leverage of touch points
6. Ecosystem culture and network effects
7. Leverage of different actors in the system
8. Optimized cost structure and expanded value streams

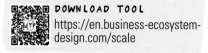
DOWNLOAD TOOL
https://en.business-ecosystem-design.com/scale

Solve the Problem of Many

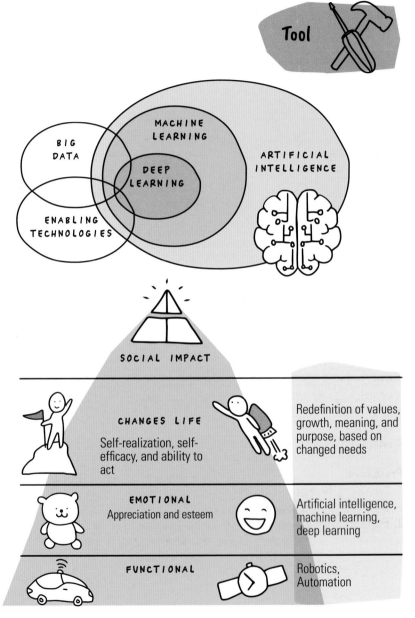

Various enabler technologies make it possible to reach a large number of customers. They deal mostly with elementary needs such as the desire for social contact (Facebook) or mobility (Uber). Based on a core functionality, business ecosystems expand their offerings and build on existing experiences and functions (UberEats, UberMoto, etc.). Successful and scalable offerings in business ecosystems deliver basic elements and values that cover the four types of needs: functional, emotional, life-changing, and those with a greater social impact. The more elements a value proposition contains, the greater customer loyalty and the greater the exponential growth of an ecosystem.

The question, "Which problems can be solved for many people?" helps the design thinking for business growth team to:
- advance the value proposition on the basis of clearly defined needs;
- check where new technologies such as robotics and automation can help to generate functional added value for customers;
- make use of methods of deep learning, machine learning, and artificial intelligence along with enabler technologies.

Procedure:
1. **Commitment:** Which needs ensure that the product, service, function, or experience is used on a recurring/daily basis?
2. **Community:** How is added value generated for the community? And how does the customer community generate added value for the business ecosystem?
3. **Data:** What data about the customers is available? How can data for the algorithm and automated processes that create value be collected?
4. **Implementation and promotion:** Is the offer so simple that children and seniors understand it?

Expansion of the Value Proposition

Tool

An expansion of the value proposition in many cases needs further digitization steps, new skills, and governance concepts. Expansion follows similar steps as the design of the actual business ecosystem. Existing value propositions are digitized and become a part of the ecosystem offering, or else experiences and functions are added in accordance with new customer needs. When expanding the value proposition, it is important to ensure that the relevant actors can make their contribution to the innovation of the business ecosystem. They must be given the opportunity to adapt their role to the dynamic changes as well. The job of the orchestrators is to provide the necessary freedom so that actors can become active even at the limits of the rules: When observing new customer behaviors or needs that seem to be recurring, for instance, they must be tested quickly and iteratively for an expanded offering so they become a part of the value proposition. In this way, successful orchestrators control the activities in the business ecosystem in the form of "leverage, innovate, expand." At this point, the cycle goes back to the first phase of design thinking, lean start-up, and the (re)design of the business ecosystem.

The expansion of the the value proposition helps the design thinking for business growth team to:
- realize sustainable growth for the entire business ecosystem;
- tie existing and new customers even more closely to the ecosystem;
- expand the offer incrementally via MVPs, with the focus always on the customer;
- integrate all actors in the system into the innovation activities.

Procedure:
1. **Leverage first proposition;**
2. **Innovate by exploring;**
3. **Expand proposition.**

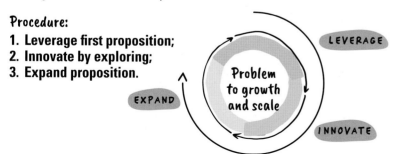

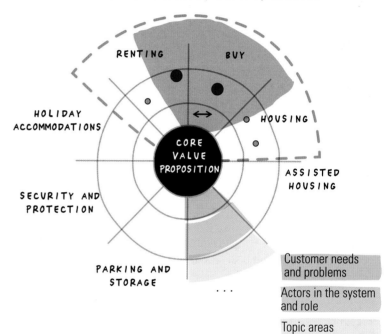

ECOSYSTEM OF "RENTING, BUYING, HOUSING"

Customer needs and problems

Actors in the system and role

Topic areas

Key

Expansion into new topic areas

Expansion with more actors who have the same skills/roles/offers, e.g. real estate portal or bank

New actors and roles in the system

↔ Identification of further customer needs for existing, supplementary, and new value propositions, e.g. contracts, moving, rating

Building the Customer Base and Community

Business ecosystems wanting to grow exponentially depend on support from their customers and should think about strategies to build communities that share successes, results, and experiences. The more varied the contact points in the communities are, the more growth can be realized. These channels are used virally for sales and marketing. In combination with the hook framework, in the best-case scenario, the customers will stay as long as possible with the offers of an ecosystem and share their experiences via other social media, which in turn draws new customers to the value proposition.

Tool

The use of the "growth loop and hook" model helps the design thinking for business growth team to:
- realize exponential growth in various forms, including the acquisition of new and returning customers/users;
- establish a system that grows by itself;
- keep the costs of growth down;
- establish recurring interaction with customers and users.

Procedure:
The procedural model consists, firstly, of the "hooked model" established by Nir Eyal. It comprises the following steps:

Trigger <-> Action <-> Reward <-> Investment

This is mirrored in the "growth loop," with "trigger" and "actions" being similar in both loops. Then come the steps:

New customer <-> Output

With regard to actions, the "growth loop" requires an external action that familiarizes a potential customer/user with the value proposition; by contrast, the "hook model" aims at establishing a habit.

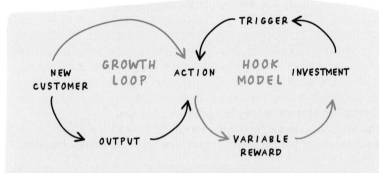

Trigger: An internal or external nudge that prompts the user to act.
Action: The customer performs the desired action in terms of the product, service, or experience.
Reward: The customer need is satisfied; at the same time, the desire to engage with the product, service, or experience repeatedly is increased.
Investment: Consists of two, the anticipation of future rewards and reasons for the customer to continue to engage with offers from the ecosystem.
New customer: Customer engages with the output and makes a decision to try out the product, service, or experience.
Output: External result that is perceived outside the ecosystem and current customer basis.

Scalable Processes, IT, Data Analytics

Technology helps to analyze routine activities/offerings in a business ecosystem on a continuous basis and to automate them so as to disrupt the traditional value chains (= continuous redesign of business ecosystems). Amazon, for instance, has been using robots for quite a while to stock and take out products and is getting closer to have its goods commercially delivered by drones. Likewise, Amazon recognized early on that a strategic option to offer cloud computing services to business customers might become a key source of earnings. Amazon Web Services (AWS), which offers access to computing infrastructure, was launched in 2006. Today, the service contributes 60% to Amazon's growth.

The focus on process automation, IT, and data analytics helps the design thinking for business growth team to:

- understand digital technologies and evaluate their impact on the ecosystem;
- build the capability of using these technologies and configure them such that they help with the scaling of IT, processes, and the infrastructure;
- establish clearly defined governance and processes for the involvement of other companies, start-ups, and technology firms;
- introduce comprehensible performance measurement and decisions for the selection of partners and technology components.

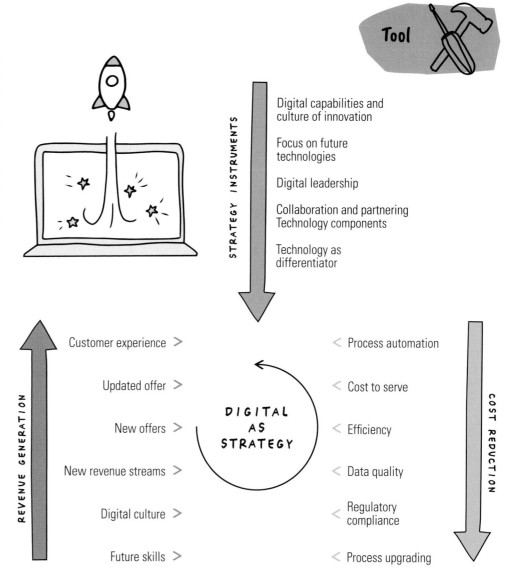

Tool

STRATEGY INSTRUMENTS

Digital capabilities and culture of innovation

Focus on future technologies

Digital leadership

Collaboration and partnering
Technology components

Technology as differentiator

REVENUE GENERATION

Customer experience >

Updated offer >

New offers >

New revenue streams >

Digital culture >

Future skills >

DIGITAL AS STRATEGY

< Process automation

< Cost to serve

< Efficiency

< Data quality

< Regulatory compliance

< Process upgrading

COST REDUCTION

Leverage of Digital, Physical, and Hybrid Touch Points

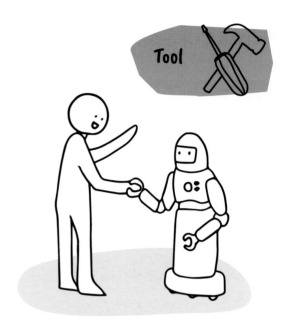

Tool

Before exponential growth becomes possible, digital maturity must be achieved, which allows interacting as a business ecosystem in a hybrid and digital world. The combination of physical and digital interaction is especially important for offers in which trust is a key element. Content generated by customers and boosted by external network effects helps scaling. Successful business ecosystems use this strategy as a motor for customer acquisition. The "Waze" traffic app, for instance, connects GPS data with real-time traffic input from customers; rudimentary gamification is used to make the process more entertaining and interesting. In addition, information is provided about physical offers at gas stations, restaurants, and DIY/hardware stores along the route. In North America, Waze is one of the most popular apps for commuters.

Leverage of digital, physical, and hybrid touch points helps the design thinking for business growth teams to:
- transfer offers from the physical world incrementally to the digital world;
- map optimal customer interaction according to needs (see multi-channel vs. omni-channel vs. opti-channel);
- analyze and use the data from digital interactions;
- provide offers for the customers that are tailor-made and prepared within the scope of mass customization;
- innovate in a data-driven way.

Procedure:
1. Gather information from the physical world to create a digital record of physical interaction and of the value chain where it makes sense.
2. Offer the customers the best channel for their needs instead of giving them a choice via multi-channel, which would overwhelm them.
3. Machines communicate with one another to exchange information, which enables advanced analysis, visualization, and the use of real-time data from various sources for customization and data-driven innovation.
4. Application of algorithms and automation to enable decisions and actions related to interactions with customers in the digital and physical world.

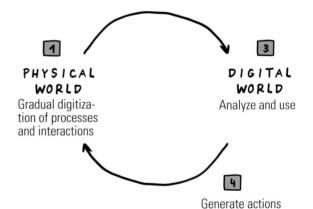

2 HYBRID WORLD

For example, use of opti-channel strategies for top-notch customer experience

1 PHYSICAL WORLD
Gradual digitization of processes and interactions

3 DIGITAL WORLD
Analyze and use

4
Generate actions

Multi-channel vs. Omni-channel vs. Opti-channel

While many companies still struggle with the concepts of multi-channel and omni-channel, exponentially growing ecosystems have already undergone evolutionary steps toward opti-channel since this approach is one of the key building blocks for scaling. Companies that have already collected data through omni-channel activities can individualize their customer interaction with new technologies (AI, big data analytics, machine learning) and offer an opti-channel that meets the needs and preferences of the customers.

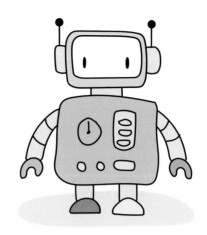

Example

MULTI-CHANNEL

- Provision of different channels (e-mail, website, chat)
- Driven by the Internet and increasingly digital customer behavior

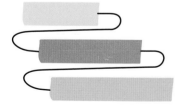

OMNI-CHANNEL

- Seamless integration of different channels
- Optimization of the channels through customer journeys

OPTI-CHANNEL

AI

- Provision of the best possible customer interaction as part of an ecosystem journey
- Use of chat and voice bots
- Personalized interaction with the customer
- Future use of emotional AI

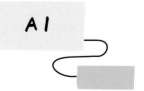
AI

EVOLUTION

Network Effects and Ecosystem Culture

Tool

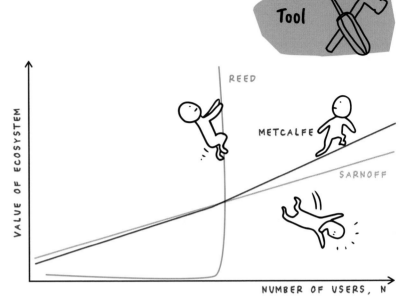

Network effects are key to scaling and exponential growth. Successful business ecosystems use strategies that are based on Reed's law. Such systems are able to grow in proportion to the size of the network (n), but usually groups are formed that scale quicker in the value (V) than others. This happens on the basis of different interrelationships among them. Centralized business networks are based on Sarnoff's Law. Here, the value (V) of the network grows proportionally to the size of the network (n). Many platforms operate according to Metcalfe's law, where the value (V) is poportional to the square of the size of the network (n).

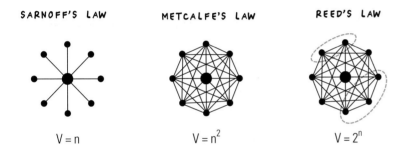

SARNOFF'S LAW	METCALFE'S LAW	REED'S LAW
$V = n$	$V = n^2$	$V = 2^n$

Ecosystem Culture based on Team of Teams

Employees who are involved in design thinking for business growth initiatives in their own company or together with other actors in the system should work as a network as much as possible so they make contacts and exchange insights and experiences. An exponential growth path is possible if the employees and teams are given the autonomy to do what they have to in the open culture that a business ecosystem requires so as to make quick and targeted decisions. Today, many companies and ecosystem initiatives are using software such as Teams, Zoom, Mural, or other collaboration platforms to support spontaneous collaboration and promote the emergence of a network in physical, hybrid, and virtual spaces.

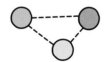

FLEXIBLE ORGANIZATIONAL STRUCTURES with clear roles and responsibilities.

NEW FORMATS FOR MEETINGS AND A COLLABORATION that is geared to acting instead of overanalyzing everything.

GREATER AUTONOMY FOR TEAMS AND INDIVIDUAL EMPLOYEES. This means that employees must be able to solve problems on their own and avoid red tape.

UNIQUE DECISION-MAKING PROCESS that continuously advances the growing ecosystem and the organizational structure.

Leverage of Different Actors in the Ecosystem

Tool

Many exponential business models are based on an unusual mix of different actors in the business ecosystem. In most cases, different types of companies from different industries collaborate so as to realize a value proposition together and benefit from the integrated value. The drone company Matternet and Mercedes-Benz are good examples of this. These enterprises have bundled their forces to design an integrated delivery solution in an ecosystem concept that is intended to change and make easier the way in which goods are procured and delivered. A transformation from a centralized digital platform toward an ecosystem supports the chances for exponential growth. Coevolution as a steady change dynamics in the business ecosystem is based on data and skills/capabilities as well as other resources of the participating actors.

The coevolution view helps the design thinking for business growth team:
- in not having to build the required resources and skills themselves but to develop them incrementally in the ecosystem with the right actors;
- in capital-intensive projects and for the purchase of assets, to distribute the burden on more shoulders;
- to establish a general change of behavior, i.e. to search for possibilities of realizing the value proposition in a business ecosystem instead of trying to build all capabilities themselves.

Procedure:
1. Identification of new market opportunity, customer problems, or inefficiencies.
2. Transformation and key issues:
   Coevolution: What is developing?/ Who makes a contribution to it?
   Mechanism: How does it develop?
   Strategy/governance: How should the evolution be orchestrated?
3. Realization and step-by-step implementation with the inclusion of integrated resources. Continuous exchange of data, information, and guiding principles for the realization of innovation and new ways of accessing markets and customers.

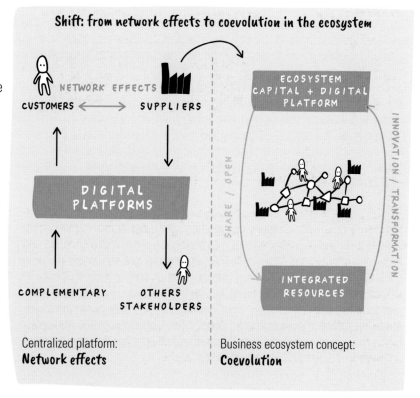

Shift: from network effects to coevolution in the ecosystem

Centralized platform:
Network effects

Business ecosystem concept:
Coevolution

Optimized Cost Structure and Expanded Value Streams

Optimization of costs and expansion of the value streams require a holistic yet tailor-made concept in the business ecosystem. However, cost management should absolutely not be allowed to encumber the growth of a business ecosystem. It is important for the growth of a business ecosystem initiative that "positive" costs be preserved, i.e. costs that facilitate future exponential growth, while "negative" costs must be reduced by strategic cost-cutting measures. To achieve this, various measures can be initiated with regard to the selection of the portfolio, required skills, the setup of the organizational and governance model, all the way to topics of operational excellence.

Procedure

Many options exist to expand the value streams, and they can be individually adapted to the system. One possibility is expansion toward value streams arising from a separate big data ecosystem. More value streams can be realized by aggregating data and making it available anonymously on marketplaces for data. In many ecosystems, data is the lubricant that allows for the development of data-driven new products, services, and functions and experiences; beyond that, there is the possibility of mass customization and providing the data of third parties for a fee (in compliance with applicable laws and regulations). Actors who are financially involved in the business ecosystem often have privileged access to the data, while other actors have limited access or need to purchase access rights. Successful initiators of business ecosystems also acquire actors or else they have a majority stake in companies to get access to important data from customers and transactions.

Tool

WHAT?

Dynamic development of the portfolio of offers	Zero-basing capabilities

WHERE?

Operating model	Sourcing of technology and infrastructure	Touch point optimization (opti-channel)

HOW?

Process excellence & automation	Future ways of working	Organizational design & ecosystem leadership	Digital as strategy	Business ecosystem design

Example

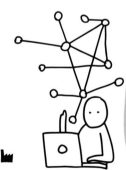

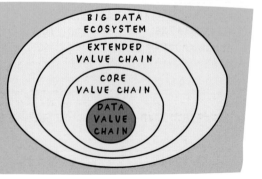

Data-driven business models combine insights from traditional and digital services and offers from the business ecosystem. The proportion of such business models is steadily on the rise. In 2020, the increase was quite noticeable. Driven by COVID-19 and lockdown measures, virtual meeting rooms were increasingly used and augmented by further services. There has also been an increase in digital twins for further optimization or to reduce costs in research and development.

BIG DATA ECOSYSTEM
EXTENDED VALUE CHAIN
CORE VALUE CHAIN
DATA VALUE CHAIN

Transition from Linear Growth to Exponential Growth

DIMENSION	LINEAR GROWTH STANDARD PROCEDURE	EXPONENTIAL GROWTH ADVANCED PRACTICES AS PART OF THE SCALING OF BUSINESS ECOSYSTEMS
DIGITAL AS A STRATEGY	Appreciation of technology as an enabler for the implementation of an ecosystem strategy and development of expertise that helps to trigger differentiation and realize competitive advantages	The orchestrator points out clear strategic goals and aspirations, followed by initiatives, to become a digital ecosystem Possesses the skills needed to develop and implement digital initiatives in coordination with other actors in the system
FOCUS ON FUTURE TECHNOLOGIES	Analysis of existing and emerging technologies for use in the business ecosystem Development of the ability to test new technologies at an early stage and check for their potential for innovation, cost reduction, and growth	Possesses the ability to understand digital technologies to evaluate their impact on the ecosystem Has the capability of using these technologies and configuring them such that they help with the scaling of IT, processes, and the infrastructure
DIGITAL LEADERSHIP	Transversal embedding of technological expertise beyond the core processes Clear assignment of responsibilities regarding technology decisions to an ecosystem team	Formation of cross-function squads and chapters for technology and innovation Special innovation labs for research and use of digital technologies in close collaboration with other actors in the business ecosystem
DIGITAL CAPABILITIES AND CULTURE OF INNOVATION	Focus is on building employee skills in the digital area Gathering innovative ideas within the organization and as part of open innovation with other actors to achieve opportunities for improvement that can be realized, which then can be implemented thanks to digitization	Close collaboration with selected start-up ecosystems; holding hackathons for problem statements in the areas of data analytics, AI, or other technologies Motivating environment for employees and other stakeholders to tackle new challenges, innovate, and make intelligent use of new enabler technologies
COLLABORATION AND PARTNERING TECHNOLOGY COMPONENTS	Awareness that new players in the market operate disruptively as a start-up or business ecosystem Focus on collaboration with well-known technology providers to extend with digitization layers and specific APIs as interfaces in marketplaces	Clearly defined governance and processes for the involvement of other companies, start-ups, and technology firms Comprehensible performance measurement and decisions for the selection of partners and technology components
TECHNOLOGY AS A DIFFERENTIATOR	Use of the technology to set oneself apart from the competitors Building first trustworthy alliances	Ability to master technologies and benchmark them The differentiation is mainly geared to the realization of outstanding innovations and customer experiences for which the respective technologies are used

To the Point !

Scaling the business ecosystem and realizing exponential growth requires the right operational model and a purposeful governance that uses all the levers to achieve the business model goals.

Exponentially growing business ecosystems by their very nature exploit all available opportunities that lend themselves for cross-market and cross-segment cooperation of the actors. They provide the cross-functional input for the further development of the value proposition, the tapping of new customer segments, and previously unaddressed customer needs.

The main goal is to solve a problem of many and, in so doing, boost the profitability of the systems with optimized cost structures and extended value flows. Opti-channel concepts support a fitting and individualized customer contact.

Scalable processes, IT, data analytics, and the use of digital, physical, and hybrid touch points help to realize the desired effectiveness and efficiency.

Further Reading Material on Design Lenses

Books have been written regarding the design lenses that are suitable to deepen the topic areas. Relevant books are available especially on the design thinking mindset, lean start-up method, and the mechanisms of scaling systems. A great deal has been written about platform economy. Only very few definitive books about the shaping of business ecosystems exist on the market up till now. According to the author's knowledge, *Design Thinking for Business Growth* is the first book that deals with this aspect holistically.

DESIGN THINKING

- Lewrick et al. (2018). *The Design Thinking Playbook Mindful Digital Transformation of Teams, Products, Services, Businesses and Ecosystems.*
- Lewrick, et al. (2019). *The Design Thinking Toolbox: A guide to master the most popular and valuable innovation methods.*
- Lewrick (2018). *Design Thinking: Radical innovations in a digitalized world* (Beck).
- Martin (2009). *The Design of Business: Why design thinking is the next competitive advantage.*
- Cross (2011). *Design Thinking: Understanding how designers think and work.*
- Brown (2009). *Change by Design: How design thinking transforms organizations and inspires innovation.*
- Leifer et al. (2014). *Design Thinking Research: Building innovation eco-systems.*
- Uebernickel et al. (2020). *Design Thinking: The handbook.*

LEAN START-UP

- Maurya (2016). *Scaling Lean: Mastering the key metrics for startup growth.*
- Maurya (2012). *Running Lean: Iterate from plan A to a plan phat works.*
- Ries (2012). *The Lean Startup: How today's entrepreneurs use continuous innovation to create radically successful businesses.*
- Van der Pijl et al. (2016). *Design a Better Business: New tools, skills, and mindset for strategy and innovation.*
- Van der Pijl et al. (2021). *Business Model Shifts: Six ways to create new value for customers.*
- Blank (2020). *The Startup Owner's Manual: The step-by-step guide for building a great company.*
- Osterwalder et. al (2019). *Testing Business Ideas.*
- Alvarez (2014). *Lean Customer Development: Build products your customer will buy.*

PLATFORM ECONOMY

BUSINESS ECOSYSTEMS

- Cusumano et al. (2019). *The Business of Platforms: Strategy in the age of digital competition, innovation, and power.*
- Parker et al. (2016). *Platform Revolution: How networked markets are transforming the economy and how to make them work for you.*
- Reillier (2017). *Platform Strategy: How to unlock the power of communities and networks to grow your business.*
- Choudary (2015). *Platform Scale: How an emerging business model helps startups build large empires with minimum investment.*
- Geoffrey et al. (2017). *Platform Revolution: How networked markets are transforming the economy and how to make them work for you.*
- Evans et al. (2016). *Matchmakers: The new economics of multisided platforms.*

SCALING AND EXPONENTIAL GROWTH

- Parker et al. (2016). Scaling Up Skalieren auch Sie! Weshalb es einige *Unternehmen packen… und warum andere stranden.*
- Eyal (2014). *Hooked: Wie Sie Produkte erschaffen, die süchtig machen.*
- Ismall et al. (2014). *Exponential Organizations: Why new organizations are ten times better, faster, and cheaper than yours (and what to do about it).*
- Ismall et al. (2019). *Exponential Transformation: Evolve your organization (and change the world) with a 10-week ExO sprint.*
- Gascoigne (2019). *The Business Transformation Playbook: How to implement your organisation's target operating model (TOM) and achieve a zero percent fail rate using the 6-step agile framework.*
- Highsmith (2019). *EDGE: Value-driven digital transformation.*

LEARN AND DERIVE APPROPRIATE ACTIONS THROUGH REFLECTION

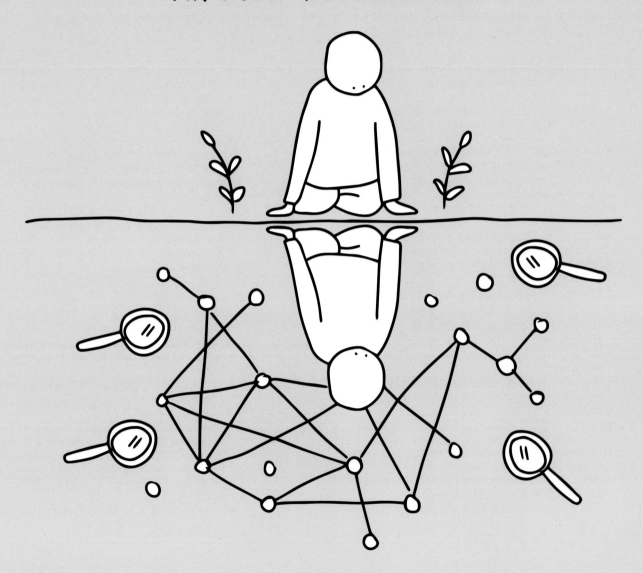

REFLECTION ON DESIGN THINKING FOR BUSINESS GROWTH

Reflection on the Initiative, Meta Level, and the Personal Attitude to the Paradigm Shift

In all agile and iterative procedural models, it has proven worthwhile to reflect on each step at different levels. In design thinking, after completing a micro cycle, for instance, or during the agile development of an MVP, after every sprint. **Typical questions are:** How well do we actually work together? How do we get along on the team? Could some things be improved? And if so, what things?

In a dynamic environment in particular, it is important for both the individual and the team to reflect at regular intervals about things and find out where the team stands and how collaboration may be improved. If you don't check regularly and discuss openly how the collaboration works, it is impossible to ensure that the team is really acting in concert and that the greater ambition of the business ecosystem is achieved. **Typical questions are:** How satisfied are we with the result of the last MVE? Have we achieved our goals? If not: Why? How can we improve collaboration on the team and with the other actors? How can we optimize the results, responsibilities, and future implementation activities within the scope of co-creation?

In addition, there is the personal reflection about the design of a business ecosystem and the associated mindshifts that demand questioning existing hypotheses and leaving the comfort zone both as an individual and an organization. **Typical questions are:** Do I really focus on solving the customer problem? Do I, as the ecosystem leader, act as an ecosystem leader within the framework of initiate and orchestrate or do I fall back into old patterns? If yes: What's the reason?

This section briefly discusses the reflection canvas for business ecosystem initiatives and describes selected tools.

PERSONAL REFLECTION

LARGER VIEW OF THE CHANGE AND THE PROCEDURE

VIEW OF THE SPECIFIC INITIATIVE

"If you want to win in the 21st century, you have to make sure you are making other people more powerful. Empower others. Make sure other people are better than you are. Then you will be successful."

– Jack Yun Ma, founder and CEO Alibaba

Key Questions about Reflection Lessons

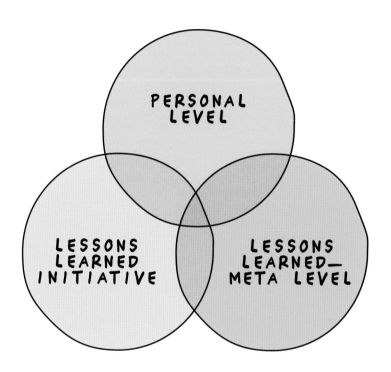

PERSONAL LEVEL

- How has your personal view of topic areas and growth changed?
- Which paradigm shift is easy to make, and where are there mental hurdles?
- How serious is your personal willingness to change for a new kind of ecosystem leadership?
- To what extent do the ecosystem design team, decision makers, and partners in the ecosystem fall back into old thought patterns?
- How can I personally contribute to the change?

META LEVEL

- What is ecosystem design?
- What are the advantages and disadvantages?
- What are the challenges entailed in the change?
- What is the difference from other approaches?
- How can different approaches be combined?
- Where are use cases in one's own environment?
- How can it be introduced across the board? What is the immediate benefit?

INITIATIVE

- What went well in the project?
- Which methods have been used? How? Why?
- What was not so good?
- What should be done differently in project work in the future?
- What are the key learnings from the initiative (positive and negative)?

DESIGN THINKING FOR BUSINESS GROWTH REFLECTION CANVAS

DESIGN LENSES
- What are the most important insights and action in each of the design lenses?

DIGITAL FLUENCY
- What digital skills and expertise were built up?
- What digital skills and expertise still need to be built up?

ECOSYSTEM LEADERSHIP
- Has the north star been communicated clearly?
- How are the teams managed?
- Where does innovation take place for the ecosystem?

MARKET OPPORTUNITIES
- What market opportunities have been realized? Where is there more potential for expanding the value proposition?

CAPABILITIES
- What new skills have been built?
- What skills are needed for the next development phase?

MINDSET
- Which mindset fits the company, values, and business ecosystem?

LESSONS LEARNED INITIATIVE
- What went well in the project?
- What methods did we apply? How? Why?
- What was not so good?
- What should be done differently in project work in the future?
- What are the key learnings from the initiative (positive and negative)?

LESSONS LEARNED— META LEVEL
- What is ecosystem design?
- Pros and cons
- Challenges
- Difference from other approaches
- Combination with other approaches
- Use cases in one's own environment
- Introduction/use in one's own environment

THINK OF POSSIBILITIES
- How has the view of topic areas and growth areas changed? What does the future market role look like?

PRINCIPLES
- According to which principles are current and future business ecosystems designed? What principles contributed to the success of the current stage in the ecosystem initiative?

DIGITAL (ENABLER) TECHNOLOGIES
- Which (enabler) technologies are used?
- Where do technology renewals need to be addressed?

BIG DATA ANALYTICS/ AI/ ML/ DL
- How is maturity in the handling of data? How do technologies such as AI, DL, and ML help with the automation of functions?

CAPITAL AND ASSETS
- How are setup, implementation, and growth financed? What assets does the business ecosystem have?

GOVERNANCE
- How is the initiative managed? Which KPIs are used to measure success?

DESIGN THINKING FOR BUSINESS GROWTH REFLECTION CANVAS

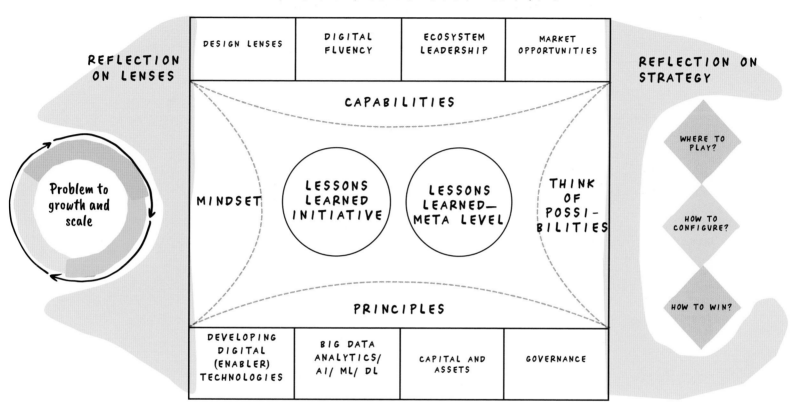

REFLECTION ON LENSES

REFLECTION ON STRATEGY

DESIGN LENSES	DIGITAL FLUENCY	ECOSYSTEM LEADERSHIP	MARKET OPPORTUNITIES

CAPABILITIES

Problem to growth and scale

MINDSET

LESSONS LEARNED INITIATIVE

LESSONS LEARNED—META LEVEL

THINK OF POSSI-BILITIES

PRINCIPLES

DEVELOPING DIGITAL (ENABLER) TECHNOLOGIES	BIG DATA ANALYTICS/ AI/ ML/ DL	CAPITAL AND ASSETS	GOVERNANCE

WHERE TO PLAY?

HOW TO CONFIGURE?

HOW TO WIN?

The reflection canvas for business ecosystem initiatives helps to reflect on current activities at the project and meta level, to learn and derive fitting activities.

DOWNLOAD TOOL
https://en.business-ecosystem-design.com/reflexion

Constant Reflection on the Entire Cycle, from the Problem Statement All the Way to Scaling

Design thinking for business growth initiatives are of a certain complexity. Constant reflection is needed to find guidance for the procedure (lessons learned—meta level) in each of the design lenses and in the transition to the next lens as well as for the specific initiative currently being worked on (lessons learned initiative). The canvas helps to reflect on one's own actions and learning. For more extensive projects, its use is also recommended during the project. In addition, an improvement loop can be started with the feedback capture grid after each canvas.

The reflection exercise helps all the teams involved to:
- collect and appraise experiences made in the project in a structured way;
- learn from experience and make use of it in the next project;
- facilitate a positive attitude toward mistakes and appreciate progress;
- identify and document the findings, make them applicable, and finally usable.

Procedure and template:
The feedback capture grid offers the opportunity of recording the current status at any time and to use the lessons learned to tackle the next phase or the next project with the learnings realized. The grid consists of four fields. Not only the things that went well are entered but also constructive criticism. And there is lots of space for open questions and ideas that have come up in the process and while working together.

I LIKE	I WISH
Things you like or find remarkable	Constructive criticism
+ ☆	
? 💡	
QUESTIONS	IDEAS
Questions that have arisen from experience	Ideas that arise from the experience or presentation

Members of the respective design and implementation teams agree on actions and improvements and implement them in the agreed form.

DOWNLOAD TOOL
https://en.business-ecosystem-design.com/feedback

Retrospective Sailboat

The sailboat retrospective is frequently used with the scrum method in the context of the reflection on a sprint. The method is also very suitable after each design lens or after one step or subproject has been completed. The sailboat can be used as a kind of debriefing after the joint facilitation of a workshop, a co-creation session, or after interviews with potential actors for a planned business ecosystem. The tool purposefully addresses accelerating, inhibitory, and environmental factors; it promotes the failure mindset in which mistakes are not seen as failures but as an opportunity to change and learn.

The retrospective helps all the teams involved to:
- improve interaction on the team and collaboration in a fast, targeted, appreciative, and structured way;
- look back and see what went well and what should be improved;
- reflect upon the question of which factors can be changed and which factors must be accepted;
- create a positive mood since all team members are listened to and can make a contribution; this in turn nurtures the mindset of self-organized teams.

Procedure and template:
1. **Opening:** Introduce the goals and the sequence of the retrospective session.
2. **Collect information:** Collect information on Post-its that are stuck to the corresponding fields of the sailboat template. Typical questions: What happened recently? What was good? What gave us some wind at our backs (WIND)? What didn't work so well on the team and slowed us down (ANCHOR)? What are the hazards and risks against which the team has no power (CLIFFS) (e.g. market, new technologies, competitors)? What shared common vision and motivation does the team have (ISLAND)? Everybody reads his or her Post-its aloud.
3. **Cluster and prioritize findings:** Select and go into greater depth about the most important topics. Get to the bottom of things, i.e. identify causes, so that not only the symptoms are tackled. The aim is also to address unpleasant issues and create the basis for improvements.
4. **Define measures:** In the last step, the measures are formulated. This means that we document precisely anything to be changed or tried out in a following iteration.
5. **Conclude the retro:** Everybody gives a brief feedback on the retro session, e.g. with a feedback capture grid. Ultimately, the group should part from one another with good feelings.

Tool

ACCELERATING FACTORS
For example: regular consultations and daily meetings

GOAL VISION
For example: Nicest insurance company in the world, and the customer will love it.

ENVIRONMENTAL FACTORS
For example: new laws

INHIBITORY FACTORS
Lack of rules, undefined roles, no suitable tools

RETRO AGENDA

GATHER INFORMATION
Goals and procedure

INSIGHTS
Develop

MEASURES
Define

CONCLUSION
Feedback on the retro

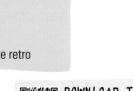

DOWNLOAD TOOL
https://en.business-ecosystem-design.com/retrospective

Give Feedback with "I like, I wish"

Feedback is needed in every iteration and every design lens. It is used for the improvement of prototypes, stories, business models, and entire business ecosystems. "**I like**," "**I wish**" are particularly suitable for sensitive projects. By maintaining a positive mood, a relationship that is based on partnership evolves between the feedback provider and the feedback recipient.
It can be used in the context of reflecting on the collaboration as well as for a specific result.
For example: "I like how you motivated us to conduct another customer survey" or "I wish not only digital channels would be used but physical ones as well."

I LIKE the various options for interaction a potential customer has in the ecosystem.

I WISH that geo data and location data would be used as well to see where the customer actually is.

Feedback in the form of "I like," "I wish" help to:
- establish a feedback ritual in which only "I like," "I wish" are allowed;
- appreciate even small successes achieved in an iteration, with a prototype or in a test;
- use reflection as the basis of continuous improvement;
- give and receive written and spoken feedback.

Procedure:
1. Communicate the rules for feedback clearly and encourage a positive mood.
2. Write the feedback down, express your thanks, and use it to improve the collaboration, prototypes, and entire business ecosystems.
3. Create space for new ideas and possibilities with "I wonder…"

I WONDER why we haven't been participating in a business ecosystem up to now.

Important: Starting a discussion as the recipient of the feedback should be avoided. It would change the mood, and the positive attitude is lost. The application of this tool aims at avoiding ad hominem criticism and maintaining a positive mood.

Any feedback should be seen as a gift. The gift must be wrapped in such a way that the positive basic mood is maintained.

DOWNLOAD TOOL
https://en.business-ecosystem-design.com/like-wish

To the Point!

Constant reflection across the entire design thinking for business growth cycle and after the individual lenses helps the team to learn at different levels, for one, at the level of the particular initiative, and secondly, in a more general sense, how to deal with major mindshifts and paradigm shifts for further initiatives or in the participation with business ecosystems.

Active reflection after individual sprints and during the transition to the next design lens supports team building and helps to remove existing hurdles that might delay the overall initiative.

With the comprehensive reflection canvas, individual milestones in terms of the technologies used, leadership, and governance concepts can be recorded.

At a personal level, reflection helps to see to what extent new mindsets are already being applied and where there is still room for change.

INSIGHTS INTO LOCAL, NATIONAL, AND INTERNATIONAL BUSINESS ECOSYSTEM INITIATIVES

EXAMPLES OF DESIGN THINKING FOR BUSINESS GROWTH

Ecosystems and Growth Initiatives Worldwide

By 2030, more than 1/3 of global sales will be generated in ecosystems. Experts assume that this evolution of business ecosystems will go so far that more than 100 different value chains will be consolidated in them. The question of whether it will all be in the hands of a few large companies, the initiators of such systems, who incrementally take a financial stake in the actors of such systems or whether such gigantic systems can also exist in decentralized structures is still open; however, the current trend seems to be that individual dominant market participants from the relevant industries are the ones who can hold their own. It is still quite exciting to watch how things will develop on the different continents. Asia is currently showing the best conditions for playing a decisive role in the field of ecosystems. Chinese companies such as Baidu, Alibaba, and Tencent, in particular, are in the process of transforming their digital business models in accordance with the business ecosystem idea. In 2020, the three Chinese companies already accounted for about 30% of China's GDP, which is more than 3 trillion euros, and this figure is rising. More and more traditional companies also are opening up and attempting to realize growth and customer access data with an ecosystem strategy. In Asia, this includes enterprises such as Ping An and DBS Bank (financial services). In Europe, initiatives by Daimler and BMW (mobility) and the Swiss Federal Railways (sustainable mobility) are well-known examples. Players such as Amazon operate internationally. Initiatives by WeWork (focus on space, living, housing), for instance, have sprung up in the United States. Numerous national and local initiatives such as Klara (SME services) and Cardossier (life cycle of vehicles) see growth opportunities in a national ecosystem play. Many of these initiatives have built their business model on innovation ecosystems as well as data and transaction ecosystems. Alongside technology, actively shaping the customer experience is key. This last chapter presents a number of examples of such initiatives. Special circumstances, such as COVID-19, have further accelerated this explosion in value creation around the world. New and changing customer needs are opening up previously untapped market opportunities for ecosystems and business growth initiatives.

Companies that have understood the evolutionary thought of business ecosystems within the framework of design thinking for business growth will take on a leading role with respect to their entrepreneurial activities and growth in the future.

Examples of platforms, ecosystem orchestrators, and ecosystem initiators

1. Tencent Group	**300**
2. Tencent: WeChat	**301**
3. Alibaba Group	**303**
4. Alibaba: Ant Financial	**304**
5. Ping An	**307**
6. DBS Bank	**308**
7. Amazon	**310**
8. WeWork	**313**
9. YOUR NOW	**314**
10. Hubject	**315**
11. Green Class	**316**
12. Klara	**317**
13. Cardossier	**318**

Snapshot of Initiatives Worldwide: 2020

EUROPE

Among the top 50 companies in Europe, there are only a few initiatives up to now that have realized a 100% digital business model, platform business model, or business ecosystem.

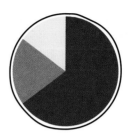

Globally, Europe covers a mere 5% of the market capitalization in currently dominant models of the platform economy.

UNITED STATES

Among the top 50 companies in the U.S., there are many initiatives that have built hybrid or 100% digital business models.

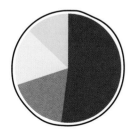

Apple, Google, and Amazon take advantage of the opportunity for exponential growth. Market shares of established companies are declining.

ASIA

Among the top 50 companies in Asia are many initiatives that have built hybrid or, increasingly, 100% digital business models.

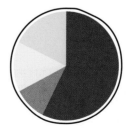

China has currently nearly 100 digital platforms with corresponding business ecosystems, with Alibaba leading the field.

KEY:
Tangible capital | Financial capital | Human capital | Intellectual capital | Ecosystem capital

Tencent Group

Over the last few years, Tencent has initialized a whole range of business ecosystems. Originally, Tencent was a company that focused on the gaming and entertainment market. Tencent's most famous initiative is an ecosystem called WeChat. At this point, it has become one of the largest ecosystems in Asia with over 1.2 billion active users. In addition to the original chat function, WeChat today offers payment services (WeChat Pay), online-to-offline (O2O) services (meitun.com), and integrated online shopping (JD. com) options. In orchestrating the ecosystem, Tencent is keen to ensure that the respective actors make a tangible contribution to the satisfaction of customer needs. The WeChat ecosystem is to become a one-stop shop for all consumers in all areas of daily life. Customer needs consist mainly of recurring interactions, e.g. chatting (= constant interaction), ordering a taxi (= daily), coordinating doctor's appointments (= monthly). In well-considered strategic decisions, Tencent takes a financial stake in other actors in the system, especially when these actors generate important data about customers that will help in the future to create a 720 degree view of each and every customer or user of the services and experiences.

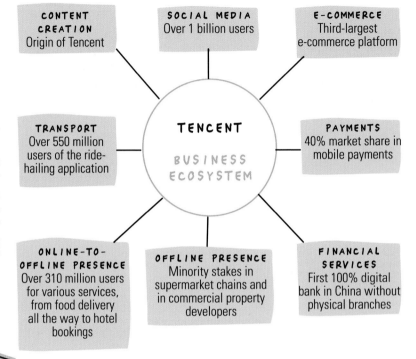

Factors of Success

- A simple mission (compass for decisions): "Improving people's quality of life through digital offers."
- Founder-managed company
- Diversified portfolio and constant expansion of the value proposition
- Innovation according to six principles: agility, openness, customer first, speed, resilience, and evolution
- Active shaping of business ecosystems

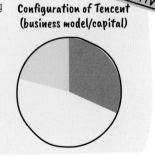

Configuration of Tencent (business model/capital)

ILLUSTRATIVE

The business ecosystem of the entire Tencent Group uses different customer access routes. They range from 100% digital interactions to online-to-offline ecosystem journeys for customers.

KEY:
Tangible capital Financial capital Human capital Intellectual capital Ecosystem capital

Tencent: WeChat

WeChat is exciting in many ways, and describing in detail how the value proposition of WeChat has developed over time would take up another book. WeChat is also an impressive example of how through customer focus and the gradual expansion of functions and experiences in MVPs and MVEs an ecosystem can be built that grows exponentially and at present

carries out transactions with over 1.2 billion people. Interaction with the users takes place in the form of over one million mini-programs teeming with 400 million active users every day (as of 2020). WeChat has taken on the governance of 1.5 million third-party software developers and 60,000 service providers.

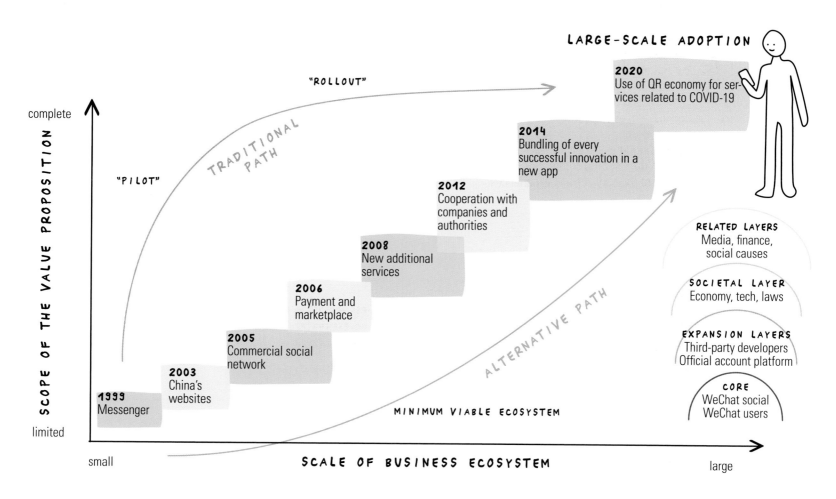

Digression: COVID-19 and the WeChat Ecosystem

The speed in which new functions and experiences of WeChat and its ecosystem were implemented during the COVID-19 pandemic was especially impressive. While in Europe, each country tinkered with an app or function for the tracking of COVID-19, China made use of the WeChat ecosystem to coordinate activities. All in all, more than 100 mini-programs related to COVID-19 were integrated.

The QR code economy played a decisive role in this. It creates a digital connection between people, things, and places in the WeChat ecosystem. The function is extremely simple; with user-friendly code scans within the WeChat ecosystem, various transactions can be carried out. The basis of this networked system consists of the official WeChat user account, mini-programs, WeChat Pay, and WeChat Work.

During the COVID-19 pandemic, these QR codes not only helped to ensure a smooth exchange of information; they also contributed toward reducing the costs of pandemic prevention and providing optimal distribution of resources, e.g. for medical care.

"Tencent health codes" were downloaded by 1 billion people and were applied more than 9 billion times during the first wave of the pandemic in China (January to May 2020), with over 26 billion users visiting in the corresponding mini-programs.

Over the same period, more than 10 billion yuan in the form of WeChat salary vouchers were announced or distributed by local governments, which effectively helped boost spending and support SMEs.

In a very short period of time, health-related mini-programs were added, and the number of users rose by 347%. More than 1,000 hospitals processed 130,000 health inquiries via the functions of WeChat Work.

As impressive is the adoption and use of the "WeChat Work multi-person conferencing tool" from January to May 2020. The service was used 220 million times to work from home. In addition, one-fifth of the schools in China use WeChat Work to reach a total of 50 million parents and their children.

INDIVIDUAL HEALTH ASSESSMENT

IDENTIFICATION

TRIPS MADE

LOCATION

BIG DATA/ ANALYTICS

INFECTION CONTACT TRACKING

HEALTH CONDITION

Alibaba Group

The rise of Alibaba began with the boom of smartphones in China. The e-commerce platform was already leading at the time. It recognized the market opportunity and made it as easy as possible for consumers to purchase goods (with a click). In no time at all, more transactions were carried out on mobile phones than on existing marketplaces. While penetration was still below 15% in 2010, today more than 90% of goods are purchased via mobile phones.

The second big transition for Alibaba came in 2014. New technologies made it possible to carry out simple P2P money transfers. Competitor Tencent launched the WeChat function "Red Envelope," to which Alibaba reacted by launching Alipay in time for for the Chinese New Year. Both services allow the user to send small amounts of money in the form of red Chinese envelopes (hongbao) to other people. This killer function radically changed the way customers use the option of the virtual transfer of small amounts of money. Through network effects and a scalable infrastructure, the volume of mobile payments grew exponentially. With Ant Financial, Alibaba covers many areas, from asset management to insurance policies all the way to loans and credit rating.

Factors of Success

- Unique business model
- Unconventional profit model
- Reliable evaluation model of the actors
- Support services for greater customer satisfaction
- Pronounced sensitivity to new market opportunities
- New transaction models (e.g. C2B and O2O)
- Holistic business ecosystem concept

Configuration of Alibaba
(business model/capital)

ILLUSTRATIVE

KEY:
Tangible capital Financial capital Human capital Intellectual capital Ecosystem capital

Alibaba's Ant Financial ecosystem pursues a different ecosystem strategy than Tencent, which opted for the most part to have one-dimensional partnerships for customized insurance solutions via their online insurance agency WeSure.

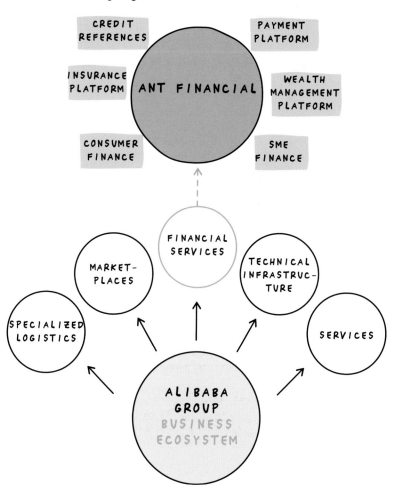

Alibaba: Ant Financial

Ant Financial might be called the fintech branch of Alibaba. Analyzing the sub-business ecosystem Ant is especially rewarding since data play a decisive role in this system. The business ecosystem has petabytes of data at its disposal, which was provided by customers and users for the most part free of charge. Other platforms such as Google or Facebook are well stocked with user data but they don't get near the dimensions Ant is aiming for. No other tech giant has the same reach and depth of data from mobile payments and the associated offline services as Ant Financial.

The data is so valuable because it provides information on user behavior all the way up to so-called live events (marriage, children, inheritance, etc.) with the greatest potential for the sale of products. With this data, Alibaba has a comprehensive view of the behavior of users. Based on this data acquisition, Ant designs, structures, and offers tailor-made financial services, from mortgages all the way to asset management and insurance policies. New technologies and intelligent business ecosystem design make it possible to bring to life the ideas of comprehensive-financing service providers envisioned in the 1990s.

Today, the use of data by Ant and other ecosystems goes beyond the distribution of comprehensive financing offers. Using AI, new premium models for policyholders are developed, for instance; at the same time, claim assessments are done in a flash with the aid of intelligent image recognition and structured loss data.

In other areas, Ant relies on other enabler technologies. Traditional passwords have been replaced for the most part by biometric data. New technologies allow identification to be carried out on the basis of face, retina, and fingerprint scans, which considerably increase the convenience for users. In this way, Ant Insurance has won over 400 million policyholders in the life, non-life, and other insurance products.

Ant Financial is a good example of how a business ecosystem can grow exponentially with cutting-edge technology and ecosystem leadership. External factors such as COVID-19 caused customer needs to change once more, meaning that interaction will most certainly take place even more in virtual worlds in the future. So it comes as no surprise that other ideas for expanding the value proposition have been moving toward personalized medicine since 2020.

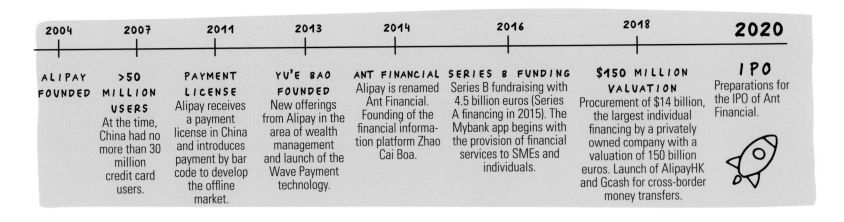

2004 — ALIPAY FOUNDED

2007 — >50 MILLION USERS At the time, China had no more than 30 million credit card users.

2011 — PAYMENT LICENSE Alipay receives a payment license in China and introduces payment by bar code to develop the offline market.

2013 — YU'E BAO FOUNDED New offerings from Alipay in the area of wealth management and launch of the Wave Payment technology.

2014 — ANT FINANCIAL Alipay is renamed Ant Financial. Founding of the financial information platform Zhao Cai Boa.

2016 — SERIES B FUNDING Series B fundraising with 4.5 billion euros (Series A financing in 2015). The Mybank app begins with the provision of financial services to SMEs and individuals.

2018 — $150 MILLION VALUATION Procurement of $14 billion, the largest individual financing by a privately owned company with a valuation of 150 billion euros. Launch of AlipayHK and Gcash for cross-border money transfers.

2020 — IPO Preparations for the IPO of Ant Financial.

The Open Business Ecosystem Strategy of Ant Financial

Ant's business ecosystem strategy purposefully relies on co-competition. The open system is made available to other financial institutions. This approach enables other financial actors to use the system design and the technology so they can address the new needs of customers as well. This opening allows Ant to realize entirely new value streams that increasingly generate more revenue than traditional financial services. Thus Ant skillfully expands activities in the business ecosystem and puts technology services for banks and insurance companies in the center of its growth strategy. And it paid off. As of 2020, Ant has a capital market valuation of more than 150 billion euros. With its ecosystem strategy, Ant became independent of conventional commissions and transactions and banks on higher margins in technology delivery. According to Alibaba, Alipay and related organizations have around 1.2 billion active users, 900 million of which are living in China.

Wealth management companies, for instance, have the opportunity to offer pension funds on Ant Fortune. As actors in the Ant business ecosystem, they also have the possibility to access data-based analyses of target customers and to publish AI-based services such as automated e-brochures for their respective customers and segments. Ant is a prime example of the fantastic potential of open business ecosystems, in which fintech is both initiator and actor in the ecosystem and the platform provided.

Globalization Strategy of the Business Ecosystem

In the longer term, Ant focuses on building out its presence globally for scaling. The aim is that customers will have the opportunity in the future to shop and transfer funds throughout the world.

Business and Data Ecosystem

Ant sees itself as a "super app" that subsumes a multitude of different functions. Data again plays a key role here, e.g. to enable suppliers access to the desired customer groups on the Ant marketing platform; to provide promotions via coupons; to create quick, simple, and cost-effective payment options; and to learn more about the customers and their behavior. Corresponding push notifications are sent to the customers through geolocation as soon as they are in a region, a city, or a store. For tourists who go shopping abroad, the app has an automatic tax refund function. In addition, the app offers the opportunity of sharing special shopping experiences via social sharing.

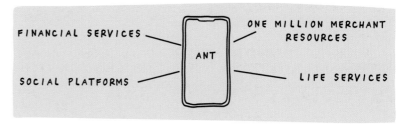

As soon as the transaction data from Alibaba's Wallet is available, Ant can offer suitable financial products that match the customers' risk profiles. These products help to check creditworthiness in real time and to provide small loans at the POS, even offering money market funds. At this point, almost 70% of the people in China use the "sesame score" as a credit ranking to gain access to personalized financial products in return.

"If you have a network of partners all sitting on the same technology stack, interoperability is not a problem. In the future, somebody using the Philippine version of Alipay can come to Hong Kong and shop at any store that accepts Alipay. That's the vision."

– Joseph Tsai, CEO, Ant

Examples of Black Ocean Strategies in the Area of Paperless Payment

In the area of mobile payment, China is ahead of all other regions on the planet, with around 47 percent of smartphone owners using a digital wallet. WeChat and Ant dominate with their black ocean strategy.

In addition, there are plans in China to connect the QR code payment ecosystem to a universal code, which will accelerate exponential growth once more, in particular, because the black ocean players have already expanded their value proposition in the QR economy over the last few years.

AI technology now also allows payment by face scanner, which is especially popular with young people in China. In early 2020, there were over 110 million Chinese users who paid with this method in supermarkets, grocery stores, shopping centers, and restaurants.

TRANSACTION VOLUME IN BILLION EUROS 77.7

UNLOCK EXPONENTIAL GROWTH

OTHERS
8%

WECHAT PAY
38%

ANT
54%

15.5

9.2

1.0

0.9

0.2

| 2013 | 2013 | 2015 | 2016 | **2017** | **2020** |

Ping An

Ping An also assumed the role of business ecosystem orchestrator in China. The insurance company has long abandoned the traditional model of simply selling insurance policies and is now focusing on the topic areas of health, housing, and mobility in its range of services. In these topic areas, products and services were developed with partners in the business ecosystem, e.g. "Ping An Good Doctor," "Autohome," and "Ping Haofang." On the one hand, Ping An is founding its own subsidiaries; on the other, it is orchestrating a number of actors who contribute to the provision of the value proposition. Similar to the WeChat ecosystem, Ping An tries to boost the frequency of interactions by using different channels. For example: Up to 30 million customers visit the Autohome platform for the purchase and sale of cars; at the same time, they are potential customers for financing and insurance products. Ping An's real estate ecosystem has become a one-stop shop for everything related to the purchase and the financing of real estate. Features such as a client-to-client rental platform help generate new customer access, which is then serviced directly by direct sales for mortgages, asset management products, and insurance policies. In the area of health, Ping An works with one of the largest network of doctors in China that are available online. The combination of online consultation, a function for ordering medicines, and brick-and-mortar hospitals attracts patients with a unique value proposition that could not be delivered by a single market participant. The online-2-offline capability, in particular, makes the system unique. With the huge volume of a multitude of data from customer information, behaviors, and preferences for certain brands, Ping An is able to match future products even better to customer needs, to predict specific life events of customers, to create better products and service bundles, and to address topics such as prevention and cases of abuse in a targeted way. The data has also become a source of income since data sets in the combination of "health, housing, and mobility" provide particular meaningful information. Similarly to Tencent and Alibaba, Ping An is expanding its range with sub-ecosystems: in the area of health with private clinics and health cloud solutions, for instance.

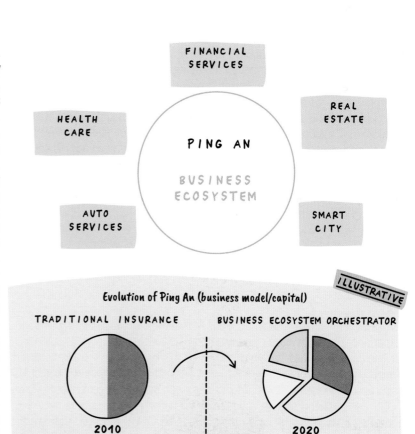

Evolution of Ping An (business model/capital)

TRADITIONAL INSURANCE   BUSINESS ECOSYSTEM ORCHESTRATOR

2010   2020

ILLUSTRATIVE

Factors of Success

- Focus on a business ecosystem that goes beyond the sale of insurance policies
- Focus on customer needs and customer experience chains
- Use of existing and new data for product and service innovations
- Investment in artificial intelligence and process automation
- Active roles as a business ecosystem initiator and an orchestrator with a focus on the monetization of data and new services.

KEY:
Tangible capital Financial capital Human capital Intellectual capital Ecosystem capital

DBS Bank

DBS Bank (Singapore) has successfully morphed from a traditional bank into a digital ecosystem player through continuous transformation. DBS banks on data, artificial intelligence, and machine learning for scaling. At the same time, the bank has capabilities that enable it to experiment with new technologies. As one of the first banks, DBS will undergo a technology shift and convert from a private cloud model into a multi-cloud model and combine the benefits of both approaches. Data plays a crucial role for DBS. The goal is to use big data analytics to gain better insights, improve the customer experience, and offer the opportunity to develop new products and services.

The value proposition of DBS is clear:

"LIVE MORE, BANK LESS"

DBS is focusing on new, 100% digital customer experiences for the entire process, from customer acquisition to transaction all the way to care and support.

Data helps to analyze customer needs in real time and to realize individual experiences through mass customization. The goal is to respond to customer events before they become obvious to the customers. The keyword is "hyper-individualization." To realize this, DBS relies on co-creation and collaboration in the respective data, business, and innovation ecosystems. The "DBS Co-Creation Program" comprises 65 partners from various sectors, including finance, health care, retail, and automotive. Together, they work on new value propositions based on current and emerging customer needs. The respective ecosystem design leaders at DBS come from a wide range of industries; many from technology companies that have already asserted themselves in an ecosystem play. Traditional bankers and industry experts are not to be found among them. DBS's "Transformation Wheel" relies on:
1. automate everything;
2. develop high-performing teams;
3. organize for success;
4. shift from "project" to "platform";
5. design of cutting-edge systems.

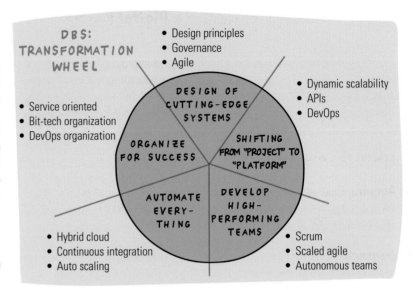

DBS: TRANSFORMATION WHEEL

- Design principles
- Governance
- Agile

- Service oriented
- Bit-tech organization
- DevOps organization

- Dynamic scalability
- APIs
- DevOps

DESIGN OF CUTTING-EDGE SYSTEMS

ORGANIZE FOR SUCCESS

SHIFTING FROM "PROJECT" TO "PLATFORM"

AUTOMATE EVERY-THING

DEVELOP HIGH-PERFORMING TEAMS

- Hybrid cloud
- Continuous integration
- Auto scaling

- Scrum
- Scaled agile
- Autonomous teams

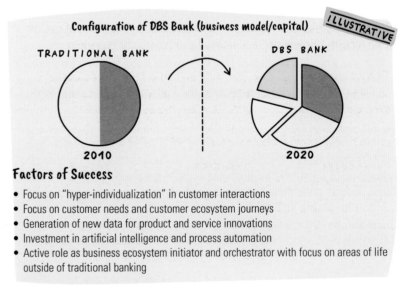

Configuration of DBS Bank (business model/capital)   ILLUSTRATIVE

TRADITIONAL BANK   DBS BANK

2010   2020

Factors of Success

- Focus on "hyper-individualization" in customer interactions
- Focus on customer needs and customer ecosystem journeys
- Generation of new data for product and service innovations
- Investment in artificial intelligence and process automation
- Active role as business ecosystem initiator and orchestrator with focus on areas of life outside of traditional banking

KEY:
Tangible capital   Financial capital   Human capital   Intellectual capital   Ecosystem capital

DBS Skills and Capabilities for a Digital Business Model

While DBS has developed customer journeys and improved existing touch points in the past, today the bank is focused on becoming invisible to the customer. The bank disappears in the consciousness, but the services from its unique value proposition bind the bank with the customer many times over.

"The winner over the next 10 to 12 years will be people who have been able to build nimbleness, flexibility, adaptability, and responsiveness into their way of working." – Piyush Gupta, CEO, DBS (2018)

To achieve this vision, DBS leverages five capabilities:

1. **Acquire:** Customer acquisition through expanded distribution, moving away from physical branches and account managers to digital marketing channels and social media.

2. **Transact:** Eliminate paper and physical forms to e-forms, e-statements, and digital account opening all the way to one-click processing of orders or end-to-end automations.

3. **Engage:** Data-driven interaction with customers in the form of customized reports, statements, and needs-based customer engagement.

4. **Ecosystems:** Initialization and participation in business ecosystems to deliver comprehensive services to the customer. Rapid connectivity with various APIs and responses to changing customer needs.

New prioritization of KPIs at DBS

50% traditional KPIs
- Shareholders
- Customers
- Employees

50% strategy
- Geography
- Regulation
- Society
- Enablers

50% traditional KPIs

20% making banking joyful
- Acceleration of digitization
- Happy customers and employees through "customer experiences"
- Value capture through digitization

30% strategy

5 Core Capabilities of the Digital Business Model DBS

ACQUIRE	TRANSACT	ENGAGE
• Increased customer acquisition through expanded distribution • Lower acquisition costs	• Eliminate paper, realize instant processing • Reduce costs	• Increase lock-in with customers based on needs, realize cross-selling through contextual marketing • Increase revenue per customer

Ecosystems: "Pipes to platforms"

Data: "Be insights driven"

In addition to the established KPIs, DBS has made the current mission a factor of success. The KPIs represent the core of digital transformation and account for 20% of the total scorecard value. Many of the experiences and features developed for customers through design thinking and initial MVPs are related to business ecosystems and expanded value propositions. The focus here is on the increasing number of customers, the majority of whom are to be served digitally.

DBS operates like a start-up. The difference, however, is that it has over 26,000 employees.

Amazon

Amazon is a prime example of a company that has by way of evolution become a dominant business ecosystem orchestrator. Amazon's digital journey began in 1995 by digitizing existing processes (selling books online). In a next step, Amazon also digitized content (e.g. e-books and Kindle format). From the strength of this marketplace, Amazon has managed to provide all sorts of physical and digital products and services all the way to B2B services in many areas today. In recent years, Amazon has increasingly focused on the design and realization of entire business ecosystems in which new network-like value creation structures have emerged through a multidimensional view of business models and the definition of new value streams (e.g. Amazon cloud services). In addition, Amazon knows how to bind customers closely through special incentives (e.g. Amazon Prime) so that they spend more time with Amazon's inclusive offerings. At the same time, this anchor effect has an above-average impact, as Prime customers generally spend twice as much on other Amazon offers as regular customers. Each business segment of Amazon positions itself to the customer with a suitable value proposition. For instance, Amazon Kindle, where consumers can simultaneously consume a wide range of products and services that are part of the Amazon portfolio on the Amazon Fire platform. In addition, the Fire platform can be used to consume other products and services outside the Amazon ecosystem, such as access to social networks, entertainment offerings, and various apps. Amazon's general openness and positioning as a middleman is driving exponential growth. Approximately 60% of Amazon's revenue comes from this intermediary business. Amazon's 40-plus subsidiaries include the pharmaceutical company PillPack, which ships individually labeled packs of medicine (labeled with the date and time to take the medicine). The advantages to the customer, in addition to free delivery, are individual packaging and instructions for taking the medicine and that dietary supplements, multivitamins, and probiotics can be added easily. Amazon is expanding its value proposition here into a huge prescription drug market, launching "PillPack by Amazon Pharmacy," a new business ecosystem.

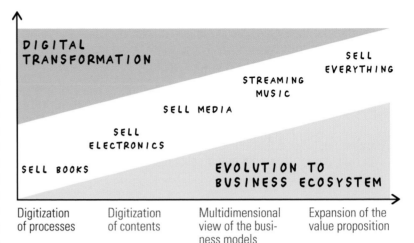

DIGITAL TRANSFORMATION

SELL EVERYTHING

STREAMING MUSIC

SELL MEDIA

SELL ELECTRONICS

SELL BOOKS

EVOLUTION TO BUSINESS ECOSYSTEM

Digitization of processes | Digitization of contents | Multidimensional view of the business models | Expansion of the value proposition

Factors of Success

ILLUSTRATIVE

- Innovation and value proposition design are two key elements in the development of new value propositions and offerings
- Strong anchor effects through Amazon Prime (solidifies loyalty to online shopping)
- Leverage of proven business models such as subscription, marketplace, pyramid model, or on-demand models
- Gradual evolution from digitization of physical processes to a holistic business ecosystem

Configuration of Amazon (business model/capital)

KEY:

Tangible capital | Financial capital | Human capital | Intellectual capital | Ecosystem capital

ECOSYSTEM VIEW OF AMAZON:
EVOLUTION FROM ONLINE BOOKSHOP TO AN ECOSYSTEM PLAY

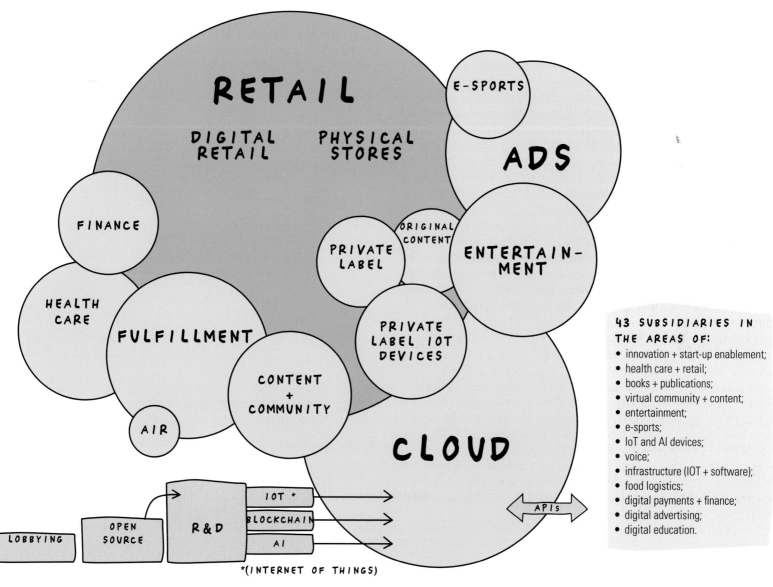

RETAIL

DIGITAL RETAIL   PHYSICAL STORES

E-SPORTS

ADS

FINANCE

PRIVATE LABEL

ORIGINAL CONTENT

ENTERTAIN-MENT

HEALTH CARE

FULFILLMENT

PRIVATE LABEL IOT DEVICES

CONTENT + COMMUNITY

AIR

CLOUD

LOBBYING

OPEN SOURCE

R & D

IOT *

BLOCKCHAIN

AI

APIS

*(INTERNET OF THINGS)

43 SUBSIDIARIES IN THE AREAS OF:

- innovation + start-up enablement;
- health care + retail;
- books + publications;
- virtual community + content;
- entertainment;
- e-sports;
- IoT and AI devices;
- voice;
- infrastructure (IOT + software);
- food logistics;
- digital payments + finance;
- digital advertising;
- digital education.

Examples of Different Ecosystem Mindsets and Value Propositions in Retail

It is also intriguing to compare different manifestations of business eco-systems in the retail sector. Traditional suppliers such as Walmart aim to improve their market position through purchasing power and efficiency. Amazon, as just described, focuses on exponential growth by opening up to many market participants and gradually expanding its value proposition. Shopify focuses on building a community and thus takes a different path than Amazon from the very outset. Several million retailers have now "moved" from Amazon to Shopify, since the winner-takes-all mentality with rigid rules of a centralized platform and the ownership and data demands of the customer interface are no longer appropriate for the times to many retailers. Initiatives like Open Bazaar go one step further and establish a purely decentralized system on the basis of new technologies. The system is primarily designed for transparency and fairness for customers and ensures that they are part of the system. The next evolutionary steps and value propositions are already emerging. Changing customer needs and a different approach to the environment and ownership have the potential for new ecosystem thinking. In addition, it will become increasingly important for initiators and orchestrators to share customer interfaces and data and to maintain transparent and fair dealings with customers and actors in the business ecosystem.

"The future of commerce needs to be owned by all of us — partners, merchants, service providers, tech enablers and shoppers. The masses, not the few. So we need you to join our movement."

– Harley Finkelstein, COO, Shopify

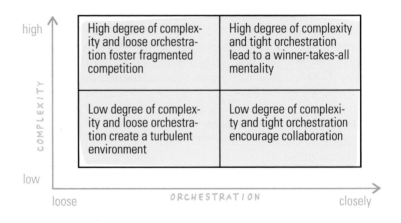

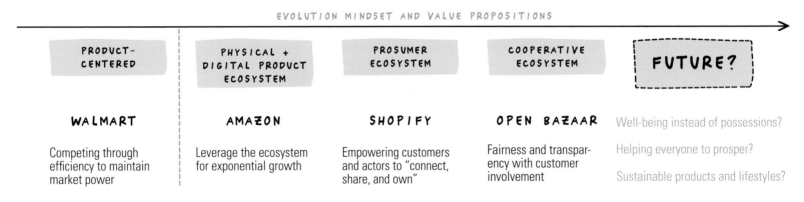

EVOLUTION MINDSET AND VALUE PROPOSITIONS

PRODUCT-CENTERED	PHYSICAL + DIGITAL PRODUCT ECOSYSTEM	PROSUMER ECOSYSTEM	COOPERATIVE ECOSYSTEM	FUTURE?
WALMART	**AMAZON**	**SHOPIFY**	**OPEN BAZAAR**	Well-being instead of possessions?
Competing through efficiency to maintain market power	Leverage the ecosystem for exponential growth	Empowering customers and actors to "connect, share, and own"	Fairness and transparency with customer involvement	Helping everyone to prosper? Sustainable products and lifestyles?

WeWork

WeWork was founded in 2010. The initial offer was simple to understand: to rent office space on flexible terms. However, WeWork's ecosystem goal goes much further. WeWork wants to equip entire areas of life with services. For this larger ecosystem ambition, WeWork has now opened a private school called "WeGrow" and retail stores operating under the name WeMRKT. In this way, WeWork communities are to be created that make it possible to organize everything from the home to the school, including transportation for the children. In other words, to establish a business ecosystem that brings everything together, namely locally in the neighborhood or in a city. Since 2010, WeWork has grown exponentially, and its vision includes everything from housing (WeLive) to fitness studios (Rise). That's part of the reason why the company and its business ecosystem now goes by the name "The We Company." The values reflect the necessary elements for a successful ecosystem player:

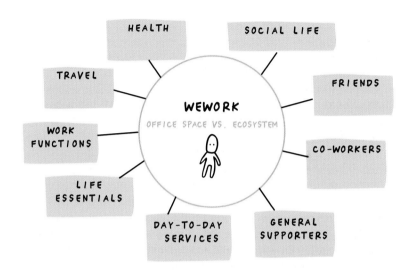

- Not selling a product but selling a vision
- Think globally
- Grow with customers
- Build a culture that supports rapid growth

From the beginning, the company had a credo of establishing their respective offerings in the spirit of a community. WeWork started by renting office space to start-ups that grew over time.

Moreover, the concept was conceived and implemented globally from the very onset. The ecosystem orchestrator and initiator does not treat The We Company corporate culture as a list of rules set in stone.

Rather, the culture is used as a tool to help the ecosystem grow, change, and evolve as needed.

"WeWork's mission is to create a world where people work to make a life, not just a living. WeLive's mission is to build a world where no one feels alone. WeGrow's mission is to unleash every human's superpowers." – Rebekah, Miguel, and Adam, co-founders of The We Company

Factors of Success

ILLUSTRATIVE

- Initial easy to understand value proposition
- Approach strongly aligned with current and future customer needs
- Expansion of the value proposition in multiple directions via MVEs
- Convincing and clearly defined business ecosystem vision

Configuration of WeWork (business model/capital)

KEY:

Tangible capital | Financial capital | Human capital | Intellectual capital | Ecosystem capital

YOUR NOW

A European joint venture is currently being initiated by Daimler and BMW, which has the potential, in its dimensions, for a rapidly growing business ecosystem. The joint venture orchestrates five pillars that together form the "Your Now" mobility ecosystem: REACH NOW (multimodal), CHARGE NOW (charging), FREE NOW (ride hailing), PARK NOW (parking), and SHARE NOW (car sharing). The future business ecosystem has the ambition of meeting the new needs of urban customers for mobility. The ecosystem has a portfolio of mobility services that is intelligent, seamlessly connected and available at the touch of a finger. BMW and Daimler are taking over the governance of the new business models with the aim of enabling a rapid and worldwide scaling of the value proposition. In this way, the business ecosystem addresses the challenges of urban mobility as well as changing customer requirements. Cities, municipalities, and other actors in the ecosystem contribute to improving the quality of life in the cities. By way of orchestration, they are carrying electric mobility forward by offering electric car-sharing vehicles and easy access to charging and parking facilities. These mobility offers, which are based on sustainability, are thus even easier to experience and use. Based on this value proposition and the current customer base of around 60 million active users, the five companies in the key regions of Europe and America want to scale globally in the future. An expansion of the value proposition with additional mobility offers based on 100% electric and self-driving fleets, which are available on demand, is conceivable. Also conceivable are services and concepts that allow vehicles to load automatically, park independently, or network with other means of transport beyond road and rail.

"We want to connect more means of transport, reach even more people in additional cities and thus improve the quality of life in metropolitan areas."– Harald Krüger, chairman of the Board of Management of BMW AG

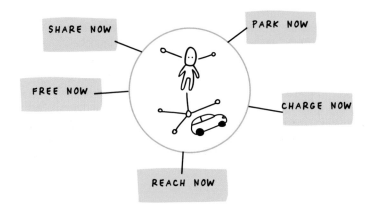

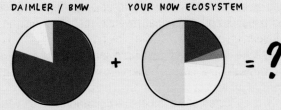

Factors of Success

- Exploit strategy based on existing products to expand market space by using start-up companies and initializing an ecosystem
- Value proposition based on the basic need simply to go from A to B
- Design of new end-to-end offerings within the "Your Now" ecosystem
- Step-by-step expansion into new areas and portfolio elements
- Two strong, established, and prestigious brands as a branding element of the business ecosystem

KEY:
Tangible capital | Financial capital | Human capital | Intellectual capital | Ecosystem capital

Hubject

Hubject is a business and transaction ecosystem with over 760 actors in 43 countries. Hubject has been building a nationwide retail network for electric vehicles (EVs) since 2012. It was originally launched as a joint initiative of Bosch, EnBW, Siemens, RWE, Daimler, and BMW. The core value proposition of the intercharge network – "Accelerating the emobility ecosystem through business services and a customer-focused approach" – includes offerings for charging station operators, traction power providers, energy suppliers, fleet operators, car sharing companies, service card providers, and even car manufacturers. In 2020, over 250,000 charging points on four continents were connected to Hubject's open platform.

Hubject deliberately pushes "coopetition" for the mobility market across four industries: automotive, technology, energy suppliers, and telecommunications providers. In addition, Hubject cooperates with regional and national companies to maintain the charging infrastructure. End customers can access thousands of charging stations through ecosystem orchestration and conveniently reserve them from their smartphone, with billing similar to roaming on the mobile network. Hubject also offers participating actors numerous benefits and additional revenue models, which in turn have a positive impact on ecosystem capital. In addition, Hubject has considered multiple revenue models for the participating actors as part of a multidimensional view of the business models. Data again plays a decisive role here. For example, dynamic data from the charging stations in the intercharge network is collected and evaluated. Digital interaction with the end customers and the activation of the respective charging stations takes place via QR codes or with RFID cards, NFC technology, or plug-charge solutions. Hubject networks various actors in this ecosystem, who together offer the end customer a unique experience. The individual actors benefit from scaling, innovation, and a cutting-edge IT infrastructure provided by Hubject.

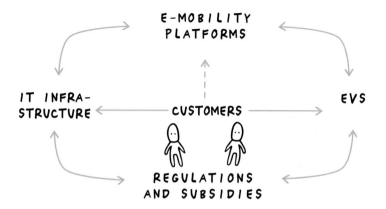

Open and networked market for e-mobility. Cooperation between charging station operators and traction current providers.

Factors of Success

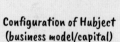

- Participation in a new growth market of e-mobility
- Core value proposition with multiple added values for actors and end customers
- Simplification and automation of processes and payment procedures
- Fast scaling by way of simple interfaces and powerful IT
- Open system with conscious decision for "coopetition"
- Strong growth of ecosystem capital through network effects

Configuration of Hubject (business model/capital)

KEY:

Tangible capital | Financial capital | Human capital | Intellectual capital | Ecosystem capital

Green Class

The Green Class ecosystem was launched in 2016 by Swiss Railways (SBB) with BMW initially as a design thinking project that designed a minimum viable ecosystem in short sprints in less than six months in the co-creation mode. The offer now consists of a public transport subscription and an electric vehicle of your choice. In this mobility concept, all customer services, road tax stickers, tire changes, taxes, and insurance are included. The Green Class business ecosystem meets customer needs for flexible and carefree mobility.

Additional services such as parking, charging on the road, car sharing, bike sharing, and cab services can also be booked. By designing this business ecosystem, Swiss Railways is responding to the changing image of e-mobility and is moving away from heavily regulated rail transport. The target segment of Green Class is primarily customers who live in an urban agglomeration or in the countryside and commute mainly to big cities. A multimodal use of transportation is part of their customer proposition, as is a more highly pronounced desire for sustainable solutions. In most cases, customers do more than five stretches of road a day. The Green Class initiative is part of more comprehensive strategic considerations of SBB: door-to-door travel along the entire mobility chain.

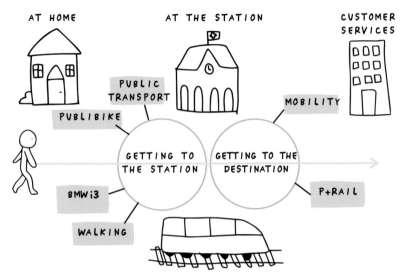

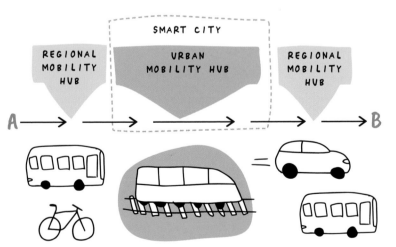

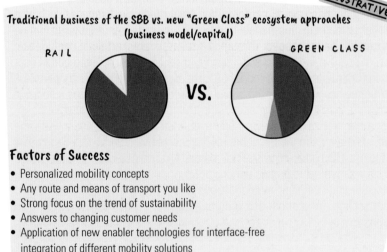

Traditional business of the SBB vs. new "Green Class" ecosystem approaches (business model/capital)

RAIL   VS.   GREEN CLASS

Factors of Success

- Personalized mobility concepts
- Any route and means of transport you like
- Strong focus on the trend of sustainability
- Answers to changing customer needs
- Application of new enabler technologies for interface-free integration of different mobility solutions

KEY: Tangible capital Financial capital Human capital Intellectual capital Ecosystem capital

Klara

Klara is a Swiss business ecosystem that has been taking over various tasks from SMEs since 2016. The business ecosystem is part of the AXON Group. Klara orchestrates banks, insurance companies, and trustees. Behind KLARA are over 100 specialists in the areas of payroll, fiduciary services, marketing, and leading-edge IT development. Klara's value proposition is focused on "more than just taking the administrative burden off people's backs – Klara makes your office easy." Within the framework of this value proposition, Klara offers payroll accounting, employee insurance, job references, sickness and accident reports, or the entire bookkeeping in a business ecosystem approach. The focus is on micro-enterprises (KLARA Business) and increasingly also private households (Klara Home), which makes it possible, for example, to manage a domestic helper easily and in compliance with the law. In addition to integrated digital services, Klara relies on a hybrid model. One of many options is to have everything set up by a specialist with the Klara setup service so that, for example, accounting works from the first moment on. Open Banking makes it possible to transfer payment data and account information easily. Individual services such as a CRM for small businesses are free of charge, while other services can be booked in small packages. Through digital assistants, artificial intelligence, data collection, and analysis, wholesale simplifications for micro-businesses are realized. Through an open ecosystem approach, various services are integrated; micro billing systems are mapped for more flexible business models, and customer interface and branding activities are managed by the respective actors themselves. Klara uses design thinking, data ideation, lean start-up, and business and data ecosystem design for the further development of the value proposition. The SME with its needs is at the center of Klara's core value proposition.

Behind Klara is a group of entrepreneurs who are convinced that managing companies or private households can be easier, faster, and more efficient.

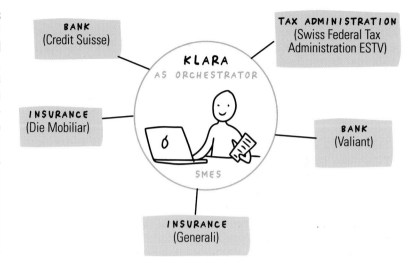

Factors of Success

- Design of offers according to customer needs
- Easy onboarding with the ability to remove inhibitions for micro-businesses through coaching and setup services
- Evolutionary expansion of the offer and use of new technologies
- End-to-end processes and digital interfaces to key partners of small businesses in Switzerland
- Application of different business models from freemium models to subscription and pay-per-use

ILLUSTRATIVE

Configuration Klara (business model/capital)

KEY:
Tangible capital Financial capital Human capital Intellectual capital Ecosystem capital

317

Cardossier

The Cardossier ecosystem was launched as an association in Switzerland in 2019. In the role of initiator and orchestrator, the association is developing a blockchain-based solution together with customers and members to map the life cycle of vehicles digitally. Members include AdNovum, the University of Zurich, the Lucerne School of Computer Science, and industry partners such as AMAG and AMAG Leasing, AXA Insurance, Mobility, Audatex, auto-i-dat AG, AutoScout24, PostFinance, and the Swiss Leasing Association. The value proposition is clear: Bringing transparency to the ecosystem around vehicles and establishing trust for all trading partners. Enabler technologies such as blockchain mean that a vehicle's data is no longer stored in different places and to different extents; instead, it is stored at several market participants in the same quality and on an up-to-date basis. Changing a data set without being authorized to do so is no longer possible. In the future, this should enable the entire history of a vehicle to be shown without gaps. The ecosystem benefits dealers and private individuals alike, public authorities such as the cantonal road traffic offices, and the Swiss Federal Roads Office FEDRO, which is also part of the ecosystem. Eleven million data sets were provided by auto-i-dat AG, an actor in the ecosystem. The next steps in the expansion of the value proposition focus on functions related to regulated processes (e.g. the import and registration of vehicles). This also includes the digital insurance certificate. Furthermore, Cardossier is working on concepts to map service and repair entries and make them traceable and transparent.

What Are the Advantages of Blockchain?

With blockchain technology, you can perform trustworthy transactions without intermediaries. Distributed ledger technology (DLT), as used in the Cardossier example, ensures that transactions are registered in many places and, once verified, are virtually impossible to change. For example, the complete life cycle of a vehicle, including the kilometers driven, workshop visits, vehicle drivers, and even location data, can be recorded on a blockchain. This is important information for leasing companies as well as used car buyers. The ecosystem provides trust.

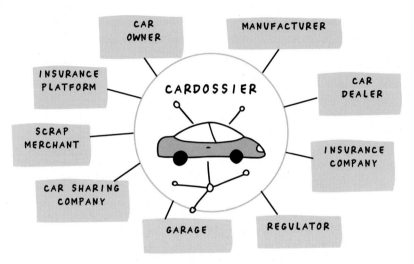

Factors of Success

- Digitization of physical assets using blockchain technology
- Increasing efficiency in an ecosystem with many actors and little transparency
- Database for new products (e.g. for on-demand insurance, pay as you drive, parametric insurance, peer-to-peer insurance)
- More transparency and data security for private customers
- Automated processes (e.g. facilitated claims management, contracting, document exchange all the way to forgery protection)
- Ecosystem with seamless customer experience based on trustworthy technology

ILLUSTRATIVE

Configuration Cardossier (business model/capital)

KEY:
Tangible capital Financial capital Human capital Intellectual capital Ecosystem capital

To the Point !

The examples show different degrees of maturity and approaches in the development of centralized business networks, platforms, and business ecosystems for the realization of business growth.

There is a tendency of large systems to acquire a dominant market position. Some of them, such as Alibaba and Tencent's payment solutions, have already successfully implemented a black ocean strategy.

National and regional ecosystem initiatives address the specific requirements in each region. They often have established customer access, a trusting relationship with the customer, or an infrastructure needed for the business ecosystem.

Actors usually take on different roles in the ecosystem. It is crucial for success to develop the respective role in the ecosystem, just as the respective ecosystems evolve dynamically.

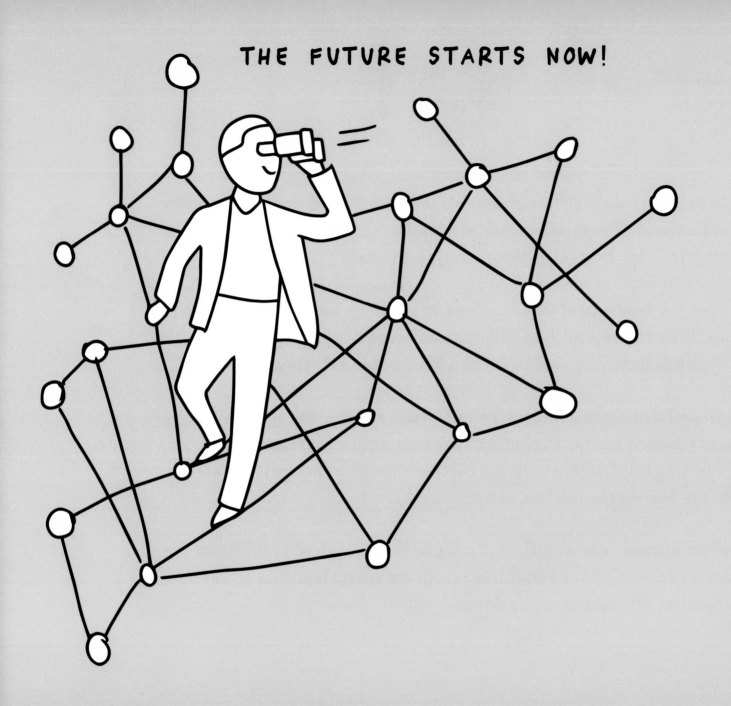

A FINAL WORD

Reflection and Outlook

Design thinking for business growth and thinking of business ecosystems is of a transformative and evolutionary nature. New ecosystems will erode existing and known boundaries, enabling companies to realize new market opportunities. On the other hand, new system boundaries and challenges will emerge. It is also noticeable that thinking and acting in ecosystems, especially for future development, already exists in many places but is not equally distributed across all industries and continents. In recent years, we as end consumers have already experienced how the formerly separate sectors of media, telecommunications, and IT merged into a superior system that allows us to consume the news in real time on our mobile devices at any time and in any place.

In many industries, decision makers still think in terms of customer/supplier relationships and venture at most a first small step toward participation in an industry marketplace or similar initiatives. For a certain number of companies, nothing will change in the short to medium term and business ecosystems will not be a major issue, since the existing business model, linear supply chains, and the strategic orientation as an integrated company works excellently for these companies. However, as digitization has increasingly accelerated in recent years and is establishing itself in all areas of life, it is to be expected that similar developments are in the offing for these companies as well. The mixing and dynamics of industries and capabilities will therefore not only be relevant to companies that want to respond to changing customer requirements or push into previously unoccupied market spaces. It is rather an overarching global phenomenon that is accelerating the paradigm shift in terms of business models and growth.

In addition, new game-changing technologies allow such systems to be organized without a central unit, i.e. there will also be an increasing shift toward decentralized business ecosystems.

The shaping of a unique value proposition with different actors includes opportunities to open up new marketplaces and marketing channels or to react to the disruption of one's own industry, existing value chains, or of individual intermediaries and to help shape these new systems actively.

Ecosystem thinking enables a systemic view of organizational and technological phenomena beyond traditional company, value chain, or network boundaries. Business ecosystem design requires that business leaders and the design and implementation teams think differently and accept the upcoming disruption, change, and transformation. With the initialization of and participation in new systems that emerge through design thinking for business growth, VUCA (volatility, uncertainty, complexity, ambiguity) is not a buzzword but a tangible reality.

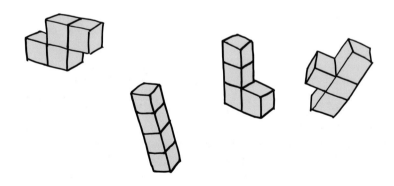

Those who want to build an ecosystem with design thinking for business growth should first ask themselves in which areas of the customer's life they want to satisfy needs and, in the second step, how other actors can help to cover this value proposition in the best possible way.

The various examples of growth and ecosystem initiatives have shown that state-of-the-art information technology has become one of the authoritative enablers to deliver products, services, and experiences in an ecosystem play. An ecosystem offers the opportunity for direct or indirect sales, to leverage customer data for tailored offerings, and to develop additional revenue streams. The lubricant of ecosystems, data, is a key element here. It seems that in some industries, online-2-offline undertakings are particularly important, i.e. the combination of the physical and digital worlds. A variety of different resources and skills are needed to initialize, build, or orchestrate systems. Ecosystems can scale globally or emerge for a region or for just one country. The examples of existing ecosystems have also shown that even niche providers and small players can successfully make such initiatives work with a well-thought-out approach.

The main aim of this book is to replace the horizontal and vertical structures that are entrenched in the cognitive repertoire of many business leaders and managers with a new way of thinking about business models, ecosystems, and growth.

The paradigm shift in the design of business models and growth described in this book has increasing relevance in current management theory and in the view of organizations and their environment as a system. Business ecosystems provide space for new approaches and procedural models. Characteristics such as the interdependencies of actors for the delivery of a core value proposition, coevolution, nonlinear behavior, and systems trimmed for scalable, systemic opportunities and challenges need flexible models. In contrast to classic market thinking, business ecosystems have customers and users, co-competitors, and actors who take on the role as initiators, orchestrate the system, or contribute to the creation of the value proposition. Ecosystem leadership also requires a new culture of collaborative working, a shift from control and command to initiate and orchestrate. Since these systems are complex, it has proven successful in their governance to give the teams, which are networked across company boundaries, as much autonomy as possible so that they can work transversally—from the ascertainment of customer needs to the design of the business ecosystem to scaling.

Only those companies that innovate strictly on the basis of customer benefits in a business ecosystem play and demand the same from other actors will succeed and achieve exponential growth.

New technologies are a fundamental driver and enabler of ecosystems. Unlike in the traditional economy, where companies need to make expensive physical investments to expand their business models, in the world of digital ecosystems, companies can grow quickly through a clever combination of data, software, and appropriate ecosystem configurations. The connections between the actors not only generate new intellectual capital but, above all, ecosystem capital! Hybrid models of physical and digital interaction currently appear particularly attractive. The best examples are the ecosystem orchestrators Amazon and Alibaba.

As to the future, it is becoming apparent that business ecosystems will achieve a high degree of disruption. New value propositions, business models, and forms of collaboration are emerging. The ambition to grow exponentially and the use of network effects will increase the speed at which such systems spread. Likewise, various trends and megatrends are affecting the positive development of business ecosystems. One is generation Z (share of the population > 25%), 100% of whom already own smartphones today and take digital interaction for granted with its simplicity and automation. In addition, new technologies allow us to analyze people's behavior and influence it in a sophisticated way. By gaining deep insights into human decision-making, it is possible to create better and more compelling value propositions that enable customers to lead healthier lives, define appropriate retirement planning measures, or simply make sustainable decisions. Through "emotional AI," systems learn to recognize human emotions, e.g. by analyzing eye movements, facial expressions, and the tone of voice. Insights about behavior in combination with emotions open up completely new possibilities to address subliminal needs or to activate certain actions of customers. We will also see new types of customer interaction in business ecosystems, via speech as well as in the form of "human augmentation" in which virtual reality is emulated and used in a targeted manner. For example, an avatar acts as a digital advisor that can simultaneously maintain eye contact with thousands of customers while adjusting its tone of voice and choice of words based on data about each customer's preferences. All these new technologies will have an impact on how people think as well. The new wave of AI, robots, and self-driving cars will have a far-reaching impact. New market spaces for business ecosystems will also emerge in the area of work-life integration. Boundaries defining topics such as designing work and leisure and lifelong learning will blur, enabling entirely new value propositions for different people and preferences. Here we can envision a future in which people can choose how the three activities mentioned above need to be balanced again and again according to their current life circumstances in a kind of portfolio approach. It's exciting, and for the future it means participating actively in these developments.

Various trends and megatrends reinforce the need to think of business ecosystems, act, and interact with customers within the scope of design thinking for business growth.

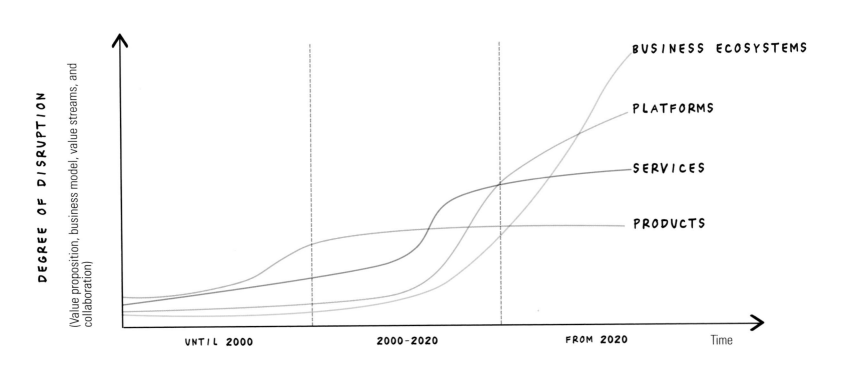

Design thinking for business growth and participation in business eco-systems requires three important prerequisites in addition to the major mindshifts and key factors:
- Opening to the outside;
- Transparency about skills and values;
- Willingness to change and acceptance of new market roles.

In addition, it is important to include the innovation ecosystem and data, information, and knowledge ecosystems in the design of a business ecosystem. Companies that are already actively operating in these manifestations of ecosystems today usually have good connections to actors and market participants, which can help realize a common value proposition.

Business ecosystems can be developed and scaled through four design lenses, within the framework of design thinking for business growth. Embedding them in existing strategy tools facilitates managing and evaluating the ecosystem as a strategic initiative.

Closing Words

PROF. LARRY LEIFER

- Professor, Stanford University
- Founding director, Stanford Center for Design Research
- Founding director, Hasso Plattner Design Thinking Research Program at Stanford

Business ecosystem design is a hot research topic in my LAB at the Stanford Center for Design Research (CDR). Having talked a lot about the different types of ecosystems over the last few years, we are currently gathering the evidence on what has worked, what has not worked, and what the root causes are for both.

As a final compliment to this extraordinarily timely book on design thinking for business growth, it should be emphasized that Michael Lewrick has worked intently on the evolution of the design paradigm over the last several years. Through his research and iterative improvement of his procedural model with various ecosystem initiatives, he has been able to explicitly address WHERE, WHEN, HOW, and WHY some ecosystems thrive and others simply wither over time.

Ecosystem design as part of design thinking for business growth needs the right mindset, suitable methods, and tools. However, it will take a few years until this mindset has arrived in all universities, companies, and with the respective decision makers so the fruits can be harvested.

Larry Leifer

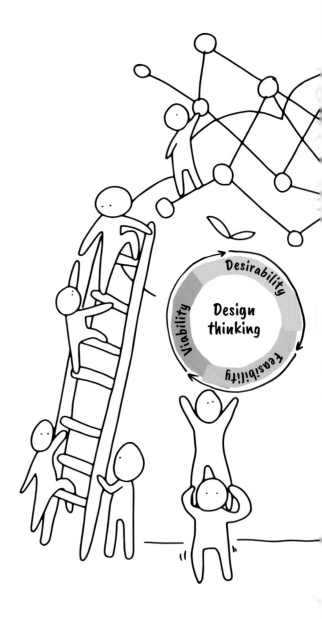

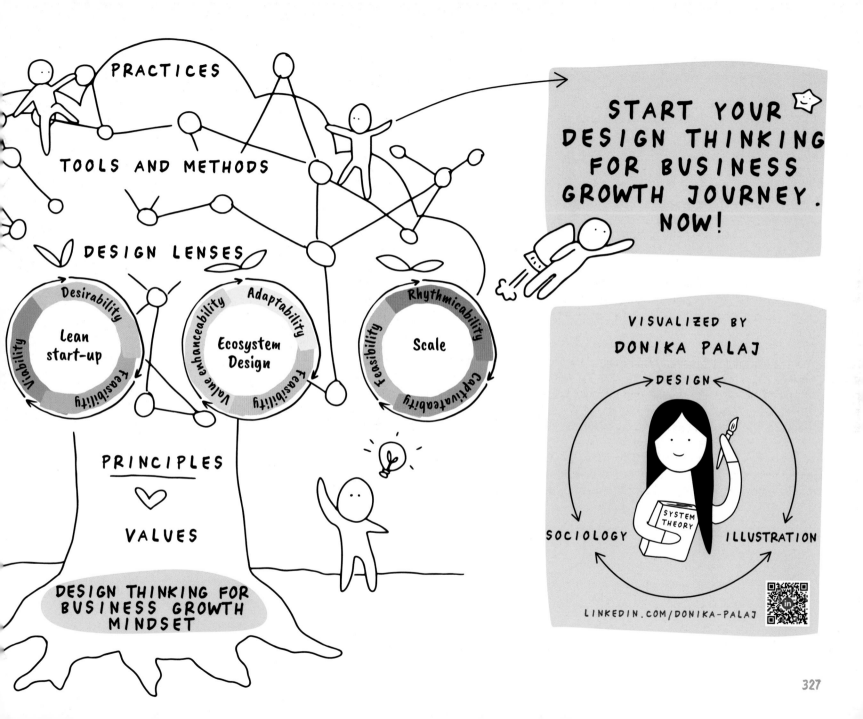

PRACTICES

TOOLS AND METHODS

DESIGN LENSES

Lean start-up — Desirability, Viability, Feasibility

Ecosystem Design — Adaptability, Value enhanceability, Feasibility

Scale — Rhythmicability, Captivatability, Feasibility

PRINCIPLES

VALUES

DESIGN THINKING FOR BUSINESS GROWTH MINDSET

START YOUR DESIGN THINKING FOR BUSINESS GROWTH JOURNEY. NOW!

VISUALIZED BY DONIKA PALAJ

DESIGN

SOCIOLOGY

SYSTEM THEORY

ILLUSTRATION

LINKEDIN.COM/DONIKA-PALAJ

INDEX
AND
BIBLIOGRAPHY

Index

Bibliography

- Adner, R. (2006), "Match your innovation strategy to your innovation ecosystem," *Harvard Business Review*, 84(4), pp. 98–107.

- Adner, R. (2012), *The Wide Lens: What successful innovators see that others miss*, London: Penguins Books, Limited (Potentially the first mention of the "Minimum viable ecosystem").

- Adner, R. (2017), "Ecosystem as structure: An actionable construct for strategy,"*Journal of Management*, 43(1), pp. 39–58. DOI: 10.1177/0149206316678451.

- Adner, R., and Kapoor, R. (2010), "Value creation in innovation ecosystems: How the structure of technological interdependence affects firm performance in new technology generations," *Strategic Management Journal*, 31(3), pp. 306–333.

- Adner, R., and Kapoor, R. (2016), "Innovation ecosystems and the pace of substitution: Re-examining technology S-curves," *Strategic Management Journal*, 37(4), pp. 625–648. DOI: 10.1002/smj.2363.

- Albers, S., Wohlgezogen, F., and Zajac, E. J. (2016), "Strategic alliance structures: An organization design perspective," *Journal of Management*, 42(3), 582–614. DOI: 10.1177/0149206313488209.

- Altman, E. J., and Tushman, M. L. (2017), "Platforms, open/user innovation, and ecosystems: A strategic leadership perspective," In J. Furman, A. Gawer, B. S. Silverman, and S. Stern (Eds.), *Entrepreneurship, Innovation, and Platforms* (Advances in Strategic Management, Vol. 37). Bingley: Emerald, pp. 177–207.

- Alturi, V., Dietz, M., and Henke, N. (2017), "Competing in a world of sectors without borders," McKinsey Quarterly, https://www.mckinsey.com/business-functions/mckinsey-analytics/our-insights/competing-in-a-world-of-sectors-without-borders.

- Arnheim, R. (1969, new edition 1997), *Visual Thinking*. Berkeley, Los Angeles: University of California Press.

- Autio, E., and Thomas, L. D. W. (2019). "Value co-creation in ecosystems: Insights and research promise from three disciplinary perspectives," In S. Nambisan, K. Lyytinen, and Y. Yoo (Eds.), *Handbook of Digital Innovation*, Edward Elgar Publishing.

- Baars, J. E. (2018), *Leading Design*, Munich: Franz Vahlen GmbH.

- Baert, C., Meuleman, M., Debruyne, M., and Wright, M. (2016). Portfolio entrepreneurship and resource orchestration," *Strategic Entrepreneurship Journal*, 10(4), 346–370. DOI: 10.1002/sej.1227.

- Baldwin, C. Y. (2012a), "Organization design for business ecosystems," *Journal of Organization Design*, 1(1), pp. 20–23, DOI: 10.7146/jod.6334.

- Baldwin, C. Y. (2012b), "Organization design for distributed innovation," Harvard Business School Working Paper (12–100), pp. 1–12.

- Baldwin, C. Y., and Clark, K. B. (2000), *Design rules: The power of modularity*, Cambridge, MA: MIT Press.

- Bansal, P., Kim, A., and Wood, M. O. (2018), "Hidden in plain sight: The importance of scale in organizations' attention to issues," *Academy of Management Review*, 43(2), pp. 217–241, DOI: 10.5465/amr.2014.0238.

- Barnett, M. L. (2008), "An attention-based view of real options reasoning," *Academy of Management Review*, 33(3), pp. 606–628. DOI: 10.5465/amr.2008.32465698.

- Beckman, C. M., Haunschild, P. R., and Phillips, D. J. (2004), "Friends or Strangers? Firm-Specific uncertainty, market uncertainty, and network partner selection," *Organization Science*, 15(3), pp. 259–275. DOI: 10.1287/orsc.1040.0065.

- Berger, W. (2014), *Die Kunst des Klugen Fragens*, Berlin: Berlin Verlag.

- Beylerian, G.M., Dent, A., and Quinn, B. (2007), *Ultra Materials: How materials innovation is changing the world*, London: Thames and Hudson.

- BIA Advisory Services, "Location-targeted mobile ad spend to reach $29.5 billion in the U.S. in 2020," press release, June 16, 2016, accessed February 26, 2019, http://www.biakelsey.com/location-targeted-mobile-ad-spend-reach-29-5b-u-s-2020.

- Birkinshaw, J. (2019, August), "Ecosystem businesses are changing the rules of strategy," *Harvard Business Review*.

- Birkinshaw, J., Bessant, J., and Delbridge, R. (2007), "Finding, forming, and performing: Creating networks for discontinuous innovation," *California Management Review*, 49(3), pp. 67–84, DOI: 10.2307/41166395.

- Blank, S. G. (2013), "Why the lean start-up changes everything," *Harvard Business Review*. 91(5), pp. 63–72.

- Blank, S. G., and Dorf, B. (2012), *The Start-up Owner's Manual: the Step-by-Step Guide for Building a Great Company*, Pescadero: K&S Ranch.

- Bloomberg News, Feb. 12, 2003, https://www.nytimes.com/2003/02/12/business/company-news-rand-mcnally-files-for-bankruptcy-with-recovery-plan.html.

- Brown T. (2016), *Change by Design*, Vahlen Verlag.

- Brown, T. and Katz, B. (2009), *Change by Design: How design thinking transforms organizations and inspires innovation*, New York: HarperCollins.

- Brusoni, S., and Prencipe, A. (2013), "The organization of innovation in ecosystems: Problem framing, problem solving, and patterns of coupling," In R. Adner, J. E. Oxley, and B. S. Silverman (Eds.), *Collaboration and Competition in Business Ecosystems* (Advances in Strategic Management, Vol. 30), Bingley: Emerald, pp. 167–194.

- Buchanan, R. (1992), "Wicked problems in design thinking," *Design Issues*, 8(2), pp. 5–21.

- Burkhalter, M. (2020). *Allocentric Business Models—An allocentric business model ontology for the orchestration of value co-creation using the example of financial services ecosystems,* St.Gallen: University of St. Gallen, Switzerland.

- Burt, R. S. (1992), Structural holes: The social structure of competition Boston, MA: Harvard University Press.

- Carleton, T, and Cockayne, W. (2013), *Playbook for Strategic Foresight & Innovation*, Download at: http://www.innovation.io.

- Cassiman, B., and Veugelers, R. (2006), "In search of complementarity in innovation strategy: Internal R&D and external knowledge acquisition," *Management Science*, 52(1), pp. 68–82.

- Catlin, T., Lorenz, J.-T., Nandan, J., Sharma, S., and Waschto, A. (2018), "Insurance beyond digital: The rise of ecosystems and platforms," McKinsey and Company: Insurance Practice, https://www.mckinsey.com/ch/our-insights/insurance-beyond-digital-the-rise-of-ecosystems-and-platforms.

- Christensen C. (2011), *The Innovator's Dilemma*. Vahlen Verlag.

- Clarysse, B., Wright, M., Bruneel, J., and Mahajan, A. (2014), "Creating value in ecosystems: Crossing the chasm between knowledge and business ecosystems," *Research Policy*, 43(7), pp. 1164–1176. DOI: 10.1016/j.respol.2014.04.014.

- Corley, K. G., and Gioia, D. A. (2004), "Identity ambiguity and change in the wake of a corporate spin-off," *Administrative Science Quarterly*, 49(2), 173–208. DOI: 10.2307/4131471.

- Cowan, A. (2015), "Making your product a habit: the hook framework," website visited on Nov. 2, 2016, http://www.alexandercowan.com/the-hook-framework/.

- Cross, N. (2011), *Design Thinking*. Oxford: Berg Publishers.

- Crossland, C., and Hambrick, D. C. (2011), "Differences in managerial discretion across countries: How nation-level institutions affect the degree to which ceos matter, "*Strategic Management Journal*, 32(8), 797–819. DOI: 10.1002/smj.913.

- Curedale, R. (2016), *Design Thinking—Process & Methods Guide*, 3rd Edition. Los Angeles: Design Community College Inc.

- Dattée, B., Alexy, O., and Autio, E. (2018), "Maneuvering in poor visibility: How firms play the ecosystem game when uncertainty is high," *Academy of Management Journal*, 61(2), pp. 466–498. DOI: 10.5465/amj.2015.0869.

- Davenport T. (2014), *Big data @ work: Chancen erkennen, Risiken verstehen*, Vahlen Verlag.

- Davenport, T. H., and Patil, D. J. (2012), "Data Scientist: The Sexiest Job of the 21st Century," *Harvard Business Review*, October 2012 issue, https://hbr.org/2012/10/data-scientist-the-sexiest-job-of-the-21st-century/.

- Davis, J. P. (2016), "The group dynamics of interorganizational relationships: Collaborating with multiple partners in innovation ecosystems," *Administrative Science Quarterly*, 61(4), pp. 621–661. DOI: 10.1177/0001839216649350.

- den Hartigh, E., and van Asseldonk, T. (2004), "Business ecosystems: A research framework for investigating the relation between network structure, firm strategy, and the pattern of innovation diffusion," ECCON 2004 Annual Meeting Proceedings.

- Doorley, S., Witthoft, S., and Hasso Plattner Institute of Design at Stanford (2012), *Make Space: How to Set the Stage for Creative Collaboration*, Hoboken: Wiley.

- Dorst, K. (2015), *Frame Innovation*. Cambridge, MA: MIT Press.

- Duschlbauer, T. (2018), *Der Querdenker.* Zurich: Midas Management Verlag AG.

- Elder, R., "Google Maps finds a way to monetize," Business Insider, March 21, 2017, accessed February 26, 2019. https://www.business insider.com/google-maps-finds-a-way-monetize-2017-3.

- Eisenhardt, K. M., and Graebner, M. E. (2007), "Theory building from cases: Opportunities and challenges," *Academy of Management Journal*, 50(1), pp. 25–32. DOI: 10.2307/20159839.

- Elstein, A. "Map publisher Rand McNally charts a course back to glory," Crain's New York Business, Aug. 27, 2015. Accessed March 6, 2019 https://www.crainsnewyork.com/article/20150827/TECHNOLO-GY/150829890/map-publisher-rand-mcnally-is-profitable-and-ready-for-a-big-comeback.

- Erbelinger, J., and Ramge, T. (2013), *Durch die Decke Denken*, Munich: Redline Verlag GmbH.

- Fernandez, A.-S., Le Roy, F., and Chiambaretto, P. (2018), "Implementing the right project structure to achieve coopetitive innovation projects," *Long Range Planning*, 51(2), pp. 384–405. DOI: 10.1016/j.lrp.2017.07.009.

- Frankenberger, K., and Sauer, R. (2019), "Cognitive antecedents of business models: Exploring the link between attention and business model design over time," *Long Range Planning*, 52(3), pp. 283–304. DOI: 10.1016/j.lrp.2018.05.001.

- Fuller, J., Jacobides, M. G., and Reeves, M. (2019), "The myths and realities of business ecosystems," *MIT Sloan Management Review*, 60(3), pp. 2–10.

- Furr, N., and Shipilov, A. (2018), "Building the right ecosystem for innovation," *MIT Sloan Management Review*, 59(4), pp. 59–64.

- Ganco, M., Kapoor, R., and Lee, G. (forthcoming), "From rugged landscapes to rugged ecosystems: Structure of interdependencies and firms' innovative search," *Academy of Management Review*, DOI: 10.5465/amr.2017.0549.

- Gawer, A., and Cusumano, M. (2008), "How companies become platform leaders," *MIT Sloan Management Review*, 49(2), pp. 28–35.

- Gehman, J., Glaser, V. L., Eisenhardt, K. M., Gioia, D., Langley, A., and Corley, K. G. (2018), "Finding theory-method fit: A comparison of three qualitative approaches to theory building," *Journal of Management Inquiry*, 27(3), pp. 284–300. DOI: 10.1177/1056492617706029.

- Gerstbach, I. (2016), *Design Thinking in Unternehmen*, Gabal Verlag.

- Gladwell, M. (2005), "*Blink: The Power of Thinking without Thinking*," New York: Back Bay Books.

- Global Market Insights, "Mobile Mapping Market size worth over $40 billion by 2024," press release, September 12, 2018, accessed February 26, 2019 https://www.gminsights.com/pressrelease/mobile-mapping-market.

- Gray, D. , Brown, S. and Macanufo, J. (2010), "Gamestorming," Sebastopol, CA, O'Reilly Media Inc.

- Griffith E. (2014), "Why startups fail, according to their founders," In: Fortune Magazine (Sept. 25, 2014), http://fortune.com/2014/09/25/why-startups-fail-according-to-their-founders/.

- Gulati, R., and Singh, H. (1998), "The architecture of cooperation: Managing coordination costs and appropriation concerns in strategic alliances," *Administrative Science Quarterly*, 43(4), pp. 781–814. DOI: 10.2307/2393616.

- Gulati, R., Puranam, P., and Tushman, M. (2012), "Meta-Organization design: Rethinking design in interorganizational and community contexts," *Strategic Management Journal*, 33(6), pp. 571–586. DOI: 10.1002/smj.1975.

- Hannah, D. P., and Eisenhardt, K. M. (2018), "How firms navigate cooperation and competition in nascent ecosystems," *Strategic Management Journal*, 39(12), pp. 3163–3192, DOI: 10.1002/smj.2750.

- Heath, C., and Heath, D. (2007), *Made to Stick: Why Some Ideas Survive and Others Die*, New York: Random House.

- Henderson Institute (2020), "Why do most business ecosystems fail?," https://www.bcg.com/publications/2020/why-do-most-business-ecosystems-fail.

- Herrmann, N. (1996), *The Whole Brain Business Book: Harnessing the Power of the Whole Brain Organization and the Whole Brain Individual*, McGraw-Hill Professional.

- Heufler, G. (2009), *Design Basics: Von der Idee zum Produkt*. 3rd exp. edition. Niggli.

- Hippel, E. V. (1986), "Lead Users. A Source of novel product concepts," *Management Science*, 32, pp. 791–805.

- Hohmann, L. (2007), *Innovation Games*, Boston, Pearson Education Inc.

- Hoppmann, J., Naegele, F., and Girod, B. (2019), "Boards as a source of inertia: Examining the internal challenges and dynamics of boards of directors in times of environmental discontinuities," *Academy of Management Journal*, 62(2), pp. 437–468, DOI: 10.5465/amj.2016.1091.

- Hsinchun, C., Chiang, R. H. L., and Storey, V. C. (2012), "Business intelligence and analytics: From big data to big impact," *MIS Quarterly*, 36 (4), pp. 1165–1188.

- Huber, T. L., Kude, T., and Dibbern, J. (2017), "Governance practices in platform ecosystems: Navigating tensions between cocreated value and governance costs," *Information Systems Research*, 28(3), pp. 563–584, DOI: 10.1287/isre.2017.0701.

- Iansiti, M., and Levien, R. (2004). "Strategy as Ecology." *Harvard Business Review*, pp. 1–11. Jacobides, M., Cennamo, C., and Gawer, A. (2018), "Towards a theory of ecosystems," *Strategic Management Journal*, 38(8), pp. 2255–2276.

- Iansiti, M., and Levien, R. (2004a), *The keystone advantage: What the new dynamics of business ecosystems mean for strategy, innovation, and sustainability*, Boston, MA: Harvard Business School Press.

- Iansiti, M., and Levien, R. (2004b), "Strategy as ecology," *Harvard Business Review*, 82(3), 68–78.

- IDEO (2009), *Human Centered Design: Toolkit and Human Centered Design: Field Guide*. 2nd eidition. [Both available on the IDEO home page or at: http://www.hcdtoolkit.com].

- Jacobides, M. G. (2019, November), "The delicate balance of making an ecosystem strategy work," *Harvard Business Review*, pp. 2–5. McIntyre, D., and

- Jacobides, M. G., Cennamo, C., and Gawer, A. (2018), "Towards a theory of ecosystems," *Strategic Management Journal*, 39(8), pp. 2255–2276. DOI: 10.1002/smj.2904.

- Jacobides, M.G., Lang, N., Louw, N. (2019), et al., "What Does a Successful Digital Ecosystem Look Like?" (June 26, 2019), www.bcg.com.

- Jonathan Larsen, Ping An chief innovation officer, "Presentation at Platform Economy Summit" November 20, 2018, available via YouTube accessed February 28, 2019, at https://youtu.be/lGcMen4qD-M.

- Joseph, J., and Ocasio, W. (2012), "Architecture, attention, and adaptation in the multibusiness firm: General electric from 1951 to 2001," *Strategic Management Journal*, 33(6), pp. 633–660, DOI: 10.1002/smj.1971.

- Kapoor, R. (2018), "Ecosystems: Broadening the locus of value creation," *Journal of Organization Design*, 7(1), pp. 1–16, DOI: 10.1186/s41469-018-0035-4.

- Kapoor, R., and Agarwal, S. (2017), "Sustaining superior performance in business ecosystems: Evidence from application software developers in the iOS and Android smartphone ecosystems," *Organization Science*, 28(3), pp. 531–551, DOI: 10.1287/orsc.2017.1122.

- Kapoor, R., and Lee, J. M. (2013), "Coordinating and competing in ecosystems: How organizational forms shape new technology investments," *Strategic Management Journal*, 34(3), pp. 274–296, DOI: 10.1002/smj.2010.

- Kelly, T., and Littman, J. (2001), *The Art of Innovation: Lessons in creativity from IDEO, America's leading design firm*, London: Profile Books.

- Kelly, K. (1994), *Out Of Control: The New Biology of Machines, Social Systems, and the Economic World,* New York: Addison-Wesley.

- Kim, W., and Mauborgne, R. (2005), *Der blaue Ozean als Strategie: wie man neue Märkte schafft, wo es keine Konkurrenz gibt*, Hanser Verlag: HarperCollins Publishers.

- Knudsen, T., and Levinthal, D. A. (2007), "Two faces of search: Alternative generation and alternative evaluation," *Organization Science*, 18(1), pp. 39–54, DOI: 10.1287/orsc.1060.0216.

- Kumar, V. (2013), *101 Design Methods*, Hoboken, New Jersey: John Wiley and Sons.

- Lang, N., von Szczepanski, K. and Wurzer C. (2019), "The Emerging Art of Ecosystem Management," (Jan. 16, 2019), www.bcg.com.

- Leifer, L. (2012a), "Rede nicht, zeig's mir," *Organisations Entwicklung*, 2, pp. 8–13.

- Leifer, L. (2012b), Interview with Larry Leifer (Stanford) at Swisscom, "Design Thinking Final Summer Presentation," Zurich.

- Leten, B., Vanhaverbeke, W., Roijakkers, N., Clerix, A., and van Helleputte, J. (2013), "IP Models to orchestrate innovation ecosystems: IMEC, a public research institute in nano-electronics," *California management review*, 55(4), pp. 51–64, DOI: 10.1525/cmr.2013.55.4.51.

- Lewrick, M. and Link, P. (2015), "Hybride Management Modelle: Konvergenz von Design Thinking und Big Data," IM+io Fachzeitschrift für Innovation, Organisation und Management (4), pp. 68–71.

- Lewrick, M. (2014), "Design Thinking – Ausbildung an Universitäten," pp. 87–101. In: Sauvonnet and Blatt (eds.). Wo ist das Problem? Neue Beratung.

- Lewrick, M. (2018), *Design Thinking. Radical innovations in a digitalized world*, Beck Verlag; Munich.

- Lewrick, M., Link. P, Leifer, L. (2018), *The Design Thinking Toolbox*, 1st edition, Wiley.

- Lewrick, M., Link. P, Leifer, L. (2018), *The Design Thinking Playbook*, 1st edition, Wiley.

- Lewrick, M., Skribanowitz, P. and Huber, F. (2012), "Nutzen von Design Thinking Programmen," 16, Interdisziplinäre Jahreskonferenz zur Gründungsforschung (G-Forum), University of Potsdam.

- Lietka, J., and Ogilvie, T. (2011), *Designing for Growth*, New York: Columbia University Press Inc.

- Lingens, B., Miehé, L., Gassmann, O. (2020), "The ecosystem blueprint: How firms shape the design of an ecosystem according to the surrounding conditions," *Long Range Planning*, DOI: 10.1016/j.lrp.2020.102043.

- Liu, G., and Rong, K. (2015), "The nature of the co-evolutionary process: Complex product development in the mobile computing industry's business ecosystem," *Group & Organization Management*, 40(6), 809–842. DOI: 10.1177/1059601115593830.

- Lowenhaupt Tsing, A. (2015) "The Mushroom at the End of the World: On the Possibility of Life in Capitalist Ruins", Princeton Univers. Press.

- Maeda, J. (2006), *The Laws of Simplicity – Simplicity: Design, Technology, Business, Life*, Cambridge, London: MIT Press.

- Mäkinen, S. J., and Dedehayir, O. (2013), "Business ecosystems' evolution — An ecosystem clockspeed perspective," In R. Adner, J. E. Oxley, and B. S. Silverman (Eds.), "Collaboration and competition in business ecosystems" (*Advances in Strategic Management*, Vol. 30) (Vol. 30). Bingley: Emerald pp. 99–125.

- Mariotti, F., and Delbridge, R. (2012), "Overcoming network overload and redundancy in interorganizational networks: The roles of potential and latent ties," *Organization Science*, 23(2), pp. 511–528. DOI: 10.1287/orsc.1100.0634.

- Masucci, M., Brusoni, S., and Cennamo, C. (2020), "Removing bottlenecks in business ecosystems: The strategic role of outbound open innovation," *Research Policy*, 49(1).

- Mather, D. (2012), "Innovating to create an ecosystem. A write up on Adner's talk." at https://smartorg.com/innovating-to-create-an-ecosystem/

- Maurya, A. (2012) *Running Lean: Iterate from plan A to a plan that works*, O'Reilly Media, Inc.

- McCaskey, M. B. (1974), "An Introduction to organizational design," *California management review*, 17(2), pp. 13–20, DOI: 10.2307/41164556.

- Meulman, F., Reymen, I. M. M. J., Podoynitsyna, K. S., and L. Romme, A. G. (2018), "Searching for partners in open innovation settings: How to overcome the constraints of local search," *California management review*, 60(2), pp. 71–97, DOI: 10.1177/0008125617745087.

- Microsoft press release, "Microsoft to acquire GitHub for $7.5 billion," June 4, 2018, accessed February 27, 2019, at https://news.microsoft.com/2018/06/04/microsoft-to-acquire-github-for-7-5-billion.

- Moore, G. (2014), *Crossing the Chasm*, 3rd Edition, New York: Harper Collins Inc.

- Moore, J. (1993), "Predators and Prey: A New Ecology of Competition," *Harvard Business Review*, pp. 75–86.

- Moore, J. F. (1996), *The death of competition: Leadership and strategy in the age of business ecosystems*, New York, NY: Harper Collins.

- Muthusamy, S. K., and White, M. A. (2005), "Learning and knowledge transfer in strategic alliances: A social exchange view," *Organization Studies*, 26(3), pp. 415–441, DOI: 10.1177/0170840605050874.

- Nambisan, S., and Baron, R. A. (2013), "Entrepreneurship in innovation ecosystems: Entrepreneurs' self-regulatory processes and their implications for new venture success," *Entrepreneurship Theory and Practice*, 37(5), pp. 1071–1097, DOI: 10.1111/j.1540-6520.2012.00519.x.

- Naspers 2018 annual report, accessed February 28, 2019, https://www.naspersreports.com/ui/pdfs/Annual_financial_statements.pdf.

- Norman, D.A. (2004), *Emotional Design: Why we love (or hate) everyday things*, New York: Basic Books.

- Norman, D.A. (2011), *Living with Complexity*, Cambridge, London: MIT Press.

- Oh, D.-S., Phillips, F., Park, S., and Lee, E. (2016), "Innovation ecosystems: A critical examination," *Technovation*, 54, pp. 1–6, DOI: 10.1016/j.technovation.2016.02.004.

- Osterwalder, A., Pigneur, Y., Bernarda, G., Smith, A., Papadakos T. (2015), *Value Proposition Design*, Frankfurt: Campus Verlag.

- Osterwalder, A.; Pigneur, Y.; Etiemble, F. and Smith, A. (2020), *The Invincible Company: How to Constantly Reinvent Your Organization with Inspiration From the World's Best Business Models*, (Vol. 4). John Wiley & Sons.

- Ott, T. E., Eisenhardt, K. M., and Bingham, C. B. (2017), "Strategy formation in entrepreneurial settings: Past insights and future directions," *Strategic Entrepreneurship Journal*, 11(3), pp. 306–325, DOI: 10.1002/sej.1257.

- Ozalp, H., Cennamo, C., and Gawer, A. (2018), "Disruption in platform-based ecosystems," *Journal of Management Studies*, 55(7), pp. 1203–1241, DOI: 10.1111/joms.12351.

- Ozcan, P., and Eisenhardt, K. M. (2009), "Origin of alliance portfolios: Entrepreneurs, network strategies, and firm performance," *Academy of Management Journal*, 52(2), pp. 246–279.

- Palmié, M., Lingens, B., and Gassmann, O. (2016), "Towards an attentionbased view of technology decisions," *R&D Management*, 46(4), pp. 781–796, DOI: 10.1111/radm.12146.

- Parente, R., Rong, K., Geleilate, J.-M. G., and Misati, E. (2019), "Adapting and sustaining operations in weak institutional environments: A business ecosystem assessment of a Chinese MNE in Central Africa," *Journal of International Business Studies*, 50(2), pp. 275–291, DOI: 10.1057/s41267-018-0179-z.

- Patel N. (2015). "90% of startups fail: here's what you need to know about the 10%," In *Forbes* (Jan. 16, 2015), https://www.forbes.com/sites/neilpatel/2015/01/16/90-of-startups-will-fail-heres-what-you-need-to-know-about-the-10/#5e710a5b6679.

- Phillips, M. A., and Ritala, P. (2019), "A complex adaptive systems agenda for ecosystem research methodology," *Technological Forecasting and Social Change*, 148, 119739, DOI: 10.1016/j.techfore.2019.119739.

- Pierce, L. (2009), "Big losses in ecosystem niches: How core firm decisions drive complementary product shakeouts," *Strategic Management Journal*, 30(3), pp. 323–347, DOI: 10.1002/smj.736.

- Ping An, "Annual reports from 2017," http://www.pingan.com/app_upload/images/info/upload/fefe8a8e-fd10-4814-b7b2-aaecf814ff6d.pdf and 2013 http://www.pingan.com/app_upload/images/info/upload/5e41531f-63f0-4428-a00a-0625327ee293.pdfaccessed March 6, 2019.

- Plattner, H., Meinel, C., and Leifer, L. (2010), *Design Thinking. Understand – Improve – Apply (Understanding Innovation)*, Heidelberg: Springer.

- Posen, H. E., Keil, T., Kim, S., and Meissner, F. D. (2018), "Renewing research on problemistic search – A review and research agenda," *Academy of Management Annals*, 12(1), pp. 208–251, DOI: 10.5465/annals.2016.0018.

- Powell, W. W., Koput, K. W., and Smith-Doerr, L. (1996), "Interorganizational collaboration and the locus of innovation: Networks of learning in biotechnology," *Administrative Science Quarterly*, 41(1), pp. 116–145, DOI: 10.2307/2393988.

- Puccio, J.C., Mance M., and Murdock, M.C. (2011), *Creative Leadership, Skills that Drive Change*, Sage: Thousand Oaks, CA.

- Rand McNally history page, https://www.randmcnally.com/about/history.

- Rand McNally website, https://www.randmcnally.com/about/patriarch_partners.

- Ritala, P., and Almpanopoulou, A. (2017), "In defense of, eco' in innovation ecosystem," *Technovation*, 60, pp. 39–42, DOI: 10.1016/j.technovation.2017.01.004.

- Riverdale and IDEO (2011), "Design thinking for educators," Version One. [available at: http://designthinkingforeducators.com/].

- Roam, D. (2008), *The Back of the Napkin: Solving Problems and Selling Ideas with Pictures*, London: Portfolio.

- Rong, K., and Shi, Y. (2015), *Business ecosystems: Constructs, configuration and sustaining superior performance*, London, UK: Palgrave Macmillan.

- Rong, K., Hu, G., Lin, Y., Shi, Y., and Guo, L. (2015a), "Understanding business ecosystem using a 6C framework in Internet-of-Things-based sectors," *International Journal of Production Economics*, 159, pp. 41–55, DOI: 10.1016/j.ijpe.2014.09.003.

- Rong, K., Wu, J., Shi, Y., and Guo, L. (2015b), "Nurturing business ecosystems for growth in a foreign market: Incubating, identifying and integrating stakeholders," *Journal of International Management*, 21(4), pp. 293–308, DOI: 10.1016/j.intman.2015.07.004.

- Rothschild, M. (1990), *Bionomics: Economy as Business Ecosystem*, Washington: Beard Books.

- Sauvonnet, E., and Blatt, M. (2017), *Wo ist das Problem?* Munich: Franz Vahlen GmbH.

- Sawhney, M. (2011), "Orchestration processes in network-centric: evidence from the field," *Academy of Management Perspectives*, 25(3), pp. 40–57.

- Shipilov, A., and Gawer, A. (2019), "Integrating research on inter-organizational networks and ecosystems," *Academy of Management Annals*, 14, pp. 92–121, DOI: 10.5465/annals.2018.0121.

- Siggelkow, N. (2007), "Persuasion with case studies," *Academy of Management Journal*, 50(1), pp. 20–24, DOI: 10.2307/20159838.

- Simon, H. A. (1997), *Administrative behavior: A study of decision-making processes in administrative organizations* (4th ed.), New York, NY: Free Press.

- Sirmon, D. G., Hitt, M. A., Ireland, R. D., and Gilbert, B. A. (2011), "Resource orchestration to create competitive advantage: breadth, depth, and life cycle effects," *Journal of Management*, 37(5), pp. 1390–1412. DOI: 10.1177/0149206310385695.

- Spieth, P., Schneider, S., Clauss, T., and Eichenberg, D. (2019), "Value drivers of social businesses: A business model perspective," *Long Range Planning*, 52(3), pp. 427–444. DOI: 10.1016/j.lrp.2018.04.004.

- Srinivasan, A. (2017), "Networks, platforms, and strategy: Emerging views and next steps," *Strategic Management Journal*, pp. 141–160.

- Stähler, P. (2002), "Business models as an unit of analysis for strategizing," *International workshop on business models*, 45(7).

- Staeritz, F., and Torrance, S. (2020), *Fightback: How to win in the digital economy with plattforms, ventures and entrepreneurs*, LIDpublishing.com.

- Stickdorn, M., and Schneider, J. (2016), *This Is Service Design Thinking*, (6th ed.), Amsterdam: BIS Publishers.

- Strauss, A. L., and Corbett, A. C. (1998), *Basics of Qualitative Research: Grounded theory procedures and techniques* (2nd ed.), Thousand Oaks, CA: Sage.

- Subramaniam, M., Iyer, B., and Venkatraman, V. (2019), "Competing in digital ecosystems," *Business Horizons*, 62(1), pp. 83–94.

- Soykök, G. 2019, "All you need is a minimum viable ecosystem. The original MVE post that sparked Pilgrim's curiosity." https://www.linkedin.com/pulse/all-you-need-minimum-viable-ecosystem-a-gaye-soyk%C3%B6k/.

- Teece, D. J. (2016), "Business ecosystem. In M. Augier and D. J. Teece (Eds.), *The Palgrave Encyclopedia of Strategic Management* (pp. 1–4). London, UK: Palgrave Macmillan.

- Teece, D. J., Peteraf, M., and Leih, S. (2016), "Dynamic capabilities and organizational agility: Risk, uncertainty, and strategy in the innovation economy," *California management review*, 58(4), pp. 13–35. DOI: 10.1525/cmr.2016.58.4.13.

- Töpfer A. (2008), *Lean Six Sigma*. Heidelberg: Springer-Verlag GmbH.

- Uber website, accessed February 28, 2019, https://www.uber.com/newsroom/company-info.

- Uebernickel F., Jiang, L., Brenner, W., Pukall , B., Naef, T., Schindlholzer, B. (2020). *Design Thinking: The handbook*, World Scientific Publishing Co Pte Ltd.

- Ulrich K. (2011), *Design Creation of Artifacts in Society*, Published by the University of Pennsylvania, http://www.ulrichbook.org/.

- Ulwick, A. (2016), *Jobs to Be Done,* Texas: Idea Bite Press.

- Usman Haque, (2010), "Notes on the Design of Participatory Systems - for the City or for the Planet," IIT Design Research Conference 2010.

- Vahs, D., and Brem, A. (2013), Innovationsmanagement, 4th edition, Stuttgart: Schäffer-Poeschel Verlag.

- Van Aerssen, B., and Buchholz, C. (2018), *Das grosse Handbuch Innovation*, Munich: Franz Vahlen GmbH.

- Van der Pijl, P., Lokitz, J., and Solomon, L.K. (2016), *Design a Better Business*, Munich: Franz Vahlen GmbH.

- Velu, C. (2015), "Knowledge management capabilities of lead firms in innovation ecosystems," *AMS Review*, 5(3), pp. 123–141, DOI: 10.1007/s13162-015-0068-6.

- Velu, C., and Stiles, P. (2013), "Managing decision-making and cannibalization for parallel business models," *Long Range Planning*, 46(6), pp. 443–458. DOI: 10.1016/j.lrp.2013.08.003.

- Victionary (2007). Simply Materials: Exploring the potential of materials and creative competency, Ginko Press.

- Voima, P., Heinonen, K., Strandvik, T., Mickelsson, K.-J., and Arantola-Hattab, L. J. (2011). A Customer Ecosystem Perspective on Service. QUIS 12: Advances in Service Quality, Innovation and Excellence, pp. 1015–1024.

- Wareham, J., Fox, P. B., and Giner, J. L. C. (2014), "Technology ecosystem governance," *Organization Science*, 25(4), pp. 1195–1215, DOI: 10.1287/orsc.2014.0895.

- Weinberg, U. (2015), *Network Thinking*, Hamburg: Murmann Publishers GmbH.

- Williamson, P. J., and de Meyer, A. (2012), "Ecosystem advantage: How to successfully harness the power of partners," *California management review*, 55(1), 24–46, DOI: 10.1525/cmr.2012.55.1.24.

- Williamson, P. J., and De Meyer, A. (2012), "Ecosystem advantage: How to successfully harness the power of partners," *California Management Review*, 55(1), pp. 24–46.

- Williamson, P., and De Meyer, A. (2019, September), "How to monetize a business ecosystem," *Harvard Business Review*, pp. 2–4.

- Yin, R. K. (2014), *Case study research: Design and methods,* 5th edition, Thousand Oaks, CA: Sage.

- Yin, R. K. (2018). *Case Study Research and Applications: Design and methods,* 6th edition, Thousand Oaks, CA: Sage.

- Zahra, S. A., and George, G. (2002), "Absorptive capacity: A review, reconceptualization, and extension," *Academy of Management Review*, 27(2), 185–203. DOI: 10.2307/4134351.

- Zahra, S. A., and Nambisan, S. (2012), "Entrepreneurship and strategic thinking in business ecosystems," *Business Horizons*, 55(3), pp. 219–229. DOI: 10.1016/j.bushor.2011.12.004.

- Zerdick, A., Picot, A., Schrape, K., Artopé, A., Goldhammer, K., Heger, D. K., Lange, U. T., Vierkant, E., López-Escobar, E. and Silverstone, R., 2001, *Die Internet-Ökonomie: Strategien für die digitale Wirtschaft, 3. erweiterte und überarbeitete Auflage.* Berlin, Heidelberg, New York.